A Third Summer   ...tyre

Previous books by Angus Martin

History

The Ring-Net Fishermen
Kintyre: The Hidden Past
Kintyre Country Life
Fishing and Whaling
Sixteen Walks in South Kintyre
The North Herring Fishing
Herring Fishermen of Kintyre and Ayrshire
Fish and Fisherfolk
Memories of the Inans, Largybaan and Craigaig, 1980-85
An Historical and Genealogical Tour of Kilkerran Graveyard
Kintyre Birds
The Place-Names of the Parish of Campbeltown (with Duncan Colville)
The Place-Names of the Parish of Southend (with Duncan Colville)
Kilkerran Graveyard Revisited
Kintyre Families
Kintyre Instructions: The 5th Duke of Argyll's Instructions to his
    Kintyre Chamberlain, 1785-1805 (with Eric R. Cregeen)
By Hill and Shore in South Kintyre
Kintyre Places and Place-Names
A Summer in Kintyre: Memories and Reflections
Place-Names of the Parish of Kilcalmonell
Place-Names of the Parish of Killean and Kilchenzie
Place-Names of the Parish of Saddell and Skipness
Another Summer in Kintyre

Poetry

The Larch Plantation
The Song of the Quern
The Silent Hollow
Rosemary Clooney Crossing the Minch
Laggan Days: In Memory of George Campbell Hay
Haunted Landscapes: Poems in memory of Benjie
Paper Archipelagos
Always Boats and Men (with Mark I'Anson)
One Time in a Tale of Herring (with Will Maclean)
A Night of Islands: Selected Poems

A Third Summer in Kintyre
Angus Martin

The Grimsay Press

Published by:

The Grimsay Press
An imprint of Zeticula Ltd
Unit 13
196 Rose Street
Edinburgh
EH2 4AT
Scotland
http://www.thegrimsaypress.co.uk

First published in 2016

Text © Angus Martin 2016

Front cover illustration. The 'Celtic' cross on the Sailor's Grave, Inneans Bay, evening of 28 June 1981, a month before the cross was replaced. Photograph by the author.

Back cover illustration. Corrugated-iron house at Glenahanty, 8 April 2016. Photograph by the author.

ISBN 978-1-84530-158-3
All rights reserved.   No reproduction, copy or transmission of this publication may be made without prior written permission.

Contents

Subjects *vii*
Illustrations *xi*
Introduction and Acknowledgements *xiii*

A Third Summer in Kintyre 1

References *253*
Index *259*

Subjects

Wood anemones and a hazel copse at Knockbay	1
1 April: Ben Gullion	3
'Mars Bars' and a pink ribbon	7
7 October and 9 November 1991	8
8 April: To Largiebaan	10
A stone at Glenahanty	11
A stolen sheep	13
Neil McKellar	15
Geocache	16
Purple saxifrage	18
Innean Mòr and 'Bòcan' Weir	21
Rock and owl	22
11 April: A burnt car on the Learside	24
Easter egg-rolling	25
Climbing out	26
15 April: Largiebaan	27
A raven	29
December 2010: Jimmy MacDonald's raven encounters	31
Other crows	33
16 & 19 April: The Dummy's Port	36
A falcon and its prey	38
5 August 1984	41
4 June 1989	42
The Larch Plantation	44
Scottish Poetry 4	46
A visit to Iain Crichton Smith in 1969	47
The *Scottish Poetry* anthologies	49
17 April: Largiebaan	51
Lesser celandines and primroses	51
20 April: Largiebaan	53

1 May: Largiebaan	54
Australian 'Footballer of the Year'	55
Early purple orchid	56
7 May: A fish-trap at Smerby	59
Little observations	62
9 May: The Inneans	63
11-12 June 1983: Sleeping rough	64
1966: 'Tiger' falls	68
Sròn Gharbh	70
A holly sapling	71
1974: A painting of Earadale	72
13 May: Davaar Island	75
21 July 1991	77
Place-names on the island	79
The Crucifixion and Che Guevara	80
Phillippa Paterson	82
The Horse Bay	84
Quarrying on the island	84
14 May: A return to Davaar	87
Sand tracks	88
17 May: Kidney vetch	88
Off Davaar	90
18 May: Lewis connections	91
Kintyre and North Sea oil	93
19 May: A grave in the hills at Killean	95
James Macalister Hall	97
Burial of James Macalister Hall	98
Enid Macalister Hall	100
Uamh Bealach a' Chaochain	102
Charlie Greenwood	105
26 May: Spring squill	106
28 May: Craigaig	107
3 June: Largiebaan	111
Mossy saxifrage	115
5 June: Rubha Dùn Bhàin	116
Mountain avens	118

6 June: Carradale Glen	119
Deuchran	120
Lurgan	123
A 'serpent ball'	127
Breaclarach	127
Sheila Maclean	129
Hugh Maclean	131
7 June: Largiebaan	133
Rose-root and wild strawberry	133
Air Training Corps	135
Squadron-Leader John McLaren Galbraith, D.F.C., G.M.	137
10 June: Below the Aignish	138
Yellow oxytropis	139
13 June: Largiebaan	141
Colin Martin	143
23 June: Johnston's Point	147
Three curachs and two canoes	147
Two fantasies	149
Four dolphins	150
Two Scottish poets	151
McBrides in Pirnmill	154
Oyster-plant	155
Cuckoos	156
29 June: Southend	157
2 July: The Galdrans	160
4 July: Crosshill Reservoir	161
10 July: Davaar Island	162
Navelwort	163
Chris Wood	164
12 July: The Inneans and Don O' Driscoll	166
The Sailor's Grave	168
A mystery verse	172
Alan Spence	173
Meditations on botany	175
19 July: Ben Gullion	178
7 August 1988: The Inneans	178

24 July: Liberator AM915	179
30 July: The Black Loch	192
Landscapes and imagination	193
3 August: New Orleans and a skua	196
4 August: A Scotch Argus	197
7 August: The Kintyre Agricultural Show	197
Walking to Largiebaan	199
Butterflies	200
Wood vetch	202
Glen Breackerie	203
Eating an adder	204
11 August: Largiebaan	205
Leac a' Chreachainn	206
Yellow saxifrage and wood vetch	207
13 August: Largiebaan	208
A bicycle accident recalled	209
A figure in the landscape	210
3 July 1987: Richard Branson's balloon	212
15 August: Even in dreams I sound the same	213
An imaginary encounter	214
A real encounter	216
Under the Aignish	216
Milestones	219
18 August: The Aignish again	221
23 August: Learside	222
24 August: Lochorodale	223
A lost place-name	225
28 August: Tarbert	226
30 August: Kilchousland and names on rocks	229
31 August: Knock Scalbert	231
1 September: Dalbuie to Feochaig	232
5 September: Tòn Bhàn	235
Recreational fishing	239
10 September: Blaeberries and sloes	242
13 September: Balnabraid	244
15 September: Lagloskin	246

Illustrations

1. Face rock on Ben Gullion, 2015. — 3
2. Amelia, Sarah and Judy Martin at Knockbay, 1991. — 7
3. Angus Martin and John Brodie at the Inneans, 1991. — 9
4. John MacDonald and Barbara Docherty at the Dummy's ruin, 1982. — 37
5. The stack at the Dummy's Port, 2015. — 38
6. Angus Martin and Teddy Lafferty in Queen Esther's Bay, 1984. — 41
7. Edwin Morgan and Angus Martin, Edinburgh, 1991. — 45
8. Douglas Dunn, Matthew Griffiths and Angus Martin, St Andrews, 2016. — 46
9. Teddy Lafferty and Eileen Denney near Gleneadardacrock, 1983. — 65
10. Neil McEachran on Davaar Island, 1991. — 78
11. The Crucifixion painting on Davaar Island with Che Guevara superimposed, 2006. — 81
12. George McSporran and Phillippa Paterson, Davaar Island, 2015. — 83
13. Angus Martin and Duncan Macdougall at the grave of James Macalister Hall, 2015. — 96
14. Boulder on hillock near Tòn Bhàn, 2015. — 111
15. George McSporran below cliffs at Largiebaan, 2015. — 113
16. Jim McAlister at Lurgan, Carradale Glen, 2015. — 123
17. Chimney-head, Breaclarach, 2015. — 129
18. Air Training Corps at Largiebaan, 1957. — 136
19. Colin Martin in Toronto, c. 1910. — 146
20. The Martin family at Dunaverty beach, c. 1957. — 159
21. Campbeltown Boy Scouts' camp in the Galdrans, 1922. — 161
22. At the Liberator marker, Glenmurril Hill, 1995. — 182

23. Angus Martin and Jon Immanuel in hills above
    Glenramskill, 2015.   184
24. Amelia Martin with bicycles at Lochorodale, 2015. 224
25. Bella and Angus Martin with ox-eye daisy,
    Ben Gullion, 2003.   238

Introduction and Acknowledgements

This book is the third, and probably last, of three accounts of consecutive summers spent walking and cycling in Kintyre: *A Summer in Kintyre* (2013), *Another Summer in Kintyre* (2014) and now *A Third Summer in Kintyre* (2015). This latest contains an unusually high literary content, largely attributable to an approach made to me in the summer of 2015 by John Killick, a Yorkshire poet and editor, who offered to make a selection of my published verse and seek a publisher for it. He was as good as his word, and a Selected Poems, *A Night of Islands*, duly appeared in February 2016 from Shoestring Press, leading to several readings and signings, including at the StAnza poetry festival in St Andrews on 3 March and at Tell It Slant, Glasgow, on 31 March.

The prospect of a small revival of interest in my poetry not only got me thinking about my beginnings as a poet and about the poets and editors who helped me progress, but also encouraged me to resume poetry-writing after a lapse of three years. On 6 November 2015, the notion came to me that I might attempt a sequence of poems on the broad theme of 'Largiebaan', that area of high cliffs, outstanding Atlantic scenery and exciting botany between Machrihanish and the Mull of Kintyre, a location which features prominently in this book. While at Largiebaan in the summer of 2015 and while writing down my experiences and impressions there for this book, time and again I thought: I should be putting this into poetry. I worked night after night at these Largiebaan poems and three months later, on 7 February 2016, had seventy-three poems I considered worth preserving. I hope that the best of them will eventually appear in a book titled *Largiebaan: A Place and a Mind*, and that, in whatever time remains to me, I may find more poetry to express, and so end my 'career' as a writer where it began in the mid-1960s.

As in *Another Summer in Kintyre*, the locations of place-names mentioned in the text can be found as Ordnance Survey grid references in the index, bracketed alongside the names themselves. I have not, however, provided grid references for large areas, such as villages.

For assistance with this book, sincere thanks, in alphabetical order, to: Ian Bailey, Lewis; John Bannatyne, Campbeltown; Shirley Bannatyne, Campbeltown; Catherine Barbour, Southend; the staff of Campbeltown Public Library; Jon Immanuel, Israel; Teddy Lafferty, Campbeltown; Iain McAlister, Campbeltown; Jimmy MacDonald, Killeonan; John MacDonald, Campbeltown; Murdo MacDonald, Lochgilphead; Duncan Macdougall, Glenbarr; Robin Fulton Macpherson, Norway; George McSporran, Campbeltown; Amelia Martin, Glasgow; Bella Martin, Tarbert; David Martin, USA; Judy Martin, Campbeltown; Barbara Matheson, Glasgow; Doug Mitchell and Kelly Toohey, Canada; Don O'Driscoll, Kinlochbervie; Les Oman, Campbeltown; Bill Pursell, Canada; Duncan Pursell, Australia; Ruth Reid, Glenbarr; Agnes and Allister Stewart, Campbeltown; Alastair Thompson, Canada; and William Watson, Campbeltown. Special thanks to Agnes Stewart for having read a draft of this book and spotted errors which I'd missed.

Apologies to anyone I have inadvertently left out, and apologies too for any errors this book still contains. If you spot any, let me know.

Angus Martin, 12 March 2016.

13 Saddell Street, Campbeltown, Argyll PA28 6DN.
judymartin733@btinternet.com

A Third Summer in Kintyre

Wood anemones and a hazel copse at Knockbay
December 2015 was wet and windy, and outings were few. The 22nd was the seventh anniversary of Benjie the dog's death, and I'd hoped to visit our old haunts at Knockbay, but persistent rain kept me at home. Most of that day was spent in my 'study' – a chaotic den overloaded with books, files and papers – and while in there I noticed a pocket notebook which had fallen on to the floor. Out of curiosity, I opened it before putting it back in its box, and the date at the top of the random page was 24 April 2013.

The entry was brief, but what a nostalgic charge those few words carried in gloomy mid-winter: 'Back from Germany & in Knockbay wood in sunshine looking at wood anemone. Wood sorrel growing with it. Glad to be back.' My wife Judy and I had spent a week at our friend Hartwig's home near the Black Forest, and on the day after we returned I'd gone into town to do some shopping and kept going until I'd left the town behind me.

'Knockbay wood' is the little hazel copse beside the track to Crosshill Loch, at the concrete bridge, and that's where George McSporran and I first noticed the white flowers of *Anemone nemorosa*. I checked for a first reference in the battered copy of the New Observer's *Wild Flowers* which I keep in my rucksack and annotate with reasonable diligence. The date there was 15 April 2011, and I could hardly believe I was 59 years old before I noticed the flower; but my journal for that year confirms the fact, and records that, curiously, both George and I had independently seen and puzzled over the flowers the day before, he in the morning and I in the evening.

Did they first appear there in 2011 or had we missed them in earlier years? It seems we missed them, because when

Agnes Stewart lived at Kilkerran Glebe in the 1980s and '90s, she often used to walk her dogs after lunch, and 'admire the Wood anemones at that wee hazel wood'.

'Anemone' and 'Windflower', an alternative name, are both, Geoffrey Grigson points out, borrowed from *Anemone coronaria* of Greek legend: 'They seem to fit our species well; the flowers do hang and nod and shake in the wind, although to the Greeks, Anemone, or Daughter of the Wind, probably signified something altogether different.'[1] The Gaelic names, *flùr na gaoithe* and *lus na gaoithe*, also evoke wind.[2] I can't say that I associate wood anemone with motion in the wind – harebell, for me, is the dancer – but I do associate it with spring and with that hazel copse at Knockbay, where I first saw it.

In 2015, I resolved to watch for wood anemones at Knockbay, and asked Agnes Stewart to let me know when they appeared in the Wee Wud at Glenramskill, which she passes several times a week during her daily 'constitutional'. On 29 March, she and her husband Allister had a look at that wood, and, through binoculars, identified four or five little anemones, 'out in all the wind', as she remarked. Wind there certainly was; it blew hard throughout the last three days of the month, bearing lashing showers of alternate rain, hail and snow – 'out like a lion', indeed! She subscribes, and with better judgement than I, to the wind association: 'They are indeed well named "wind flower".'

On 1 April, three days after Agnes's sighting, and at the end of a walk with daughter Sarah's dog, Chomsky, I decided to check the hazel copse at Knockbay for wood anemones. As I expected, there was none, indeed no flowers of any kind, apart from a few cross-leaved golden saxifrage, which are so modestly attired they scarcely qualify as flowers at all. On 9 April, after a short walk on Ben Gullion, I was on my way back to Kilkerran graveyard, where I'd left my bike, when I remembered I was meant to be checking for the flowers. I wasn't expecting to find any, but found two, inside the wood. Both were feeble and I knew I'd want to return in the hope of seeing more vigorous specimens.

1 April: Ben Gullion

Though Chomsky didn't know it, we were heading for a double hillock on Ben Gullion, which in 2001 I named 'Marilyn', after Marilyn Monroe. The name was a pun on 'Munro' – a mountain over 3000 feet – with an added element, which should be obvious from the topographical description. On the south side of the western hillock, there is a rock feature which resembles a man's face. At the beginning of *Another Summer in Kintyre*, I discussed natural rocks which resemble human faces, but omitted this one because when I visited it in 2014 to photograph it, I failed to see it. I remembered the face as a profile, but when I looked at the profile, it wasn't convincing and I decided that heather growth had obscured the lower part.

1. Face rock at 'Marilyn' on Ben Gullion, 2 April 2015.

I was prepared that day to cut back the heather in order to reveal the profile, but as I approached the rock I suddenly saw the face looking at me. I had discovered that the effect is more striking frontally, and, since I had no camera with me, I returned the following day and, from below the rock, took a series of photographs from different angles. The best of them is reproduced on page 3.

I believe it to be the 'daddy' of all Kintyre rock profiles, and, on my way uphill on the 2nd, I pondered what name I might give it. I quickly settled on 'Arthur', for Arthur Miller, the American playwright who was Marilyn Monroe's last husband. The face is in an obscure and little-visited area of Ben Gullion, close to the march with Kilkerran, and I wonder how many other hillwalkers have noticed it. Few, I'd say, though I like to think that over the millennia of human presence in Kintyre, innumerable individuals have seen its craggy features.

I recently bought, in a charity shop, a book titled *Simulacra*, '... intended to reassure those who see faces and figures in rocks, trees, clouds and damp stains on walls'. The book, by John Michel, contains 196 illustrations of simulacra – 'shadowy likenesses to familiar objects' – and many are very striking indeed. There is none from Scotland, but I'd put 'Arthur Miller' up against some of them!

While plodding up to Marilyn on 2 April, following the march-fence, I noticed at my feet what, in a moment of irrationality, I perceived as a little pile of cooked spaghetti! When I looked closely at the bits, I realised that the explanation was natural, though still very curious. Something had stripped the skin from a common rush, presumably for food, and left the spongy white pith. I'd never before seen that, and when I returned home and told Judy she undertook a little research and identified a common vole as the likeliest candidate; and, indeed, there had been vole burrows round about. Here's a thought – back in our great-grandparents' time, country children might have the job of skinning rushes, but it was the pith they wanted, for twisting into wicks for the little oil-lamps called 'cruisies'.

On the top of the western hillock of Marilyn, there's a flat rock which, I instinctively know, thousands of people over thousands of years have sat on. It's coated in scurfy grey lichen, so clearly few people use it now. It doesn't take a great effort of imagination to visualise the kinds of people who would have sat there: hunters in pursuit of game; gatherers in search of the blaeberries and crowberries which still carpet the hill; herds, many of them little children, watching over their grazing stock from the useful height; warrior-bands; cattle-thieves; fugitives and destitutes; and, last of all, ramblers like myself, enjoying a day's leisure. Of course, to see the landscape as they saw it, the coniferous cover, imposed in 1979, has to be imagined away.

I've written several poems about woodlice – 'slaters', as they're locally known – and one of them was written at that rock on 27 April 2008. Woodlice prefer darkness and dampness, but this one was out in the spring sunshine, '... descending charily/ a tilted square of lichened rock'. My disruptive presence was probably the cause of its movement, and if I'd considered that possibility at the time, the poem might have taken another direction. As it happened, I focused on the thought that the creature would probably spend its entire life on that hillock, '... seeing and hearing nothing I admire/ spurning indeed the very sun in heaven'.

George McSporran and I sat on that rock on 4 April, a day when mist clung to the upper hill. We followed, for as far as it went, an old track we call the Peat Road, which the tree-planting on Ben Gullion in parts obliterated; elsewhere on the hill, nature itself has been erasing the route, but sections survive in isolation, visible to those who know what they are looking at. That first part has been incorporated into an unofficial mountain bike route, which runs downhill off the official middle bike trail. Several of the forest routes which George and I opened up last century, and enjoyed privately, more or less, have been appropriated in recent years by bikers, attracted to them for reasons not dissimilar to our own.

On our way up, I remarked to George that despite the bikers' adoption, and improvement, of 'our' routes, I'd yet to see even one cyclist on any of them. A few minutes later, that hitherto elusive cyclist appeared, speeding downhill and then coming to a sudden halt. Chomsky began barking furiously at the strange apparition in biking apparel, but he'd met him before on Ben Gullion. The biker was Jimmy MacDonald and we joined him where he'd stopped. He said he would accompany us back the way he had come, to restart his descent, and also warned us of other bikers on the hill. Sure enough, two more appeared while we were chatting with him on the middle trail, and before we cut through forest to follow the march-fence up to Marilyn.

I was on the Peat Road the following day, alone with Chomsky, and encountered yet another cyclist, who likewise halted and then pushed his machine back uphill to start again. I didn't recognise him, but when I mentioned I'd met Jimmy there, he asked if I was Angus Martin. What could I say but 'Yes'? He told me he was Craig Morris, a colleague of Jimmy's at the swimming-pool.

That afternoon, Sunday 6 April, I gave Marilyn a miss and instead sat near Fin Rock, which is lower on the hill, and one of my favourite spots in Kintyre.[3] By then, Chomsky, whose home is in Glasgow, had been with Judy and me for eight days, and I'd had him on Ben Gullion daily. Let loose on the hill, he ran about constantly and I judged that he was beginning to run out of energy. Sure enough, when I sat for lunch, he lay at my feet and scarcely budged during the hour we spent there. On his last day in Campbeltown, I took him on to the ridge overlooking Kilkerran graveyard. I sat in sunshine beside a rowan, one of several which, when they first appeared on the skyline some ten years ago, I mistook for human figures. To a branch of the tree I tied a broken boot-lace I found in my rucksack, to mark a first visit there.

'Mars Bars' and a pink ribbon

The little wood at Knockbay, which consists of no more than a score of trees – all of them old, and most of them dying or dead – meant nothing to me for many years. I'd pass it by going to and returning from Crosshill Reservoir and might pull a few nuts – there was seldom more than a few – from the trees beside the track, or lift them ripened from the ground and break them open with a stone.

2. L-R: Amelia, Sarah and Judy Martin eating 'Mars Bars' in the hazel wood at Knockbay, 3 November 1991. Photograph by the author.

On 3 November 1991, a small event occurred in the wood and is preserved in a photograph I took. I liked the photograph from the moment I first saw it, but years would pass before I consciously connected the photograph with its location. I had dated the slide, but when I checked my journals for an account of that day, there was none: the record jumped from 7 October to 9 November. However, I remember what was happening in the photograph. My wife Judy and daughters Sarah and Amelia were sitting eating a 'Mars Bar' each. Jimmy MacDonald was also present, but isn't in the photograph. He'd 'phoned that morning to suggest a walk on Ben Gullion and we said we'd meet him. He offered to bring sweets and duly appeared with 'Mars Bars', but we'd eaten one apiece before anybody realised that Jimmy, our benefactor, hadn't one for himself!

Jimmy, Amelia and the little hazel wood were reunited almost twenty-three years later. On Hogmanay 2014, Amelia and I decided to stroll along Kilkerran road before dark, and turned up the track to Knockbay. We met two chatting dog-walkers, Ross Robertson with Arlo and Jimmy with Kosi, and, having exchanged a few words with them, carried on as far as the wood, by which time darkness was almost down. In a pocket of the jacket I was wearing I carry a tangle of cake ribbons which I save for occasional route-marking or sentimental remembrance, and handed Amelia one of them, inviting her to tie it to a tree to mark our presence there at the year's end. She did as I suggested and we turned for home.

7 October and 9 November 1991

I probably didn't take my rucksack with me on that walk to Ben Gullion on 3 November 1991, so there would have been no journal either, and presumably nothing happened that day that I considered worth recording later. But the entry before the blank was 7 October, a hike to the Inneans with John Brodie, a fellow-postman.

When I went to bed the previous night, I didn't imagine I'd be going far in the morning, but the wind and rain had abated by then and the sun shone for most of that day. If my daughter Sarah hadn't wakened me, I'd probably still have been in bed when John arrived for me shortly after eight o' clock. As it was, by the time I was ready to leave, an hour had passed. He left his car at the foot of the Bruach Dearg, after an unsuccessful attempt to drive up the badly rutted brae. We headed into Gleann Eadar da Chnoc, by the track past

Gartnacopaig, and stopped for lunch mid-way through the glen, at the ruined shepherd's cottage.

As we were preparing to leave the Inneans, we saw someone with two dogs coming down into the bay, and through binoculars I recognised Agnes Stewart, with Jess and Fly. When I suggested photographs to mark the unexpected encounter, Agnes produced a new camera, which I described in my notes as 'fully automatic'. She took one of John and me, then I took one of John and her, and then there was a moment of farce. As I was walking towards her to hand her back the marvellous new camera, 'I slipped spectacularly in my treacherous four-year-old welly boots and landed on my back ... but still gripping her camera'. That the camera, by my instinctive reaction, was undamaged, was proven by the photographs she later sent me, each with the date printed on it.

3. *Angus Martin and John Brodie at the Inneans, 7 October 1991. Photograph by Agnes Stewart.*

Many of the 'old school' of hikers preferred to have their destination to themselves, and, if they saw another party already there, might bypass the place in disgust. In a letter she wrote to me the following day, Agnes remarked: 'I had a lovely day yesterday, & though it may sound ungracious, I was glad that you & John were leaving as I arrived at the bay. It's always nice to have it to oneself. I didn't loiter long – just ate my "piece", took some photos of the magnificent waves & headed out.'

On 9 November, I set out for the Inneans alone, but the day was windy and cold and after lighting a fire on the shore at Craigaig and brewing a pot of tea, I turned back and took the 3.30 bus at Machrihanish back to Campbeltown. At Fionn Phort in the Galdrans, on my way south, I had encountered the brothers Peter and John Kelly from Machrihanish village, beside a heap of logs they had sawn from a tree – plane, they thought – washed ashore during a gale the previous week. I photographed them and then chatted for a while.

8 April: To Largiebaan

On the day after Chomsky's departure, I decided to turn my back on Ben Gullion for a more challenging walk. I took the 12 o' clock Southend bus to Auchencorvie and from there headed along the Homestone road. Minutes later I was in conversation with Robert Brown, who was working in his garden. We talked mostly about natural history, but had switched to other subjects when Jimmy Robertson and Kenny Durnan appeared in their council 'freighter'. I spent the spring and summer of 1978 as a dustman and offered up a memory from that time.

I was one of a crew of three, and we had a sideline in 'scran', which was essentially recycling before the practice was officially adopted. Anything that could be sold on, such as copper wire, would be set aside, along with objects we ourselves fancied. One of the crew on another 'freighter' had a nice collection of ornaments he'd rescued from the mechanical maw, and I still use, as grass-cutters, old sheep-shears the farmer at Escart left at the roadside with his rubbish. At that time, paper and cans were worthless, as were glass bottles unless they were returnable. Once a week, when we were emptying the bins in Glen Breackerie, we'd wash our collection of bottles in the burn at Dalsmirren bridge, so that they were gleaming when we exchanged them for cash with sympathetic shopkeepers. One warm afternoon, after we'd finished the bottle-washing, we lay on the grass at the bridge with a transistor radio playing and all fell asleep. Panic broke out when somebody wakened and realised the time – we were seriously behind schedule!

I remember that day for another reason. Before I fell asleep, I heard from the radio a song which excited me so much I noted the title and the name of the band: 'Vacant Possession' by The Movies. I bought the album, *Bullets Through the Barrier*, and one other of the five albums the band recorded, *India*. None of them is, or evidently ever will be, available on CD, but in 2015 an eleven-track compilation of rescued material, titled *Remix*, was made available as a free download on The Movies' website, so something of the band's fine musical legacy survives into the digital age. It was one of the band members, Jon Cole, who found singer-songwriter Sandy Denny after the fall from which she died in April 1978,[4] while I was emptying dustbins in Kintyre.

Robert, too, had a sleep story. A father and son from Drumlemble were thinning turnips on a farm near the village, with the farmer himself. The drills were long, and, at the end of one stint, all three paused for a rest ... and fell asleep. They woke to the sound of the farmer's wife bringing the cows in for their evening milking, and when the farmer realised what had happened, he began beating the father about the head with his bunnet, as though it was all his fault!

A stone at Glenahanty

At Glenahanty, I went straight to one of the gables. I have two flat metal boxes designed to hold slides, and for decades I had ignored these boxes, believing they were full of rejects. Last winter, however, I decided to open them, and was appalled to find that the thin foam rubber lining on the underside of the lids had degraded into a sticky mess resembling brown candy floss, and that some of it had gone on to the slide-mounts. I cleaned the lids and then turned to the slides. I soon established that the transparencies themselves were undamaged, but would it have mattered, anyway? These slides were discards. Or were they? I began looking through them and discovered many duplicates, but also many I'd forgotten I had, some of which now interested me. Values change with time, and here were images which, thirty years on, clearly meant more to me than they had at the time I was amassing and assessing them.

One of them in particular intrigued me. It was captioned: 'Glenahanty old house, with stone weight suspended from roof at gable and Bruach Dearg in the background, 17 July 1983.' The use of stones to help keep thatched roofs in place during gales was common practice, but this one had been attached to a corrugated iron roof. I hadn't noticed it since taking the photograph, over thirty years ago, and wondered if it was still there. It was, but it had fallen to the ground, though the wire was still hanging from the gable. I had a look in the stone ruins and noticed, scored in a byre wall, when the plaster was still soft, '1952', the year I was born.

In 1921, a visitor to Glenahanty remarked on the transition from thatch to metal roofing: 'Much of the beauty of Glenahanty has been lost since I saw it first. Then the houses were thatch-covered and ferns grew out of the walls; now it is roofed with the less romantic, if more sanitary, corrugated iron.'[5] These traditional houses were later abandoned, and replaced, further back from the road, with a cottage built entirely of corrugated iron, which, unlike the stone-built steadings, is now falling apart.

An evocative photograph of Glenahanty, published in the *Campbeltown Courier* in 1938, shows the old steadings with smart corrugated-iron roofs and skylights, the same roofs that are on the buildings to this day. The picture was taken below the road and also shows grazing cattle in the foreground and a conifer-free hill in the background.[6] There is even a painting of the old steadings, something I wouldn't have expected to see. When I first saw it, in December 2015, looking from the street into the gallery space of Coastal Design, Campbeltown, I wasn't sure that I was seeing what I thought I was seeing, but the identification was confirmed. The artist, Ronald Togneri, had placed the red-roofed steadings close to the top of the painting, an arresting perspective which unconsciously imitated that of the 1938 photograph. The sloping grassy sweep of the foreground was occupied not by cattle, but by two tiny figures – his grand-daughters – and the colourful scene at once put me in mind of rural France (with which countryside I am, admittedly, familiar only from pictures).

A stolen sheep

A family named McMath – Anglicised as 'Mathieson' – farmed Glenahanty, in unbroken succession, from the seventeenth to the early twentieth century. Donald McMath, the last of the name there, and a venerable Gael, died in 1909,[7] and was succeeded by a nephew, Neil McKellar, whose mother was Mary Mathieson. Neil used the names 'McKellar' and 'Mathieson' interchangeably, an inconsistency I'll examine later, but in the following account he is 'Mathieson'.

At Campbeltown Sheriff Court in 1913, he pleaded not guilty to a charge of sheep-stealing. There was only one sheep – a wether hogg, or castrated yearling – involved, but the case generated much controversy and the court was crowded.

Mathieson was accused of having stolen the sheep on 10 October 1912 from Kilwhipnach farm. The farmer there, David Reid, testified that in September he had bought twenty-two black-faced hoggs from Robert MacQuilkan, farmer in Low Ugadale, and put them 'into a field by the public road leading over the hill to Southend'. On 10 October, Reid's son, John, reported that one of the sheep was missing, and Reid was later told there was a wether hogg at Glenahanty corresponding to the missing animal.

When Mathieson's lawyer, Archibald Stewart, examined David Reid, he asked him: 'Who informed you that the hogg was at Glenehanty?'

Before Reid could reply, Sheriff John Macmaster Campbell intervened with: 'I do not think that is a pertinent question. If witness does not care to answer this, he need not do so.'

Witness: 'I do not wish to give the name.'

Stewart: 'Do you mean, my Lord, that witness is not bound to answer the question?'

Sheriff: 'I do not think that he is bound to answer that question.'

Stewart: 'I would like that to be noted, my Lord. I would like the witness to be withdrawn to argue the point.'

When Reid had left the court, Stewart argued that the question was an important one, because he believed the informant would be called later as a witness and he might be able to demonstrate whether the informant was credible or not. The Sheriff ruled that if Mr Stewart were to ask the witness 'whether A or B or C was the informant, mentioning a name', then the question would be permissible. Reid was then recalled to the witness-box, and Stewart asked him: 'Did Lachlan MacNeill tell you that Mathieson had a wether hogg?' Reid's answer was 'Yes', and he explained that MacNeill was 'a large sheep farmer, and he was familiar with most sheep markings in Kintyre'.

The informant's identity was clearly a sensitive point, MacNeill being a neighbour of Mathieson's and a member, like Mathieson, of a long-established Glen Breackerie farming family. MacNeill, who farmed Amod and Gartnacopaig, told the court that he himself had 'missed two gimmers' which he suspected he might find at Glenahanty. He went there with his shepherd in Gartnacopaig, John Campbell, and James Reid, Culinlongart. Mathieson was 'agreeable to the inspection', but complained that 'there was a great deal of noise being made about the two gimmers he had', and warned that 'if there was any more of it he would make the parties answer to their betters for it'.

On 14 January, David Reid also went to Glenahanty, to examine the sheep suspected of being his, and Mathieson 'showed the hogg quite willing[ly]'. But Reid was convinced, from the lug-marks – two splits on the near ear and four half-splits on the off ear – that it was one of the sheep he had bought from Robert MacQuilkan, who was with Reid and the Campbeltown inspector of police that day. MacQuilkan confirmed that the lug-marks were his, adding: 'This is an unusual mark, and there is not another the same in Kintyre.' So much 'keel' (red ochre) had been applied to the fleece that he was inclined to think it was intended to obliterate the original markings.

In Sheriff Macmaster's judgement the 'real test' was: had Mathieson 'established any really satisfactory explanation for his possession of the sheep'? He had not, and there was 'no doubt' that the hogg belonged to David Reid. The verdict, therefore, was 'guilty'. Mathieson's lawyer, Archibald Stewart, asked for leniency and reminded the court that the accused had been married only eight months. 'The whole amount at issue,' he continued, 'was at most 5s worth of goods. Considering the time this charge has been hanging over the accused's head, he thought the ends of justice would be served by giving a dismissal.' Macmaster Campbell thought otherwise and fined Mathieson £3 or twenty days' imprisonment.[8]

Later in the day, my walk would take me to Innean Mòr, where another sheep-stealer lived, in the eighteenth century. There was neither fine nor imprisonment for him – he was hanged.

Neil McKellar

Regarding Neil's Mathieson/McKellar identity, in his first census appearance, at the age of six, in 1871, he is 'McKellar', and in the following three censuses, up to 1901, he is

'Mathieson'. In the 1913 court case, he was 'Neil McKellar Mathieson' and when registered in Campbeltown poor roll in 1929, he was 'Neil Mathieson McKellar'. He appears to have lived his entire life at Glenahanty.

The records I have for his mother, Mary, are no more helpful. Within the same census period, 1871-1901, she was at Glenahanty as housekeeper to her brothers, Archibald and Donald, and appears uniformly as 'Mathieson'. In 1871, she was 'married', in 1881 'married', in 1891 'unmarried' and in 1901 a 'widow'. When she died at Glenahanty on 22 December 1911, she was 'widow of Dugald McKellar',[9] and in Neil's poor roll entry his father is 'Dugald McKellar, shepherd'. Yet, I found no trace of a Dugald McKellar, at Glenahanty or anywhere else.

Neil was admitted to Campbeltown Register of Poor on 24 April 1929, suffering from 'acute gastritis' and 'swollen legs', and awarded £1 a week. He was described as a 'farmer' at 'Glenehanty Farm', born 4 January 1865, and married 6 June 1912 in Campbeltown. His wife was Mary Martha Doyle from Wigton, aged 35 in 1929, against his 64. They had five children. He died at Glenahanty on 7 May 1929, thirteen days after 'going on the parish'.[10] The immediate fate of his poor widow and children is not recorded.

Geocache

Past Largiebaan, I looked under the Kintyre Way stile, wondering if the 'geocache' box would still be there. It was and I opened it and took out the notebook. My entry on 11 March 2014 had been the first in the book, and I saw that I'd be first in the book again in 2015. I also saw that I was almost last in the book in 2014. About fifteen minutes, I guessed, separated that final entry and mine.

On 5 November 2014, I took my sister Barbara's nephew from Skye, Lewis Docherty, and his wife, Zoe, to Largiebaan. They had recently married and were staying with Barbara at Drumlemble as part of their honeymoon tour of Scotland.

Soon after we left the last strip of forest and were on the open moorland, heading towards the cliffs, a couple appeared ahead of us, coming in our direction. They were from Derbyshire and, by an amazing coincidence, were also on honeymoon. Walking the Kintyre Way in November certainly wouldn't be the choice of many honeymooning couples, but the weather that week had been fairly benign, and that day was sunny. I told them about the geocache box and made a mental note to check it on the way back for their names. I did so and found 'Angela' and 'Roland' and the comment: 'What a treat.' There was someone else out there that day, but we didn't see him. The day before, I'd offered Jimmy MacDonald a lift in Lewis's car, but he planned on leaving earlier by bicycle, and his destination was Rubha Dùn Bhàin, south of where we'd be. At Glenahanty, I noticed a message from him, scored with a stick in a patch of mud. By the time Lewis, Zoe and I reached the cliffs, the sun had disappeared behind haze and the air had turned chilly. The big flask I'd filled with tea proved to be damaged – I should have recognised the problem when the tea heated the outside of the flask as soon as I poured it in – so we didn't even have the comfort of a hot drink.

The first entry of 2015 was soon to be joined by another, and, again, the two would be separated by about fifteen minutes. I was sitting on the stile transcribing parts of the geocache notebook when I heard voices. A man, a woman, a young girl and two dogs were approaching from the west. The woman told me a fox had just crossed the track in front of them, but I hadn't seen it. I asked her if she was on holiday and she replied that her mother lived in Tarbert and her name was Ann Thomas (the artist). They had come from Machrihanish and Ann Thomas would collect them at some point on the Glen Breackerie road.

Among the objects deposited in the box, I noted a Paracetamol tablet, a girl's photograph and a small bone-shaped dog treat, to which cache I literally added my 'tuppence worth' in the form of a coin. A week later, I transcribed a message, dated 9 April, from Susan and Lorna, who 'loved Innean Glen & Bay' and left a copy of the lyrics of 'Campbeltown Loch' and 'Mull of Kintyre' printed on blue laminated paper, with the invitation to 'please take'. I declined the offer. Catherine Gallagher had deposited a boarding-pass for the Cairnryan-Belfast Stena Line ferry dated 29 May 2014, 15.30, which I admired as 'a genuine article of memorabilia fixed in time and place'. (I found out later that Catherine was travelling to Ireland for her cousin Jillian's wedding.) On subsequent walks to Largiebaan, I discovered that the geochache box was gone.

Purple saxifrage

The breeze was strong on the cliff top, as it generally is, so I sat below the top, as I generally do. I cut down at the first green slope I came to, and within a minute or two had found an inviting spot sheltered by a rock with little clumps of purple saxifrage (*Saxifraga oppositifolia*) flowering from cracks and ledges. I didn't realise I was sharing their space until I was preparing to leave, otherwise I would have savoured their nearness. It's wonderful to reflect on how these modest harbingers of spring endure for year upon year through storm and flood and snow, rooted on rock in one of the most exposed coasts in all Kintyre. Or perhaps it isn't so wonderful, since it is 'one of the hardiest arctic-flowering plants' and 'vies for the accolade of being the most northerly reaching, having been recorded from the north coast of Greenland at Cape Morris Jessup ...'[11] M. H. Cunningham and A. G. Kenneth, in *The Flora of Kintyre*, remark (p 22) on 'a beautiful pink variant ... in the Largybaan area ...' The flowers round about me were indeed pink and beautiful.

Geoffrey Grigson, in *The Englishman's Flora* (pp. 202-3), noted that it took two hundred years to find a dozen species of saxifrage in the British Isles. Purple was discovered in 1668 on Ingleborough, the second-highest mountain in the Yorkshire Dales, by the English naturalist John Ray. By the early nineteenth century, 'though the rock garden was not born, the vivid, purple-flowered *Saxifraga oppositifolia* had been taken from its mountain crags and snow to London, where at Covent Garden plants could be purchased at a shilling or two shillings each'. We may be certain, I think, that none from Largiebaan was ever sold into captivity at Covent Garden.

Two other saxifrages, which flower later than the Purple, may be found at Largiebaan, the white-flowered Mossy (*S. hypnoides*), which I'd see later that spring, and Yellow (*S. azoides*), which I had seen in previous years and would see again in the summer.

While I ate the last of my provisions and finished the tea in my flask, I began looking about me and realised that I'd sat in that same spot once before. Judy and Jimmy MacDonald were with me that day, which was memorable because Jimmy was bitten by a spider there. Judy was now in Glasgow and I thought of her. I also thought of Agnes Stewart, as I had promised her I would; her Largiebaan days appear to be over, unless an elixir of youth magically comes her way. On the day after my visit to Largiebaan, I e-mailed her with a brief account of my time there, and she replied ruefully: 'I made the mistake of reading your email before I went to bed and ended up at Largiebaan all night, looking for the three different saxifrages. Midnight thoughts can be very queer.'

Constant presences, on the slope below me, were seven nanny goats, grazing peacefully in a slow upward progression. I took off my boots to allow my feet a little freedom. Occasionally, after a long hike, my toes feel as though they have been smashed with a hammer, sensations doubtless connected with ageing. I was a little anxious about how my leg muscles would cope with this first demanding hike of the year, but next morning, after an unusually sound sleep, I actually felt energised.

I was facing north, across a vast stony amphitheatre, which shepherds called the Corrie, to the rock wall of the Aignish, which dips towards the sea from over a thousand feet. I noticed an intrusive form on the skyline close to the top of the Aignish, and trained my binoculars on it. When magnified, it turned into a sheep, but, as I scanned the terrain, a light-coloured bird shot across my field of vision, and I followed its progress south until, mere seconds later, I lost it against the background of boulders and scree. It was a peregrine falcon, and about half-an-hour later I glimpsed a kestrel, which appeared from the south and would presumably have followed the ridge I'd occupied, but, seeing me there, swung away and within seconds was lost against the broken landscape.

I began contemplating that landscape, streaked with scree and dotted with huge rocks. Each rock, large and small, as it broke off and rolled and bounced down the slope, would have been an event, which, mere seconds later, when it came to rest, became just one static stone amid multitudes. When the time came to leave my resting-place, I decided to do a transverse to the Aignish, instead of returning to the top and the Kintyre Way. Passing directly above these immense runs of scree, I marvelled at the quantities of stones they must contain, and I fantasised that I'd been given the time and the endurance to count every stone in that amphitheatre. I'd start from the south and work my way north, numbering every loose stone I could find. At the conclusion of my labours, years or decades later, what number would I have reached? Would it be in the hundreds of thousands, or might there be millions of stones there, each one of them a traveller, if only once, in its own time?

The word 'scree' and its Gaelic cousin, *sgrìodan*, are from Norse *skriða*, a landslip on a hillside.[12] There are plenty of screes in Kintyre, yet only one place-name containing the element, the hybrid 'Sgreadan Hill', north of Glenlussa. *An Scriodan*, on the north coast of Arran, comprises big sandstone blocks which were dislodged around the year 1700, causing a 'concussion' heard miles away in Kintyre and Bute.

Another Arran place-name, *Scribhinn Clann an Deamhan*, 'Scree of the Devil's Children',[13] echoes a place-name on the south side of Davaar Island, the Devil's Riddlings, a slope whose stones 'fell through' the Devil's riddle.[14]

Innean Mòr and 'Bòcan' Weir

From the top of the Aignish I rejoined the Kintyre Way and followed the narrow twisting track down to the ruins of Innean Mòr. The route passes through the old township, and one of the way-markers actually stands inside the remains of a building.

It was to this remote settlement in 1709 that John Weir drove the sheep he and an accomplice had stolen from William Fleming in Garvachy, near Oatfield. His Gaelic nick-name *Bòcan* is still used in Kintyre for a repulsive or unlucky person, and he was probably both, certainly the latter, because he was hanged for his crimes.

His wife was Mòr McConachie, who must have belonged to Innean Mòr, which in 1691, as 'Indinmore', was leased to Malcolm and Alexander McConachie. The neighbouring settlement, on the north side of the glen, 'Indinbeg' – for Innean Beag – was leased in that same year to another McConachie, Duncan 'Oig' (Gaelic òg, 'young'). McConachie, however spelled, is *MacDhonnchaidh*, 'Son of Duncan', but many, perhaps even all, McConachies in Kintyre at that time were really Campbells.[15] Weir's sheep-stealing accomplice, Neil MacIlglash – *MacGhilleGhlais*, 'Son of the grey or sallow lad', and later Anglicised as 'Gray' – belonged to Innean Beag, which may be translated as 'Little Cove', while Innean Mòr is 'Big Cove'.

The preceding might be considered too stodgy for digestion, but it's there as a reminder that in most parts of Kintyre at that time the English language and culture were alien, and that any English-speaking – or Scots-speaking – traveller might as well have been in the Atlas Mountains for all the chance he would have had of making himself understood.

In October 1709, Weir and MacIlglash set off 'under cloud of night' to Garvachy and drove away the thirteen sheep by a 'mountain way' to avoid being seen. On the following night, Weir killed two of the sheep and concealed three others alive 'in a hole upon the lands of Inanmore'; the other six were never found. Fifteen gentlemen and farmers formed the jury at Weir's trial in Campbeltown, and their verdict, on 23 June 1710, was 'guilty'. On 15 September, he was 'hanged on ane gibbet until dead'.[16] To modern sensibilities, Weir's execution doubtless seems an outrage; but to the eighteenth century victim and his family, the loss of these sheep may also have been a matter of life or death. Oh, and the sheep butchered or thrown into a hole on Cnoc Moy are unlikely to have advocated mercy either, had they been given the language to articulate their feelings.

Rock and owl

On my way up the Inneans Glen, by the Kintyre Way, I saw what might have been the ghost of one of the Garvachy sheep, but as I approached nearer to it, it became a large perching raptor or owl, and momentarily – the reaction was so fleeting it hardly registered – I felt an inexplicable stab of apprehension. The shape of a bird was there, with the head turned to the south and its beak distinct. The illusion was created by late sunlight on the rock, which was coated with grey lichen, giving it a whitish appearance. More factors than just light must, however, have contributed to the illusion – time of year, time of day, and the cloudless sky were all, I suspect, crucial to the effect, because I've passed that rock a hundred times or more and never, until that evening, even noticed it.

A few minutes after I had photographed the rock and resumed my journey, by a queer coincidence I saw, beside the track, the remains of a freshly killed raptor, or so I assumed. There were no signs nearby of the bird's having been plucked, only a broken-off section of vertebrae, with the legs attached to it, and every scrap of flesh removed. The hard yellow pads on the talons intrigued me, and I gingerly touched one.

On the following Monday, Judy e-mailed the photographs I'd taken to Jimmy MacDonald for identification. His immediate response was, 'Looks like a Barn owl to me', but he said he would forward the images to Neil Brown, who monitors and rings the barn owl population in Kintyre. Ten minutes later, a second e-mail confirmed the identification, with the additional detail that 'because the talons have no notches in them, it's probably a bird hatched last year'. How far had these remains been carried from the location of the kill, and what species of raptor had made the kill? I'll probably never know, but from rock to reality was a remarkable step.

Further on a bit, there was another odd sight: at the meeting of streams, a pile of charred wood. A fire had been lit in a pleasant grassy spot, but it was close to the head of the glen and I wouldn't have expected a camp there. Then a memory clicked. As an explanation, this may be nonsense, but it's as close as I'll get unless someone actually admits to having camped there. About three weeks before, returning by bus from Glasgow, I overheard one end of a mobile 'phone conversation. The young man in the seat in front of me was talking to a friend in Campbeltown, and I didn't pay much attention to the conversation until I heard him suggesting they set out for the Inneans as soon as the bus arrived. He was confident the trip would be feasible, but this was mid-March and the bus wasn't due in until after six, and I thought to myself: it'll be dark before you're even half-way there. The friend, too, seemed unenthusiastic and a squabble broke out. The friend appeared to resent having the organising role imposed on him, and was particularly annoyed by a request for a warm woollen jumper. That conversation was followed by several others, each testier than the previous. The outcome of the debate is unknown to me, but my fellow-passenger was met off the bus by his friend, with a van, and if the Inneans had finally been agreed on, perhaps the remains of the fire I saw marked the furthest point the pair reached that night.

By the time I was approaching Ballygroggan steading, darkness was closing in and I knew I'd have an hour to wait in Machrihanish village before my bus came at 10.35. I imagined, as I plodded along, that someone would give me a lift home, and someone did. There was a white van parked beyond the steading, with a man loading an all-terrain vehicle into the back of it. I spoke briefly to him and carried on. While I was filling water into bottles at the outflow trough past Ballygroggan Cottage, the van stopped, and the driver, who was Scott McAllister, leaned out the window and asked if I'd like a lift. I confessed to him I'd been fantasising about such an offer and climbed into the front beside his sister. He dropped me off at my house, nearly two hours before I'd have arrived by bus.

11 April: A burnt car on the Learside

On my way down the Learside by bike, I had a nasty surprise at Sweetie Bella's Quarry – a burnt-out estate car. I tried to construct a feasible explanation. Had the car been stolen and then torched? 'Joyriding' on the single-track, hilly, winding Learside road didn't seem likely. Was it an old, unwanted vehicle somebody chose to destroy in a remote spot? The absence of number plates, back and front, gave this theory some credence. Or had the vehicle contained incriminating evidence of some kind and been burnt to conceal that evidence? Yet, there were no signs of police involvement. And how long had the car lain there? I hadn't been on the Learside in three weeks. This was definitely not a sight one would expect to encounter on the quiet romantic Learside of Kintyre!

I took a couple of close-up photographs of the car, and then climbed above the quarry to frame it with the First Water in the background. I'd taken only one photograph there, when a red car appeared from the north and stopped. I knew the driver and we exchanged a few comments on the wreck. When he remarked that the fire had been caused by an electrical fault in the engine, I realised that he knew more than I did. 'Do you know whose car it is?' I asked him. 'Mine!' he replied, and explained that he was now in a borrowed car.

I asked him if he'd like his photograph taken beside the burnt car. His reply was an emphatic 'No!'

His story was that he had been on the shore that morning picking wilks and noticed smoke rising from the quarry. Realising it was coming from his car, he hurried back to the road and 'phoned the fire brigade, which arrived thirty-five minutes later, too late, of course, to save the vehicle. He said that his insurance company had arranged for the wreck to be towed away that afternoon, but on my way home, just before dark, it was still there.

Later in the year, I was surprised to chance on a newspaper report headed 'Alarming Motor Accident: Car Ablaze on the Learside Road'. The year was 1928, when that road would have been little better than a cart track (it was improved in 1947, when an eight-acre site at Ru Stafnish was acquired to build the radar station on). The driver was D. Rankine Scott, son of a Campbeltown tailor, who was home on holiday from India, where he held 'a high position in the banking world'. He was returning to Campbeltown from Southend, when, on Corphin brae, a dog ran in front of the car. He swerved to avoid the animal, and, seeing that the car was going to hit a stone dyke, he jumped out, and just as well because it burst into flames on impact and burned so intensely that only the chassis and wheels were left.[17]

Easter egg-rolling

While wheeling my bike up Corphin brae, I noticed eggshell fragments on the road and remembered the Easter egg with a pirate's face painted on it I'd noticed stuck on the fence at the same place on 27 April of the previous year. I also noticed something glinting on the road and lifted it. It was a little six-petalled pink plastic flower which had been stuck to an egg for decoration. I picked up two others and put all three in a pocket for later disposal, thinking back to the tiny pink flowers of the saxifrage I'd seen at Largiebaan three days earlier – natural, beautiful and not for sale.

On my way out to Largiebaan on 8 April, on an incline of the road past Homestone I'd noticed broken eggshells, and on my way home after my day on the Learside I saw further evidence of egg-rolling, this time near the top of the road down to the Second Water. Lying in a ditch were the remains of two boiled eggs, each with 'hair' attached – yellow pleated wool on one and white free-hanging wool on the other – and a shattered painted face.

All of these impressed me as manifestations of the ubiquitous car culture. Instead of walking into the countryside to find a hillock or sloping field, drive to a lay-by on a hilly road, park and then roll the eggs. Still, I suppose it's gratifying that the tradition continues, even if the boiled eggs are never eaten by the children, who doubtless prefer the chocolate versions.

Climbing out

My destination on 11 April was the Dummy's Port, and I left my bike as usual in the quarry above Corphin ruins. I'd last been there on 18 March, and, seeing sheep grazing around the ruins, I decided, to avoid disturbing them, to cut straight down to the bottom of the field and follow the fence to a stile. There was a distinctive little headland before me as I descended the field. I'd never particularly noticed it before, but it looked inviting, so I crossed the fence on to its grassy summit. From there, I could see on to the shore, and, noticing driftwood, decided to look for a route down, and identified one. It was slippery and overgrown with briers, but took me on to the shore. Having cut a load of logs, I continued south to the Dummy's and returned to the road by the wilk-pickers' track I usually follow.

Once again, I descended from the headland, equipped this time with secateurs as well as a bush-saw. Having filled a rucksack with logs, I decided that, instead of climbing out from the Dummy's, I'd attempt a direct route, but not the one I'd descended on: I wanted one that was dry and mud-free.

I scanned a little cliff on the south side of the headland and identified a diagonal route which looked feasible. I set off, lugging an ash branch, and was about a quarter of the way up when I heard my name called. Having turned my head at once towards the shore, I had no time to be astonished.

I saw Sandy McSporran and Lee Holland, and a climbing companion of theirs, Davie McAllister. They could see what I was doing, but what were they doing? Sandy explained that they were walking the coast from Polliwilline to Campbeltown. I brought out my camera and took a couple of photographs of them below me, and then urged them to press on, as daylight would be fading in a few hours. They were already gone before I thought to advise them, 'If I'm not home before dark myself, you'll find me here, dead or alive'.

The remark would have been meant as a joke, but, as I soon discovered, the joke had a grim underside. The route turned out to be steeper and harder than I'd anticipated, and I've never been confident on terrain which is both precipitous and unfamiliar. Parts of the slope were covered with dense mats of dead bracken, and I couldn't tell how much solidity was below them. There were three particularly awkward stages of the climb, and I was only too aware that, should I fall, there was progressively further to fall! I had guessed that a row of trees ahead of me on the skyline signified the top, but I guessed wrongly. There was yet another difficult stage, with a sheep-track leading left and another leading right. I chose the left-hand one and finally reached the top. Was I glad to see that fence in front of me!

15 April: Largiebaan

I returned to Largiebaan with big plans. I'd climb down to the shore at the Aignish and find a nice piece of driftwood to take home with me for the fire; on my way down, I'd photograph one of the big screes from underneath it, with my back to the sun, so that the light was favourable; and I'd look more closely at purple saxifrage colonies. Only one of these plans was fulfilled – I saw saxifrages, but they were same ones as before, close to the cliff top – because I'd been wildly optimistic in my expectations. I cycled that day and was slowed by a strong westerly breeze the whole way to Glenahanty, where I left the bike. The wind was even stronger on the cliff tops, but by then I'd run out of time and already decided to defer a descent to the shore until later in the summer, when there would be more daylight and I'd have the other two saxifrage species to search for.

On my way up the Bruach Dearg, I lost the force of the wind and decided to stop for lunch. I sat above the ravine and burn on a grassy slope yellow-starred with lesser celandines. While sitting there, I was startled by a sudden noise from the road. I imagined that some animal was running by, but when I turned my head I glimpsed a young man descending on a mountain bike. The noise I'd heard was his braking on the stony brae and the skid of a wheel. He had curly red hair under his helmet and I wondered who he might be. Later enquiries identified him as George Cowan.

As I passed Gartnacopaig, Ewan Johnstone emerged from the building and without preamble asked me if I'd ever come across a photograph of the replica ship's bridge and bow which had been built in the 1930s at the front of the steading. It was the idea of John McNeil – locally nick-named 'Sugar Neil' – who bought Gartnacopaig from Sanda Estate in 1926. McNeil owned the Colonial Ironworks in Govan and was a descendant of the MacNeills in Amod[18] (p 14). The view from the teak deck of the 'ship' was out over Glen Breackerie, and Ewan recalls sitting there with Peggy Harvey in the 1960s; but the structure was deemed unsafe soon after and dismantled, leaving only a big metal upright, with bits of rotting wood attached to it, which can still be seen at the roadside. Access was from the back door of the farmhouse, and steps led up on to the structure, with room enough underneath to park a car. The answer to Ewan's question, regrettably, was that I had never seen a photo of the structure; but I would like to, and so would he.

We were joined a few minutes later by Barry Gelder, Southend carpenter, who revealed that I was only the seventh person he'd seen on that road since the New Year, though doubtless a few had passed unnoticed; I, for one, a week earlier.

Passing Largiebaan, I reflected that in my own lifetime the farm had needed three shepherds – and the same number at Ballygroggan – but has been unoccupied since Archie Ronald moved out in 1990 after twenty-four years. He lived in one of the two wooden bungalows – only one remains – which, when at the framing stage, sceptics condemned as 'hen-hooses'; but Archie himself remembered them as 'very warm and dry'. In his penultimate year at Largiebaan, he told me, he gathered, sheared and dipped about 2000 sheep with only occasional assistance from a son.

He remembered the Largiebaan shepherds during the Second World War as Angus Gillies and his sons Willie and Colin, along with Duncan MacDonald (to whom I referred in *Another Summer in Kintyre*, p 121). By then, High Glenadale was unoccupied and its ground merged with Largiebaan's. In the 'old days', Archie said, one of the Largiebaan shepherds would assume the duty of fetching provisions, and his 'hirsel', or sheep stock, was consequently smaller than the others'.[19] In the original stone-built shepherds' house nearby, an earlier shepherd, John Beattie, was born and died, aged 70, in 1935.[20]

A raven

I spent ten or fifteen minutes finding a spot below the cliffs which would afford some shelter from the wind, and finally chose a little hollow where I could sit with my back to a rock. The wind was so strong, I doubt if there was a calm corner anywhere on that coast. It was the best I could find, and I noticed, as I settled into it, that it was close to the spot I'd occupied a week earlier, with its spacious view north towards the Aignish. Where I now huddled, I could see, to my right, a bit of the Atlantic, and, directly ahead, a bit of the sky.

Out of that bit of sky, a raven (*Corvus corax*) glided right over the top of me, looking down as he passed. Again he passed over me, and, as I was describing his behaviour in my notebook, he came a third time, from the south and unseen, and startled me with a loud croak. I knew then that he had seen the bread crusts I was throwing away, or, at least, that he was associating me with the possibility of food. I'd been going to save the rest of the sandwich for later, in case I felt hungry on the way home, but decided to leave it, too, and broke it up. As I was preparing to leave, I heard a curlew call and climbed to the top of the crag I'd been sheltering under, in the hope of seeing the bird. I didn't, but saw the raven perched on the skyline, watching and waiting.

As I headed across the open ground and away from the cliffs, I kept looking back in the hope of seeing the raven make his move. To my delight, I saw him skim the ridge and drop straight into where I'd been ten minutes earlier. I almost left it at that, but decided to return to the spot and settle the question conclusively. There literally wasn't a crumb left there. Since he was still around, in a fit of generosity I tore up a sweet pastry, the last of my provisions, and left the bits for him.

I was at Largiebaan again two days later, and again the raven came looking for food. I'd been sitting for about forty minutes without having sighted him, and was wondering at his absence, when I saw a fleeting shadow on the grassy slope below me. I looked and saw him between me and the sun. He reappeared against the sea in a long unbroken glide which took him behind the Aignish and into the Gulls' Den. I didn't at first see him return to my spot, but heard the faff of his wings in the still air. I had brought a packet of four out-of-date rolls with me and tore up and scattered two of them. A couple of minutes after I moved off, he landed on the tip of the crag above my resting place. I kept looking back to see when he'd drop on to the food, but he was content to bide his time. My transverse towards the Aignish took me to a hollow and I slid into it and crouched out of sight, as I supposed, watching him with binoculars through two clumps of grass. He finally descended to the food, lifted a scrap and flew a short distance away to tear it up and eat it. He didn't, as I'd expected, return immediately for more, but flew towards me, had a look into my hiding place, and, presumably satisfied that I posed no threat, turned back and set about the rest of the food, at which stage I ended my observations.

December 2010: Jimmy MacDonald's raven encounters

During an intensely cold spell in December 2010, Jimmy MacDonald had a couple of close encounters with Largiebaan ravens, presumably the same pair. He was huddled on the cliffs, in freezing conditions, hoping for an opportunity to photograph raptors, but, apart from a distant fox and an occasional hooded crow, he had seen no life. To compound his misery, his flask had broken and soaked the contents of his rucksack, sandwiches included. In disgust, he had thrown the spoiled sandwiches some twenty feet on to the scree behind him, consoling himself with the certainty that the soggy bread would feed some creature.

Soon afterwards, 'the near-silence of the December afternoon was broken by the noisy whistling wing-beats of a Raven passing close overhead'. A female had arrived on the scene, to be joined, seconds later, by a male, which, as it flew past, scrutinised first Jimmy and then the wasted food. Jimmy didn't expect any immediate action from the birds, and assumed that they would return to claim the food after he had gone. The male alighted on a crag, about 300 feet to the north of him, and sat there for about twenty minutes, 'preening, croaking and watching the coffee-stained sandwiches'. Then, to Jimmy's surprise, it took off, flew straight towards him and dropped on to a rock about 30 feet from where he sat.

'I slowly moved the camera into position and snapped off a few decent shots as the Raven seemed to weigh up what to do next. In amazement, I watched the large bird hop clumsily from boulder to boulder, until eventually it was close enough to secure its prize. It quickly filled its throat pouch with a quite amazing amount of soggy bread, then flew off to a distant knoll, where it was quickly joined by its mate.

'In a few minutes it was back, and once again went through the whole cautious routine of getting close enough, before gobbling down as much as it could, and departing. This time I was ready for it, and got some far better images than I had the first time ... and spent the rest of the afternoon photographing this hugely impressive corvid from very close quarters.'

Jimmy was back at Largiebaan about a week later. There was snow on the ground and the air was bitterly cold. Soon after his arrival, the two ravens appeared, as though they recognised him and associated him with food. He had packed some old bread and cheese, hopeful of securing more photographs of the birds, but by then the sun had gone behind cloud. None the less, he threw the food behind him, this time a little closer, and waited.

> Almost as soon as the bread had left my hand, the male came sailing in, alighted 20 feet away, and wasted no time in hopping over to his prize and once again filling his throat pouch. As before, the female kept her distance, but he was amazingly bold. At one point, he was within 10 feet of me, all the time fixing me with his dark eyes, just in case I made any sudden threatening movements.
>
> At such close quarters, I could hear a strange sound coming from the bird, quite indescribable, but almost like a sub-song in much smaller songbirds. If you have ever been close to a rookery, you may have heard the inhabitants quietly creaking and whistling to one another. You have to be very near, but they do it, and so do Ravens.[21]

Other crows

The only other crows likely to be seen out there are 'hoodies', with their grey on black colouration, though in recent years jays (*Garrulus glandarius*), a spreading species in Kintyre, have appeared in the coniferous forests near Largiebaan.

Choughs (*Pyrrhocorax pyrrhocorax*) nested in caves along that coast until the early 1980s, when the entire population, by then reduced to a few pairs, disappeared. With their red bills and legs and chiming call, they are delightful birds, and, as insect-eaters, the most innocuous of all crows. Had the choughs survived a decade or two longer here, they would, I feel, have been classed as a species worthy of active conservation. I regret their absence, yet count myself fortunate to have seen the last of them. In *A Summer in Kintyre* (pp. 50-53 & 231), I discussed the species and possible causes of its loss, but predation wasn't one of the factors I considered. It may not be relevant in this case, but combine protection of raptors with an already diminished chough population and there might just be a link. The same link might apply in the case of golden eagles and mountain hares, which were once common around the Mull and now appear to be either extinct there or depleted to near-invisibility (I have never seen one anywhere in Kintyre). Of choughs, Dugald Macintyre, gamekeeper and writer, remarked that peregrine falcons found them easy prey and that he'd seen their 'lovely red bill and feet many times at the "plucking post" of a peregrine'.[22]

Choughs also bred, further back, on the Learside, and we catch a glimpse of them in Captain T. P. White of the Ordnance Survey's *Archaeological Sketches in Kintyre*, published in 1873. When he walked around Auchenhoan Head to visit Saint Kieran's Cave (probably in 1866) he noted (p 104) that from the 'weird caverns' on the headland 'rock jackdaws and pigeons flit scared at the intrusion'. His 'rock jackdaws' were choughs and his 'pigeons' were rock doves, which are also now absent from that stretch of coast.

There is a small rookery on the edge of Kinloch Green, across the road from my house in Saddell Street, and I have been feeding its members for many years. In 2014, however, Judy and I observed the emergence of bolder behaviour from the birds. One of them took to perching on the telephone wire which leads into the kitchen, and, mere inches behind the window glass, inviting us to feed it. Only the top part of the window opens, so we were lobbing food out to it through that gap, and just as it became adept at catching the food, we became adept at pitching it accurately. Other rooks adopted the same tactic and there are now probably eight or nine which use the wire for privileged gain. At times a queue will form, with four or five birds vying for attention. Patience generally prevails within the assembly, but sometimes a dominant bird will chase off the others. Compared with herring gulls, some of which are vicious in their dismissal of rivals, the rooks on the wire are gentle, and a warning jab of the beak in the direction of an unwanted competitor is demonstration enough. Should a scrap of bread, or whatever, be too big to swallow whole, some rooks will catch it and hold it between claw and wire and tear it into manageable pieces. But one individual, at least, will bat away unwelcome scraps with its beak, and accept only what it can immediately swallow. An old club-footed rook comes daily, and he, of course, is unable to grip the wire, but we try to ensure that he gets his share by other means.

Jackdaws (*Corvus monedula*) are also avid recipients of welfare, and they get their share by sheer nimbleness. If there is a jackdaw around, any scrap, momentarily overlooked by gulls and rooks, will be seized with unerring accuracy and carried off. On 25 March, a jackdaw which was almost blind arrived to feed on the roof below our window. I had never seen it before (in that condition, anyway). Both eyes were diseased and the bird's facial feathers were matted with coursing discharge. It was so blind that, when it landed, it was pecking hungrily at splashes of gull excrement. It managed to secure a few scraps of bread amid the clamour on the roof, and flew off without having been attacked by any other bird. Two days later, opposite the West Coast Motors garage, I saw a bird flattened on the road. It was a jackdaw, and the conclusion was obvious. Death, for that poor bird, must have been a merciful release. A road is not a natural constituency for any bird in death, so, being squeamish at times, I asked Judy if she would move the corpse. She lifted the remains on a shovel and buried them in our back garden. I remembered that a daffodil bulb I'd found in Alexandra Park, Glasgow, and brought home with me, still hadn't been planted, so I put it into the earth with the bird. Daughters Sarah and Amelia lived close to the park at the time, but both would be moving to other parts of Glasgow, and I took the bulb, dislodged anyway, as a memento of Dennistoun. It also became an adornment on the grave of a bird I noticed only in the last days of its life, when it became conspicuous by its infirmity.

Hooded crows (*Corvus cornix*), from their long history of persecution, were rarely seen near human habitations, but in recent years they have nested in Campbeltown, and the spread of coniferous afforestation during the past fifty years has provided them with unlimited safe nesting sites all over Kintyre. In my own lifetime, their status has gone from 'rare' to 'common', a proliferation which sheep farmers contemplate with understandable alarm, for, alike with ravens, they will prey on new-born lambs and distressed ewes, picking the eyes from living victims. In almost thirty years, up until 21 May, I had seen only one hoodie in the back garden of 13 Saddell Street. On 21 May, when the bird appeared at feeding time, my immediate reaction was that I didn't want it around, not least because resident sparrows and blackbirds were tending fledglings, which hoodies will catch and eat. As it transpired, it didn't return until later in the summer, when it became just one of the crows, neither more nor less aggressive. Its first visit gave me one abiding memory of its intelligence. I was breaking up and throwing out the tough ends of a brown loaf, and each piece the crow secured was taken straight to a tub, half-filled with rainwater, in the backyard. The bird dropped the bread into the water, let it float a while, then retrieved and swallowed the moistened morsel. I'd never before seen any bird do that. I later noticed it hiding food in caches around the backyard and even on the stairs leading up to our door.

16 & 19 April: The Dummy's Port

My niece Barbara Matheson was in Kintyre visiting her mother for a few days, and I suggested a walk. We each had four spare hours in the afternoon, and I suggested the Dummy's Port as a destination. Since we'd be using Barbara's car, I recognised an opportunity to bring home a load of firewood the easy way, but I had a feeling, too, that Barbara would relish a return to a stretch of coast I reckoned she hadn't walked for some thirty years.

She left her car at the Second Water and we walked up the brae to the quarry above Corphin, and then descended to the Dummy's, and back by the shore to the car. As walks go, it was a dawdle, but, with the prospect of a drive back to Kirkcaldy and an immediate return to nursing the following day, she was more interested in relaxation. We reminisced for a while on our visits to the Dummy's in the early 1980s with John MacDonald, in particular the meals cooked over driftwood fires, but mostly she was content to sit in the calm of the afternoon and enjoy doing nothing. On our way back along the shore, we saw a peregrine falcon, which revived a memory from the '80s, but I shall return to that when I return to the Dummy's three days later.

I went by bike this time and, before heading south to Ru Stafnish for firewood, I sat under the stack on the south side of the ruined fishermen's hut to eat lunch. Someone, probably a wilker, had placed a red plastic fish-box there as a seat, and that became my seat too. Had I not been passing the box on my way to the shore since 2013, I'd have known anyway it had been there for years from the moss colonies overgrowing the handles. The stack is an imposing feature of the shore and must have had a Gaelic name which was lost, and perhaps names too in earlier languages.

4. John MacDonald and Barbara Docherty (now Matheson) eating at the Dummy's ruin during a sleety shower, 1 May 1982.

A falcon and its prey

5. The stack at the Dummy's Port, 19 April 2015. Photograph by the author.

I was thinking back to an encounter I had with a peregrine falcon there more than thirty years before. Unusually, I didn't record it at the time, but, also unusually, I remember it vividly. I'd been sitting in the Dummy's Port and decided to stretch my legs. I hadn't gone far when I was startled by the whoosh of a bird passing rapidly over my head. I looked up at once and saw a second bird, a falcon, bank away suddenly and disappear; but the first bird, a racing pigeon, was there in front of me, perched on a rock shelf. It had clearly been targeted by the falcon and, aware of the threat, had tried to outfly the raptor, and succeeded, possibly thanks to my unwitting intervention. The pigeon was in a state of total shock. I returned to it, two or three times, before I left the shore, with scraps of food I imagined I might tempt it with, but it sat in rigid indifference. I assume it would have resumed its journey after I had resumed mine, but its owner, if he ever saw it again, would have won no prize in that race.

In the 1980s and '90s, evidence of falcon kills of racing pigeons were quite common, and I amassed a small collection of rings from the legs of birds which lay with the feathers and other scattered inedible parts, but since the turn of the century neither racing pigeons nor their remains are much in evidence. I had a walk around the stack and, on the seaward side, recognised the very rock face on which the pigeon had found refuge.

The earliest report of a ringed pigeon kill I've noticed in local newspapers was in June 1896. While walking in the hills, John McLean, son of the shepherd in Blary, Barr Glen, noticed a heap of feathers and other remains. An enamelled ring, on the right leg, bore the year '1894', the number '174' and the initials 'W.S.F.C.', and one of the feathers on the right wing was stamped 'West of Scotland Glasgow Flying Club'.[23]

A week later, the same newspaper reported that Robert Ferguson, gamekeeper, Point House, had captured 'three fine specimens of the peregrine hawk at the Mull of Kintyre. The birds, which are full-fledged, were forwarded by steamer to the south of England, where they will be trained for hawking'.[24] That business transaction would possibly earn Robert a jail sentence nowadays; at that time, however, peregrines, like all other raptors, had no legal protection, and, without their 'sporting' value, their fate would have been death.

Kintyre falcons had a high reputation, and there was a headland on south-west Kintyre whose birds were especially valued. One nineteenth century Ayrshire falconer named Ballantyne – reputedly a pupil of the last Royal Falconer of Scotland – came regularly to Kintyre for young birds and stayed at Keil House, Southend, with James N. Fleming, who was jailed after the crash of the City of Glasgow Bank in 1878. On one of the visiting falconer's raids on the special headland, he got stuck on the cliff. He could neither be hauled up nor let down to the bottom, and had to remain on a ledge until a longer rope was fetched from a long way off. One of Fleming's sons recalled that the young falcons were kept 'at hack' in the Keil kennels, that is, they were free to fly about, but were always fed at a regular hour in their quarters. If one of the birds failed to return at the set time, it was at once denied further liberty, 'because missing a meal meant that the bird had killed, and, unless taken up ... would soon have been lost. I can remember the birds well, though I was quite a young lad at the time, and I also remember them being brought in from hawking, carried by a "cadger", with their hoods and jesses on.'[25]

An interesting account of the care of falcons captured on 'Yleandavar' – Davaar Island – has survived from 1690. The birds were 'heried', or harried, on 25 May of that year and delivered to John Hood by Alexander McNachtan, 'faulconer'. Dugald Campbell of Glensaddell, 'Bailye of Kintyre', paid Hood 'Sex pund twelve shilling' for feeding and tending three 'young haulks' and 'the old tersell' – tercil, a male peregrine – which had clearly also been captured, with its offspring, and was 'hurt in the wing'. Hood supplied a receipt of payment at Campbeltown on 20 June, when presumably the birds were handed over.[26]

5 August 1984

I also remembered an incident on the stack involving Jimmy MacDonald, which I did record. The date was 5 August 1984, when he would have been nine years old. I was actually writing in my journal when the drama began. I heard him shout, and, sensing his fear, climbed straight up the stack to him. I managed to calm him and then coax him down, step by step, though I had a fright myself on the way down. He descended without difficulty, but was shaken and complained of a headache.

6. *Angus Martin and Teddy Lafferty in Queen Esther's Bay, 5 August 1984. Photograph by Jimmy MacDonald.*

It was an eventful and a sociable day. At Glenramskill, we had met Margaret McGeachy, son Duncan, daughter Wendy and two visiting relatives, heading for Davaar Island; at Kildalloig, we encountered Allister Stewart on his bicycle; and in Queen Esther's Bay we found Teddy Lafferty. He was finishing a second cup of tea when we joined him, and

I drank a cup of his brew. Before we continued south, half-an-hour later, I took a couple of photographs of Teddy sitting on his fish-box, then handed the camera to Jimmy, who took one of Teddy and me sitting together, 'the result of which', I noted, 'will be interesting'. It was a creditable composition and perhaps indicative of Jimmy's photographic talents which would emerge some twenty-five years later. On the shore at the Second Water we found a group of picnickers, to one of whom, by then married with children, 'I used to have a strong attraction', a little personal detail which, had I not committed it to my journal, I would certainly have forgotten.

On our way home, we picked a load of mushrooms from roadside fields, and, in the Ardshiel Hotel, ordering a drink for Jimmy and me and describing the day's mushroom-gathering to Isobel Mitchell and Harry and Catherine Lavery, a stranger, whom I'd noticed looking intently at me, came up to the bar and described some fungi he'd seen on the Island of Mull. I wasn't familiar with the species, but I invited him to join Jimmy and me in the back room. His name was Tom Baird and he lectured in photography at the Maryland Institute College of Art in Baltimore, U.S.A. We chatted for an hour and would have met again, perhaps for a hike, but he was leaving Campbeltown next day for Edinburgh and the Festival. I corresponded with him briefly but never saw him again, though, while writing this book, I searched the internet and found some of his photographs.

4 June 1989

The title poem of my first collection of poetry, *The Larch Plantation*, was written at the Dummy's Port on Sunday 4 June 1989, while waiting for Teddy Lafferty to arrive. I'd met his sister Fiona that morning and she told me he was 'only going to the Dummy's', to which I replied that 'only' was hardly appropriate, since the Dummy's was close to the limit of Teddy's range in a day's walking. Teddy, I knew, would have set off hours before me, but I had decided to cycle and expected to either find him at the Dummy's or be there when he arrived.

I cycled as far as the Second Water, concealed my bike in bracken on the south side of the burn, and walked the shore to the Dummy's. I arrived about 3 p.m., and Teddy wasn't there. As I mused in my journal: 'If he comes, he'll be too late to stay long. No doubt he has stopped in Queen Esther's Bay; maybe he's going to stay put; maybe he's on his way. Anyhow, I'm happy enough to have the place to myself.'

I almost started building myself a fire-place on the shore, but noticed one Teddy had made from four stones atop a grass-covered rock to the north of the ruin, and used it to cook a meal of 'Burgamix' – a dried vegetarian mixture – and baked beans. Since I hadn't brought oil, I had to keep adding water to the frying-pan to prevent the burgers sticking and burning, but for convenience I was using sea-water and the result was a rather salty meal, which induced a fierce thirst.

It was a bright day, and, when I arrived, windless, but a northerly breeze sprang up later. While I was sitting on the shore, a red-hulled fishing boat, which I identified as 'CN 123', steamed south. Note in journal: 'I've a hunch it might be the *Antares*.' Reading that entry twenty-five years later, the name leapt out at me. 'CN 123' was, indeed, the *Antares*. In the following year, on 22 November, while fishing northeast of Arran, her trawl-warps were snagged by a submarine, *HMS Trenchant*, during a naval exercise. The *Antares* of Carradale was dragged under, and skipper-owner Jamie Russell and his young crew, Dugald John Campbell, Stewart Campbell and Billy Martindale, were all drowned.[27]

I actually wrote two poems on the shore that day, 'The Larch Plantation' and one about Teddy's non-appearance, which I later judged to be a dud; but here's a bit of it: 'I came to a deserted shore:/ no driftwood blaze, no rucksack/ with its contents spread around it,/ no gesture of unhurried recognition ...'

While I was working on my poems, I heard voices and then saw three men descending from the hill, so I shifted and sat among boulders on the lower shore, so well concealed that I heard one of them – a reprobate I had no desire to meet – remark, as he stood at my smoking fire, 'Somebody camping'. They were there to pick wilks, and two of them were obviously 'greenhorns' to judge by the questions they were asking the smoke-analyst. Two headed south and one north, and I was alone again; but it was time for me to leave, anyway.

I had a 'phone call from Teddy the following evening to explain his non-appearance, Fiona having mentioned her chat with me. He was delayed by tide at Auchenhoan Head and had to wade around the foot of the cliffs, so decided he would content himself in Queen Esther's Bay, as I had surmised. Later on, we must have missed each other narrowly, because he arrived home about 6.30 and I arrived at 6.40.

The Larch Plantation

Nineteen eighty-nine was a very productive year for me as a poet – I was focused and on form – and many of the poems in *The Larch Plantation* belong to that year. There wasn't much to the title poem, except perhaps atmosphere. I dedicated it to Teddy, the man I waited for in vain. Had he arrived, the poem would almost certainly not have been written, because, with very few exceptions, my poems are realised in solitude. The larches which inspired the composition stand above the shore, and when the wind rose after I arrived there, I began to hear them stir. Here is the poem in its entirety.

> When the north wind forays
> among the larches –
> greener than all the greens assembled here –
> I hear the sound of water boiling,
> but really it's only the wind
> stirring surfaces as the sun travels north.

The Larch Plantation was published in 1990, and in the following year earned for me a Scottish Arts Council Spring Book Award of £750. I believe my work had, at that time, an influential female advocate, but who she was I have never discovered. There are now so many literary prizes, it is tempting to dismiss them entirely as commercial devices, tainted by cronyism, but I certainly enjoyed my moment of recognition and still remember it with pleasure. With my wife Judy and infant daughters, Sarah and Amelia, I attended a ceremony in an Edinburgh book shop. The other recipients included Norman MacCaig and Edwin Morgan, and the cheques were presented by Douglas Dunn – three of Scotland's most distinguished living poets at the time. When we all assembled to be photographed – Alison Kennedy and Gerald Mangan were also in the line-up – I took the opportunity to remind Edwin Morgan that he had been instrumental in the publication of the first poems of mine to appear nationally.

7. Edwin Morgan and Angus Martin in conversation at the Scottish Arts Council Spring Book Awards in Edinburgh, 1991. Photograph by Antonia Reeve Photography.

8. *Twenty-five years later, L-R Douglas Dunn, Matthew Griffiths and Angus Martin at the StAnza poetry festival, St Andrews, 3 March 2016. Photograph by Bill Henderson.*

Scottish Poetry 4

'Profile' and 'Hallowe'en' were accepted for *Scottish Poetry 4* in 1968, when I was 16 years old. Earlier in the year, on 31 October, I'd hitch-hiked to Oban with a sheaf of poems to show to Iain Crichton Smith, one of the finest Scottish writers of his generation, and prolific both in Gaelic and in English. I managed to find out where he lived – in Combie Street – and arrived at his door without warning, not a considerate way to treat anyone likely to be striving to reconcile creativity with full-time work. What he made of me and my juvenilia I will never know, but he was considerate enough to suggest I try *Scottish Poetry* with some poems, and gave me a spare copy of the third anthology, which he signed.

As 'A. S. Martin', I sent off some poems and was thrilled to receive a note from one of the editors, Edwin Morgan, saying

46

that two had been accepted. Recently, I found in a box of old papers the 'advice' from the University of Edinburgh, dated 14 December 1968, which accompanied a cheque for £4 4s – the first money I ever earned from writing, and at 16 years old too!

These *Scottish Poetry* anthologies were quite the nicest poetry books I have ever seen: compact, hard-covered and beautifully designed. I lost my copy of number 4 many years ago, but in 2010 was given one by someone who knew I was looking for a replacement, and I marvelled at the company I'd kept: George Mackay Brown, Tom Buchan, Douglas Dunn, Robin Fulton, Robert Garioch, Alan Jackson, Norman MacCaig, Hugh MacDiarmid, Edwin Morgan, Iain Crichton Smith ... enough said!

A visit to Iain Crichton Smith in 1969

The following year, on 11 October, I was in Oban with a bus load of Campbeltown Grammar School football and hockey teams, and, after their games against Oban High School had been played, I went off on my own to visit Crichton Smith again. In my diary, written up that night, I reassure myself that I 'didn't barge in on him', and entered his flat 'only on his assurance that I wasn't likely to disturb him by staying to talk'; but I had again turned up at his door uninvited.

He showed me in and we sat together at an electric bar heater. As happened on my earlier visit, he immediately asked what books I had with me. The answer was a manual on shorthand – I was then junior reporter on the *Campbeltown Courier* – and F. Scott Fitzgerald's *Tender is the Night*. I found him 'a very easy person to tune into – very friendly and interested in one's own comparatively unimportant activities. That's not to say he won't discuss his own work – he can & does, with conviction and sometimes surprising candour'.

He spoke enthusiastically about 'the Silent Film era', and mentioned he had bought a television set solely to watch *The*

Golden Silents, a BBC series Michael Bentine presented in 1969 and '70. I glanced around the room and saw the set, 'brand-new and very stylish and modern'. He fetched a large, lined ledger-like book, in which poems were written in block letters, and read one of them aloud. I couldn't make out a lot of what he said, but when he finished the poem, he explained that it took its inspiration from television. Actors walking resembled 'ghosts nearing the Styx', and, when he switched off his set, 'he imagined the shrinking and eventually disappearing figures as ghosts departing the world'. He mentioned that the BBC producer Douglas Eadie had visited him and proposed that some Scottish poets 'should have film technicians put at their disposal and be allowed to make a film, rather on ad-lib lines'.

Turning to literature, he asked me how I rated the talents of Stewart Conn, Norman MacCaig, Tom Buchan, Douglas Dunn and David Fergus. My responses aren't on record – I doubtless knew little about some of them and nothing about others – but when he asked me which English-language poet outside of Scotland I most admired, my answer was Robert Lowell, and I discovered that he too considered 'The Quaker Graveyard in Nantucket' a masterpiece.

He mentioned a first detective story which he had written and was revising in the expectation that his publisher, Gollancz, would accept it for publication. He had recently been in the offices of the *Glasgow Herald* and had suggested casually that, as he was reading a lot of detective fiction, the newspaper might consider sending him review copies of newly-published novels in the genre. He had received 'eight or so' titles the previous week and 'read them and wrote up the review in two days'.

It may have been during that visit that Crichton Smith, an inspirational English teacher in Oban High, told me he had written his first novel, *Consider the Lilies*, during a summer holiday. A novel written in six weeks – I could hardly believe it! But he confessed that he was too prolific for his own liking and would prefer to produce less work, if less would mean higher quality, and he clearly believed it would. He seemed to consider his facility with language a handicap in his pursuit of excellence.

We corresponded for years and I kept his scrawled letters, imagining that one day they'd be published as *Letters to a Young Poet*, but years later they were all buried in the town dump at the Durry, along with hundreds of letters from other writers, some famous then, some still famous, and some now forgotten. This is how that personal calamity came about. I'd been sorting through piles of letters one night, separating the special from the ordinary and packing them into bin-bags. I left the bags outside my bedroom door, intending to move them into the loft for safekeeping when I rose in the morning, but, by a cruel chance, next morning was also when the Crosshill Avenue rubbish was collected, and my mother, assuming the bags held what they were designed to hold, left them out for the 'bin men'. By the time I woke, they were in the back of the 'freighter'. I 'phoned the Town Council offices in a frantic state, hoping my bags with their precious contents might somehow be retrieved, but was told I was too late.

In January 1974 I dreamt about receiving a letter from Crichton Smith. It consisted of several pages, but he had written only one of the pages and I didn't know who had written the others. There was writing on the back of the envelope, too: 'If I were a spoon, I'd cream your mind.'

A few extracts from real Crichton Smith letters survive as transcripts in diaries, and this is one of them, dated 23 October 1969: 'Poetry is a funny thing: one takes a step forward and a few back. For a long time, I was writing trash and then I'd write one good poem. But, there's no doubt about it. In your case it's worth persevering. I like very very much the last verse in "The Way the Wind Blows". Only a poet could have written it. Keep at it.'

The *Scottish Poetry* anthologies

'The Way the Wind Blows' would appear in *Scottish Poetry 6*. I'd forgotten where the poem was published until I saw a copy of the anthology in a Glasgow charity shop, saw that I was in it, and bought it. As usual, I pitched time and place into the future in the hope that the record might interest someone, even – or especially – me. From the flyleaf, I see that the date was 24 November 2011 and that Judy and I attended, that evening, Scottish PEN's annual Naomi Mitchison Memorial Lecture at Glasgow University, Denise Mina the speaker. The event was poorly attended, but among the audience we recognised and spoke to Campbeltown-born author Moira Burgess, herself a Mitchison scholar.

Re-reading the poem forty years later, I was unmoved, as I knew I would be. It seemed a mere procession of dead words across the page. During that earliest creative phase, from about 1967 to '73, I enjoyed a remarkable facility with language. Poems poured out of me, two and three a day, for weeks at a time, but, as I judged later, they were deficient in maturity of vision, juvenilia in other words. Yet, dozens were published, many of them by Robert Nye, poetry editor of *The Week-end Scotsman*, a distinguished critic and a poet himself. He would promote my poetry again, in the mid-1980s, when I resumed the practice after a break of ten years; the front page of *The Scotsman*'s week-end supplement of 23 August 1986 was devoted entirely to a spread of my poems, with accompanying photographs, a compliment I'd forgotten had been paid to me until a friend, Jim Macmaster, reminded me of it and I looked for and found a copy of the newspaper. By then I was 'Angus Martin', but looking back to my earliest phase, it's as though these poems were written by someone else, whose vision I no longer recognised or valued; and so they were – his name was A. S. Martin.

Recently, in a diary of 1972, I found the transcript of a letter from a girlfriend with whom I had an especially troubled relationship. It was so troubled, and the troubles so uncomfortably unresolved, that I still revisit the bombed landscape of our war, looking for, and finding, shining memories of *détente*. When an emotional legacy is overwhelmingly dark, it's easy to miss the little lingering stars which signal 'happy times'. She was a student at Edinburgh University at the time: 'Dear Angus – I've been looking for books for an essay on *Paradise Lost* and I noticed a girl carrying *Scottish Poetry 2*. On further search I discovered *Scottish Poetry* Vols. 1-6. Have you seen the new one? I like your poem about the wind in it. I feel fierce pride and a wave of absurdity at the thought that you may be, and probably are, studied in this establishment. Finding the poems, I felt hope for everything and ridicule for the stupid academics with their Ph.Ds. in this and that ...'

17 April: Largiebaan

This was a perfect spring day – calm and sunny – in a week of such days, and Judy fancied accompanying me to Largiebaan by bike. We set off at 12.15, but immediately encountered problems. One of the gear cables on her bike had snapped months earlier and hadn't been repaired, and when Eddie Kerr cycled passed us with ease near the Flush, I shouted after him: 'Can you give us a tow, Eddie?' Judy's bike was seriously underperforming, and so, to be honest, was she; she hadn't done much cycling all winter and was out of condition, and she'd already put in several hours of strenuous gardening while I was lying in bed. Mid-way along the Homestone road, we agreed that Largiebaan was no longer feasible for both of us, so we parted. I carried on, while she spent an hour on Cnoc nan Gabhar, 'Hill of the Goats', enjoying the peace and the extensive views. I left my bike, as usual, at Glenahanty, and walked without a break to the cliffs and sat near to where I'd been two days earlier, but this time with a view across the Big Corrie to the Aignish.

Lesser celandines and primroses

I was surrounded, where I sat, by the lovely yellow stars of lesser celandine (*Ficaria verna*). On that coast, it is both the earliest of the spring flowers and the most abundant. I opened my copy of the New Observer's *Wild Flowers* (p 1) to see what dates and locations I'd noted, and found, for 17 April 2011, the following: 'Inneans Glen carpeted and also coast north. With Judy.' It was four years to the day since I'd written that note and I felt a pang of sadness that Judy wasn't with me to share the botany, and the beauty, of Largiebaan. Four years earlier, 'The strongest impression of the day was the carpets of lesser celandine brightening the slopes of the glen, their yellow, however, when one would look closely, frequently mixed with the blue of dog violet, the other most abundant spring flower.'[28]

The earlier Latin name for lesser celandine was *Chelidonium minus* – from Greek *chelidon*, a swallow – 'bycause that it beginneth to springe and to flowre at the coming of the swallow', as Rembert Dodoens (in Henry Lyte's translation) explained in 1578. Coincidentally, that very day I saw my first swallow of the year, flying over the cliffs, though it was some weeks later than the celandines. An earlier popular name for the flower, 'Pilewort', identifies its 'rootes and graines' as a supposed cure for haemorrhoids, 'which being often bathed with the juice mixed with wine, or with the sick man's urine, are drawne togither and dried up, and the paine quite taken away'.[29] I could have been doing with a concoction of the same, when, at the end of my journey home, I eased myself off the saddle of my bike!

While sitting looking at the Aignish, half-a-mile to the north, I noticed a splash of yellow. I trained my binoculars on the spot and saw a patch of flowers, and when I scanned other grassy facets of the cliffs I saw that they too were speckled with the same flowers, thousands of them. They could only be primroses (*Primula vulgaris*), but so many there? I was silly to doubt the evidence of my own eyes, but I wanted to be sure, and, after finishing lunch, I set off across the Big Corrie, scree-hopping my way towards the Aignish, until I was close enough to confirm the identification. The primrose was one of five species I found in the corrie, the others being lesser celandine, common dog violet, wood sorrel and purple saxifrage. I was back on the top an hour later, at 6 p.m., and home at 8.15, good going for me.

At Largiebaan, I saw my first wheatear of the spring (Jimmy MacDonald beat me by a month) as well as my first swallow, and on my way there saw my first warbler, a willow, in a tree below Gartnacopaig. As I looked at it through binoculars, it leapt from its branch to snatch a big meandering fly out of the air, and I reflected on how suddenly a life can be ended.

20 April: Largiebaan

I was back at Largiebaan with Judy three days later. We took the 1 p.m. bus to Machrihanish and walked there by the Kintyre Way. Two days previously, Jimmy and Katrina MacDonald had sat above the Inneans Bay, at the road-marking boulder on Beinn na Faire,[30] and watched a white-tailed eagle for about twenty minutes. Jimmy described 'an absolutely huge bird', which appeared to be about two years old. These eagles, which were exterminated in Scotland and then reintroduced, have been extending their range southwards and are being seen increasingly off the west coast of Kintyre. Will a pair ultimately nest near the Mull? Local ornithologists doubtless hope so; shepherds may be less enthused by the prospect. Neither Judy nor I has ever seen a white-tailed eagle and we were hoping that the bird Jimmy watched might still be around, but if it was we didn't see it. In fact, bird sightings were strangely few that day. Even the scrounging raven failed to appear.

Certainly, I sat in a different spot that day with Judy, but the raven's all-seeing eyes would have spotted us anywhere in that vast terrain, and perhaps intuited that two humans might mean even more food. The slog from Innean Mòr up to the Aignish took us an hour, by which time we were ready for a rest and a cup of coffee. I'd planned to occupy my usual spot, but as we were descending the ridge to reach it, I noticed a grassy hollow just below the ridge and we decided we'd sit there instead. The breeze was strong, but when we dropped below the ridge, its force diminished.

The place seemed familiar, and I remembered, after looking around me for a few minutes, that I'd sat there with Murdo MacDonald, Sandy McMillan and my daughter Amelia, and that we saw flowers which none of us recognised. I had been scanning the terrain with binoculars and happened to notice specks of colour on a rock face no great distance to the north. I told Judy about having been there before and who was with me and that we'd met with a strange flower, but I couldn't remember the name of it. Several days later I found an account of that day. The date was 21 March 2012 and the flower was purple saxifrage, already discussed on p 18.

Sandy photographed some of the flowers and e-mailed the images to me. When I forwarded them to Agnes Stewart, she responded as follows: 'I was amazed the first time I saw it. It was some years ago on a dullish day, when it seemed almost to shout out at me from the rocks near the top of the Big Corrie. The *Flora of Kintyre* mentions it being at The Gap, or near The Gap, but although I have looked, I have never seen it there.' Had I remembered the flower's identity, that day with Judy, I'd have gone across to the rock face and looked for it. I went back on 1 May, as recounted below, but saw no sign of it, and when I checked other locations I found the plants withered.

We left the cliffs at 6.50 and walked the Homestone road, reaching Auchencorvie with about ten minutes to spare before the last bus from Southend appeared just before 10 p.m. To our surprise, the driver, Gordon Duncan, said he'd been watching for us on the road, because Jackie Morrison, the driver of the bus which took us to Machrihanish, had told him of our plans for the day. That's what I call service!

1 May: Largiebaan

I set off for Largiebaan by bike. I was in a busy time, with commitments pressing – such is 'retirement'! – but decided

I had to get away, and the weather forecast for that day was good. But when I paused on a bend of the brae past Lochorodale to remove the thick jersey I was wearing, I noticed that the Arran mountains were snow-topped, and felt a coolness in the easterly breeze catching me there.

Shortly afterwards, at 2 p.m., I heard my first cuckoo of 2015 and congratulated myself on having been granted the assurance of another year of life ... well, maybe! I normally hear the first call in the last week of April, but owing to commitments which kept me indoors, and the generally poor weather that week, I hadn't been anywhere a cuckoo was likely to be. I'd heard cuckoo reports, however: the first was Dugald McKendrick, Glenramskill, on 21 April, Allister Stewart on the 25th, at Corrylach, and his wife Agnes on the day after at Auchenhoan.

Australian 'Footballer of the Year'

I hadn't gone far along the Glenahanty road when I saw a man sitting in a quarry up ahead. 'I see you've taken the easy way!' he called to me. I dismounted and at once met the challenge, arguing that there was nothing 'easy' about pushing a bike up long hills, and adding that I'd be on foot from Glenahanty to the Largiebaan cliffs, and back. Doubtless it was a 'wind-up', and it worked! The joker was Tommy MacPherson, a keen walker whom I see occasionally in remote places. Now in his mid-seventies, he is still going strong. As I do at times, he uses local bus timetables to plan his walks. On that day, he had gone to Southend on the 12.00 bus, walked through Glen Breackerie, and would catch the bus back to Campbeltown at 4.25 from Auchencorvie.

I can't claim to know Tommy well, but, in common with most local football enthusiasts, I do know that he was once Australian 'Footballer of the Year'. It's an interesting story. He worked in Argyll Colliery at Machrihanish after he left school, and played, with distinction, for the local junior side, Drumlemble. After moving to Glasgow in 1960, to work as a fitter at Dalmarnock Power Station, he played with such junior clubs as Bellshill Athletic and Blantyre Victoria. After three years in Glasgow, however, Tommy decided to emigrate.

Soon after he sailed, his father noticed an advertisement placed in a Scottish weekly newspaper by a Melbourne football club, George Cross, which was seeking to recruit players. Tommy Snr. replied to the advertisement, enclosing newspaper cuttings – Tommy had trials with senior clubs Kilmarnock and Berwick Rangers – and when his son arrived in Australia, he was met 'at the boat' by representatives of George Cross, who offered him not only signing-on terms, but also several jobs to choose from. 'He eagerly accepted and quickly became a mainstay in the team with some brilliant play at left half.' After sixty games for the club, his honours included an Australian Cup-winner's medal and, of course, Australian 'Footballer of the Year', 1965.[31]

Early purple orchid

Purple saxifrage had departed, but there was another purple-named flower out. The wind was north-westerly, and I knew that finding a sheltered corner would be difficult. I tried the customary hollow under the cliff top, but couldn't settle there and decided to follow the top down a bit until I found a more satisfactory retreat. That's when I saw the early purple orchid, a single flower tucked in below the top of the cliff. It wasn't 'purple', though; it was more scarlet, and so bold in appearance that its function seemed to be to announce the species' presence there. I looked down and saw a few more in scree, but there weren't many, and half-a-dozen was the total for the day. It looked decidedly exotic out there on that rocky coast, and I mused later that 'If it grew there in concentrations, like mats of bluebells, it would be an absolute marvel on the cliffs'. These were the first orchids of any kind I'd seen that year. (I was on the Largiebaan cliffs, with Murdo MacDonald and Jimmy MacDonald, four years to the day, 1 May 2011, when early purple orchids provided our 'most interesting observation' of the visit.[32])

I looked for *Orchis mascula* in *The Flora of Kintyre* and found (p 45) that 'A beautiful pink variant has been seen at Largybaan'. In botany, not only does colour vary in some species, but also botanists' perception or description of colour, and illustrated guides don't always help, since colours, when printed, don't necessarily appear true to nature, which takes the meditation back, I suppose, to individual perception. Yes, I am confused, but I'll stick with 'scarlet'!

Three days later, I met Agnes Stewart at the Wee Wud at Glenramskill. As I approached on my bike, she was standing in the road gazing into the wood, admiring, as I well knew, its fine unfailing display of marsh marigolds and wood anemones. While we were discussing the orchids I'd seen at Largiebaan, I remembered I had my little camera with me, containing photographs of the flowers. As I showed them to her, I suddenly recalled that we'd already discussed *Orchis mascula*, after Judy identified them on the verge of the Moss Road near the airport. I was sure that outing on the bikes must have been two, maybe even three years before, but when I checked my journals the date was 12 June 2014 – less than a year!

This orchid was a legendary aphrodisiac, and Geoffrey Grigson in *The Englishman's Flora*, first published in 1958, remarked that 'love potions' were being made from it in Shetland and Ireland 'until recently'. Doubtless its properties were also known in Kintyre, and perhaps it was the aphrodisiac of choice in a little story I recorded in 1977 from Calum Bannatyne, a retired shepherd who would have heard it in Strone from Mrs Archibald Todd, who was Agnes MacNeill, a member of the Gaelic-speaking family in Amod (p 14).

A girl in Glen Breackerie had a notion on a ploughman and brewed a concoction which she took to him disguised as tea. The belief, Calum explained, was that 'if ye could make a tea o' this ... an' get the man tae drink it, he wid make love tae ye'. This girl, who was seventeen years old, took the brew to the man while he was ploughing, and subsequently had a son to him. Calum, however, had a rational interpretation of the tale: 'But it wis quite easy tae see it. If you wir offered tea an' tasted this taste o' "tea", ye knew damnt well there wis somethin' in it. If she wis tryin' that on ye, what wid ye do on her? Ye wid say, "All right, here ye are, here goes". Widn't ye?'[33]

I had admired these early purple orchids, but my interest went no further than the aesthetic. For previous generations, the interest was different. A plant might be admired, but the main question would be whether it was edible or otherwise useful. Our forebears, and not so far back, at that, often went hungry, which explains the recurrent deaths, of children especially, from eating poisonous roots and berries. I have never wondered, when looking at orchids, what the part of the plant underground might look like, but Geoffrey Grigson knew:

> Dig up an Early Purple Orchid and you find two root-tubers in which food is stored, a new, firm one, which is filling up for next year's growth, [and] an old, slack one which is emptying and supplying the present needs. The symbolism of the kinds of *Orchis* with undivided tubers could hardly be overlooked. Sympathetic magic made them venereal, for which there was support even in the sober Dioscorides, spring-head of all wisdom in the *scientia scientarum* of botany. Orchis meant 'testicle'.[34]

Grigson has a lot more to say on the subject, but I'll turn now to his long list of local names, which itself testifies to the past importance of the plant. There are almost a hundred of them, from all over the British Isles, not including Gaelic names, which he omits. The list goes from Aaron's beard to wake Robin, with many strange and poetic forms in between, such as adder's mouths, bloody bones, fried candlesticks, kettle-cap, poor man's blood, soldier's jacket and underground shepherd. Grigson is hard to catch out, but I believe he is mistaken in one of his interpretations. 'Puddock's spindles', he says, is a Perthshire name meaning 'kite's legs',[35] but in Scots a 'puddock' is a frog or toad and 'spindle' is surely just that – the stick which held the spun wool or flax in hand-spinning. Significantly, one of the Gaelic names for the early purple orchid is *cuigeal-an-losgainn*, 'the frog's distaff', another allusion to spinning.

Another of the Gaelic names for the early purple orchid, *clachan-ghadhair*, is literally 'hound stones', but means 'hound testicles', a reference to the dual tubers; 'dog stones', which Grigson recorded from Somerset, has the same sense. There is a certain aptness in the name, because I was bitten by a dog that day on my outward journey. The dog in question wasn't of the *gadhar* type – a lurcher or greyhound-foxhound cross – but a collie, which attacked in true collie fashion, from behind and with a bite to the back of the leg. Its teeth penetrated thick corduroy and long johns, punctured my skin and caused me pain for days afterwards. A kick in the stones, had I been able to catch my assailant, might have been just retribution, but that wouldn't be me.

I didn't find out until much later that George McSporran and his son Sandy were in the hills not far from me on 1 May. They walked up Glenadale from Glen Breackerie and joined the Kintyre Way, which took them on to Amod Hill.

7 May: a fish-trap at Smerby

I wrote about fish-traps in a book for the National Museums of Scotland, *Fishing and Whaling*, published in 1995, but I didn't realise until 2013 that there was one a few miles from Campbeltown, at Smerby. I must have passed it often while wood-gathering on that shore and failed to notice it; but there isn't much to notice. The defining feature is a stone barrier built across a rocky inlet north of the ruined castle. Its function seemed obvious: to trap in the ebbing tide any fish which had swum in with the flood tide. These are the notes I made on 13 September 2013: '2nd bay N of castle – tidal enclosure – yair? – but not much area within the trap, if it is so – landward side is natural rock outcrops – seaward side has some natural rock, but at N end stones have been fitted in by hand – between the two, and running W-E, is a low barrier of rocks built there – photographs taken.' A few days later, I contacted Frances Hood, Kintyre's leading amateur archaeologist, to report my discovery. To my surprise, she had already identified the trap, and written up a report on it for an archaeological journal.

'Yair' is Scots for a fish-trap; in Gaelic the standard term is *cairidh*, which George Campbell Hay recorded in Tarbert. Hugh MacFarlane, my main source of knowledge in Tarbert when I was researching *The Ring-Net Fishermen*, didn't give me that Gaelic word, though he may have known it, but he mentioned in June 1973 the remains of a stone fish-trap in Bàgh mu Dheas, the south bay at Barmore Island.

Traps constructed of wattle – interlaced rods and twigs – would not survive, but a stone structure would, especially if looked after, as was the case at Loch a' Chumhainn on the west side of Mull. A fish-trap there is described by C. R. Wickham-Jones, in *The Landscapes of Scotland* (pp. 74-75), as 'in a particularly good state of repair', a condition she attributes to its having been 'maintained over the centuries by successive generations of one local family'. As to the antiquity of that fish-trap, and, by implication, fish-traps in general, she allows that it could 'reach back into prehistory'.

The concept of the fish-trap is particularly suited to narrow sea-lochs and other coastal inlets, of which, in Kintyre, there are relatively few. The one at Smerby utilised a natural reef parallel to the shore, and the entrapment area is small. What kinds of fish might it have caught? The answer is, just about any species found in the Kilbrannan Sound. A shoal of herring might occasionally swim close inshore or be driven in by predators, but the fish most likely to find themselves trapped would be flatfish and members of the cod family, such as saithe and pollack. These would be small fish as a rule, but there would doubtless be occasional big surprises.

In the eighteenth century, fish-traps in the Clyde estuary were condemned for their wastefulness, when too many herring were caught for the local population to eat or preserve, or immature fish were needlessly destroyed. Fish-traps certainly had to be tended, tide after tide if possible. If left unchecked, any fish stranded when the tide ebbed could be picked off by gulls and other opportunists, as well as by humans without any proprietorial interest in the trap but none the less tempted by a free meal.

A 1938 newspaper report on a 'new paddling pool' on the shore of Campbeltown Loch illustrated the principle of the fish-trap. This man-made pool – not the land-locked one which gave the name 'Paddling Pool' to the now-obsolete children's play-park at Kilkerran – had 'marooned' a shoal of immature herrings and also a sea trout, which latter probably ended up in someone's pot. Agnes Stewart recalled that paddling-pool, which was located where the concrete ramp slopes to the foreshore from the Promenade. She was taken there as a child, in the summer of 1942 or '43, and remembered it as '... all stones, and not the best place to paddle, but it's not a great problem when you are very young'.[36]

On 10 March 2016, just as I was finishing this book, an example of natural entrapment presented itself not half-a-mile north of the Smerby fish-trap ... or so I thought for about an hour! When I settled myself on the shore in late afternoon sunshine, I noticed dozens of busy gulls – most of them common – close inshore as the tide ebbed. They were diving into the sea and coming out with what appeared to be small fish in their beaks. I narrowed the prey possibilities to sand-eels, but decided I ought to attempt a positive identification before I left. It was just as well, because when I made my way to the water's edge I discovered that the gulls' prey was not fish at all, but beautiful blue frilly ragworms, swimming with a slow undulating motion. They must have been in their thousands in that expanse of draining water, and the ones I watched finally burrowed for cover in the seabed, which was a mixture of stones and sand. I'd never before seen even one ragworm, so it was an exceptional experience.

Finally: by whom would the Smerby fish-trap have been managed and maintained? The question is impossible to answer, but there must be a possibility that it was built for the use of the medieval castle-dwellers.

Little observations

Between visiting the fish-trap and the site of Smerby Castle, on 7 May, I sat for an hour-and-a-half on the shore to the north. I had difficulty finding a spot out of the wind, but finally settled on a flattish rock sheltered by a higher rock. I expunged from my mind human history and its episodic savagery,[37] and opened it to the nature of the coast: the rooted flowers and the birds that came and went as I watched and listened.

As I settled on to my chosen rock, I noticed the tiniest colony imaginable of English stonecrop (*Sedum anglicum*): three minute pink flowers growing from a crack in the mica schist. I was anxious to avoid harming them and was very careful in my movements. Before leaving, I took a few close-up photographs of the flowers, and when I looked at them later I noticed crumbs from my sandwich lying alongside the flowers, and the crumbs were bigger.

A seal came close inshore to look at me. The tide was just about full in, so the seal was no great distance from me, in water so shallow I could have comfortably waded out to it through the floating bladder-wrack. It was staring at me, and, since seals are supposed to be fascinated by music, I decided to whistle to it. I was broadcasting tuneless nonsense until I reasoned that my friend in the water might prefer a proper tune. After a few seconds' thought, Robin Williamson's lovely 'October Song' somehow emerged as my choice, but the seal was not noticeably impressed and swam away.

A sedge warbler appeared in a tree behind me and began delivering his repertoire of borrowed song-snatches, all run together and repeated over and over with rapidity and passion. I felt privileged to be listening to a little songster who had transported his magical sounds, boxed in a tiny brain, all the way from Africa. From time to time, in the background, a blackbird piped up with his unhurried notes. For years, I avowed a preference for the sedge warbler's music over the blackbird's, but now I believe the two can't be compared on equal terms – the blackbird's is 'classical' and the warbler's 'jazz'.

9 May: The Inneans

My daughter Amelia was home from Glasgow for the weekend and receptive to my suggestion of a hike. Her friend, Lucas Mati, came along, and, since he has a car, the walk started at Ballygroggan, thus eliminating the slog up Lossit brae from the bus terminus at Lossit Gate. When we arrived at the Kintyre Way car-park at Ballygroggan, there was a car already there, a black Audi which was identical to Lucas's, an odd coincidence in such an isolated spot, I thought. The car belonged to Gary Anderson, Lucas said, and we watched for him throughout the afternoon, but the only person we saw in seven hours was a middle-aged man, in the Inneans Glen, who ignored us. He was heading up as we were heading down. He had a small rucksack on his back and stopped occasionally to look at some distant object. While he was watching something, or nothing, through his binoculars, I was watching him through mine, but failed to recognise him and guessed he might be an intense ornithologist. (A few days later, I happened to meet Gary Anderson at Glenramskill and asked him where he had gone that Sunday. The answer was Craigaig, with his girlfriend and dog.)

Soon after the frigid encounter, we left the Kintyre Way and crossed on to the opposite side of the glen to sit at the boulder marking the northward turn of the old road,[38] since 2012 a favourite resting place of mine if the descent into the

Inneans Bay, or, more to the point, the climb back out, doesn't appeal. I sat there for the first time on 15 May 2012, with Jimmy MacDonald and Amelia, during a circular walk which took us from Glenahanty to the Largiebaan cliffs, and from there across the Inneans Glen up to the boulder, and back to Glenahanty through Gleann Eadar da Chnoc. That day, I photographed Amelia sitting at the boulder and was certain I had a decent image, but when I looked at the developed slide I was astonished to see that it comprised two near-identical images side-by-side – an accidental double exposure. I got my photograph almost three years later, when the two figures in the image were not Amelia, but Amelia and Lucas, with the boulder in the background.

The sun broke out for about ten minutes after we arrived, lighting up Cnoc Moy, at 1462 feet the second-highest hill in Kintyre. From where we sat, its whole north-facing aspect was right in front of us, with only the very summit out of sight. Amelia remarked admiringly on the 'turquoise' of the sun-illumined undersea sand-patch in the Inneans Bay. Soon afterwards, when the sun disappeared behind cloud, she remarked on the slanting rain-showers distant over the Atlantic, and as we walked north to Craigaig, we were caught in a couple of them.

11-12 June 1983: Sleeping rough

Between the Inneans and Earadale Point, we passed the location of my only overnight camp on that coast without a tent, but we were too high, on the old track, to see it. I cycled out the Homestone road on 11 June 1983 with provisions and equipment. (Looking back on those camping trips in the 1980s, I wonder how I could be bothered lugging the stuff I did for what was rarely more than a night's stay.) This time, however, I had left my little blue tent at home and decided to rely instead on a survival-bag Teddy Lafferty had given me. Teddy, with his mountaineering background, was familiar with these bags, which, as their name suggests, are designed for use in emergencies, for example if detained by extreme weather in the hills. Since the bag was made from plastic – orange-coloured for visibility – it rolled up into a compact bundle which took up little room in a rucksack. In certain conditions, a survival-bag might indeed by the difference between life and death, but it's no substitute for a sleeping-bag, as I later found out.

9. *Teddy Lafferty and Eileen Denney in evening sunlight near Gleneadardacrock, 13 August 1983. The background hillside in the north has been ploughed for tree-planting. Photograph by the author.*

I jump now from 11 June 1983 to 13 August 1983. An American, Eileen Denney, had come to Campbeltown for a few days during a tour of Europe, and I suggested a night's camping at the Inneans. I took my tent with me, but had only one sleeping-bag, my own, which I gallantly gave to Eileen, deciding I could make do with the survival-bag. It was a mistake; I should have borrowed another sleeping-bag. I have no written record of that trip, but I remember a night of misery, freezing inside that plastic bag, while Eileen slept soundly at my side. I'd reckoned, before we set out, that since it was summer I'd be fine, but I discovered that, under clear starry skies, summer nights can be very cold. I have a few photographs from that trip, including a couple taken near Gleneadardacrock where, quite by chance, we met Teddy heading back from the Inneans as we were heading out.

It's 11 June 1983 again, and, as Glenahanty came into sight, heavy rain began falling. I sheltered inside one of the old houses there and contemplated turning back, but the rain passed and I decided to continue. As I approached Gleneadardacrock ruin, the rain returned. This time it was heavier and lasted longer. Since the ruin is roofless, I squeezed into the fire-place, trying to make myself comfortable and at the same time keep my legs dry, and listening to raindrops tinkling musically as they hit the old cooking pots lying about on the floor. When the rain finally stopped, I resumed the hike and reached the Inneans before dark.

The place I selected for my bed was to the north of the bay, 'the hard grassy base of a rock overhang up among boulders'. I'd be lying – inside both sleeping-bag and survival-bag – across a goat-track, and I noticed that goats had been using that very spot for shelter. Gulls, presumably from the nesting sites on the Stacs to the north, were 'making a continual clamour', some of them 'flying backwards and forwards, telling me off'. I was about 60 feet above the shore, and the surf, which I'd heard long before I reached the coast, was loud. I had no doubt I'd find sleep difficult, and one 'bang' startled me just as I sat to fill in my journal at 10.54 p.m. Fifteen minutes later, there was still sufficient light in the west by which to write. By then, I was seeing the flashing of Balnacarry lighthouse on Rathlin and the lights of a coaster, close in and heading north. Before I closed my journal, I noted that my feet were wet and that I'd changed my socks, and finally: 'Windier now, and ... the appearance of these big black clouds in the west is ominous. I trust – and hope – there won't be too much rain.'

There wasn't any rain that night, but neither was there much sleep for me: 'The crashing of the waves all last night was like thunder, which had to be heard to be credited.' I overslept that morning, 'slept in while sleeping out', as I remarked in the journal. When I rose at 8, the sun hadn't yet reached into my lair, but I'd realised there was a 'magnificent' day awaiting me, and wasn't long getting out of my bags. 'I am most fortunate,' I exulted in my journal. 'The great spirit of the place has once more blessed my presence.'

Breakfast, cooked in the bay, consisted of baked beans and scrambled eggs, made with milk, margarine and finely chopped seaweed. After I'd eaten, I walked back north to the Stacs, two high, tooth-like rocks below Earadale Point. I climbed the northernmost one and quickly took a couple of photographs of fledged herring gulls. I was surprised by how relatively few chicks there were that year; just five that I could find, and a nest with three unhatched eggs in it. I noticed, with interest, the legs of baby rabbits scattered at the nests, which confirmed that herring gulls habitually catch and kill young rabbits.

In the Inneans Bay, in June of the previous year, I watched, with my nephews Malcolm and Donald Docherty, a gull swoop on a young rabbit and kill it. The bird took ten minutes to despatch the rabbit, which it then swallowed whole. None of us was moved to intercede. As I remarked in *Kintyre: The Hidden Past* (p 167): 'We were mere spectators in the world of the victim and the predator; we had eaten; the gull, too, had to eat; and the poor rabbit, in the order of nature, had to die.' I'll add here that interference with natural predation can have unwanted consequences: by the time one has scared off the predator, its prey might already be wounded, and the 'saviour' is left with a creature whose dying has been agonisingly prolonged.

When I returned to the bay, I lay in my sleeping-bag and managed about ninety minutes' sleep, interrupted by rain. I thought the shower would pass quickly, so I turned over and decided to sleep more, but a greater flurry started and I had to heave myself out of the sleeping-bag to get my camera and matches under cover.

Before I left the bay, I was visited by a dozen stirks and heifers, which I'd seen grazing on An Cirein the previous evening. The first intimation of their arrival was the sudden scattering of the sheep which had been grazing unconcerned quite close to me. The cattle made straight for my camp. At first, though curious, they were very wary of me, but they gradually edged closer, though none would lick the hand I offered. They began to investigate everything, nosing round the fire, in the kettle, poking at driftwood, sniffing the rucksack, and one of them even had a drink of beer I'd left unfinished in a cup. I went on to the shore to gather seaweed, but, seeing the beasts getting stuck into a bag, I hurried back to the camp and found that they had eaten half of my brown loaf and covered the rest in 'slevers'. I threw them the remains of the bread, which they picked up and chewed. Soon after they left me, to huddle together at the south end of the bay, I tried to light a fire to brew tea, but gave up and settled instead for a drink of milk. Then I packed my gear and headed out.

1966: 'Tiger' falls

I am back in 9 May 2015 with Amelia and Lucas, on the coast between Earadale and Craigaig, but not for long. Somewhere around there, in 1966, Malcolm Hamilton was badly injured in a fall and had to be stretchered two miles to Ballygroggan. This happened the year before my first trip to the Inneans,[39] where Malcolm and his brother Stewart were camped at the time of the accident, but I didn't hear about it until the early 1980s, by which time it had been embroidered into the fabric of Inneans lore. The stories I heard were sketchy and unreliable, and I had to wait until 2015, when I chanced on a report of the accident, to meet with a factual account. The accident happened on Sunday 11 September 1966, on the 'rock-strewn shore near Earadale

Point'. The brothers were heading for the Inneans Bay from Ballygroggan using the coastal rather than the more popular moorland route.

It was an eventful week-end on the coast. An RAF Wessex helicopter from Ballykelly in Northern Ireland had crashed into the sea off the Mull two days earlier. Two of her crew were rescued by another helicopter, but 20-year-old Samuel McGugan was missing, presumed trapped inside the aircraft as it sank. Malcolm and Stewart had been assisting Coastguards in a search for the missing man, and went to Ballygroggan farmhouse to leave a rope belonging to the Coastguard.

There were six children in the party which set off for the Inneans: Malcolm's daughter Marianne (13), son Leslie (9), Stewart's daughter Maureen (13), son Stewart (8), and two friends, Fay Martin (14) and Katrina McMillan (13). When Malcolm slipped on a steep grassy slope, he slid fifty feet, bounced off a ledge and fell ten more feet on to rocks on the shore. Stewart stayed with him while the children ran back to Ballygroggan farm for assistance. One of the shepherds there, Donald Sinclair, drove down to Machrihanish village and telephoned the emergency services.

By the time the rescue team reached the shore, after a two-mile hike over rough terrain, Malcolm was unconscious. After Dr Cameron had attended to him, the team prepared for 'the gruelling cross country return trek' to the ambulance at Ballygroggan. The stretcher was carried by ambulance men Neil MacDonald and Donald Kennedy, assisted by Police Constables D. Campbell and John McCall and Sergeant Hector MacKinnon. Malcolm, who had suffered a fractured skull and five broken ribs, was taken to the Cottage Hospital, Campbeltown, and from there transferred by air ambulance to the Southern General Hospital, Glasgow.[40] He recovered.

Malcolm was a 42-year-old miner at Argyll Colliery, Machrihanish, which would close the following year. He later worked at Campbeltown Shipyard, which itself closed after its last order was completed in 1996. He was one of a family of twelve children reared at Trodigal Cottage, Machrihanish; his father was Robert 'Bobbins' Hamilton, a fencer and drainer, and his mother was Phemie McIntyre.[41] His nick-name was 'Tiger', which I quote without hesitation, since it appears on his gravestone in Kilkerran, above the particulars of his death: died 31 January 1995, aged 71.

At the time of his accident, Malcolm and his brother Stewart had a big, roomy tent permanently pitched in the Inneans Bay, as described and illustrated in *A Summer in Kintyre* (pp. 25-26).

Sròn Gharbh

Amelia, Lucas and I stopped for ten minutes or so on Sròn Gharbh, having climbed on to it by the precipitous goat track which winds below the ridge. I was there in April 2010 with two archaeologists, one of them a vertigo sufferer, who baulked at the track. We reached the ridge by scrambling up a grassy incline, which took us a bit longer but settled the poor man's nerves.

I was concerned that Amelia might find the route intimidating, but she was relaxed throughout, and recounted, for comparison, a friend's freak-out a year before in Skye. Amelia was with four others tackling the Old Man of Storr. The path they should have been following had been erased by flooding, and an elderly couple, who were descending, advised them to go straight up a scree slope. Amelia got up all right, but one of her friends panicked, 'as it really was a sheer drop and the ground wasn't secure at all. When we eventually got to the top, which is famous for its panoramic view, it was very misty and we couldn't see a thing!'

On the ridge itself, Lucas noticed two rocks, a big one on top of a smaller one, which he immediately suggested had arrived there by human agency, and the more I looked at them, the more inclined I was to agree with him. Both glacial deposition and displacement from above came to mind as possible explanations, but the position of the rocks on the very top of the natural rock ridge, the larger one stabilised by the smaller one, tended to dispose of these theories, which left Lucas's theory. But why would anyone have gone to the trouble of lifting these rocks and placing them there? My only suggestion was, as a feat of strength, and I remembered hearing of boulders in different parts of Scotland which men would test their strength by lifting, and still do.

A holly sapling

Trees are very rare on the exposed coast between the Mull and Ballygroggan. I know of just three which are not stunted and cowering in gullies, and they are all in an area of rocky hillside between Sròn Gharbh and the burn that runs into the south end of Craigaig Bay. There are a birch and a willow, growing horizontally together out of a rock face, and a rowan. As Amelia, Lucas and I were descending towards the burn, we passed the solitary rowan, from which a nesting hooded crow flew out. (Jimmy MacDonald has told me of a 'well-grown hawthorn', which he has seen blossom in spring, on the bank of the burn that runs into Port na h-Olainn, south of Innean Gaothach.)

As we were crossing the burn, I noticed another tree, whose presence on that coast surprised me. It was holly (*Ilex aquifolium*), the first I'd ever seen out there. Madge Cunningham in *The Flora of Kintyre* (p 18), which was published back in 1979 and drew on earlier records, remarks on its absence from 'the Mull of Kintyre area' and its scarcity in south Kintyre generally. I have noticed, however, that holly has been slowly and inconspicuously colonising Ben Gullion forest during the past twenty years, though it seldom takes root in locations which promise full development. The location near Craigaig looked decidedly unpromising. The sapling is growing horizontally from the bank of the stream and if it isn't washed out in a spate, it may dislodge itself with the weight of its own growth.

1974: A painting of Earadale

I once had a watercolour of Earadale, the headland south of Sròn Gharbh, but I don't remember the painting. It wasn't framed and I pinned it to a door in my bedroom. That bedroom in 24 Crosshill Avenue is where this story begins, and I should explain that it was where friends and acquaintances often ended up after the pubs closed at 10 p.m. Looking back on my late teens and early twenties, I realise that I must have been a trial to my parents, whose bedroom was through the wall from mine. The word *inconsiderate* hardly covers it, and I recall one Hogmanay, a few years before my Father died, when my Mother took me aside and confided that he was very hurt by my habit of taking visitors straight upstairs without even introducing them. That revelation shocked and shamed me, and I made sure that, for better or worse, he met the celebratory crowd that night.

Some casual acquaintances I met in pubs would spend the night at 24 Crosshill Avenue, if they had nowhere else to go. With a scatter of pints inside me, I was hospitality personified. Entire visiting rock bands bedded down in Crosshill Avenue. One of them, I remember, was Cado Belle, which emerged in Glasgow in 1974 from the fusion of Joe Cool and Up, released the album *Cado Belle* in 1976, and disbanded two years later. Two of its members, Colin Tully and Maggie Reilly, enjoyed commercial success after the break-up. Maggie Reilly is best known for her collaborations with Mike Oldfield, and sang on 'Moonlight Shadow', which reached number 4 in the British chart in 1983. I remember that song coming on the radio in October 2003, as Judy was driving the Martin family along an *autobahn* to a holiday near the Black Forest with Hartwig and Elisabeth Schutz. When I informed my daughters that the singer they were hearing once spent a night in my house in Campbeltown their response was disappointingly cool. I also remember that Maggie Reilly went out and bought my Mother a pot-plant as a 'thank-you' for the night's accommodation. No rock star excesses with Cado Belle!

When I began researching and writing my first book, *The Ring-Net Fishermen*, in 1974, I gradually turned my back on pub culture. A former drinking companion, the late Dugald McNaughton, occasionally quoted back at me my stock remark when declining the suggestion of a night 'on the town': 'Time spent in pubs is time wasted.' After my Father's death, my Mother told me that his major anxiety for me was that I'd end up an alcoholic on street corners. The literary calling has wasted and shortened many lives, but perhaps my modest aspirations saved my life.

It's 15 January 1974 and Will Maclean's ring-net project is three months in the future. In a pub that evening I met a Grammar School teacher I'll call Donald and invited him to my room (such an invitation nowadays would probably raise suspicions of sexual intent, but back then no such interpretation applied, at least in the Campbeltown I knew). I had envisaged a lively discussion of literature and art, but what transpired was much worse than that. My guest from the outset decided that I'd taken him into my home to show off my 'prized possessions'. The trouble started when he pulled a copy of *Four Points of a Saltire* from a bookshelf. This was the book, published in 1971 by Gordon Wright, which presented a selection of poems from four Scottish poets, Sorley Maclean, George Campbell Hay, William Neill and Stuart MacGregor, and was instrumental in establishing Maclean as the foremost living poet in the Gaelic language. I had a lovely copy of Maclean's *Dain do Eimhir*, printed on blue paper with illustrations by William Crosbie, and made the mistake of showing it to Donald. I compounded that mistake by showing him an account Maclean gave me of the inspiration behind the *Dain do Eimhir* poems, written up from memory after I'd visited him at his home in Skye in 1972. This document incensed Donald, who questioned me vehemently on the source of the information and refused to listen to my explanations. I had been three pages into a letter before I went out that evening, and he accused me of having arranged the sheets of paper on my desk in order to impress visitors to the room.

When I began putting away the books we'd been looking at, muttering angrily – a clear sign that I wanted him out – he asked me to sit down. If I imagined that he meant to conciliate me, I was mistaken. He asked me, with a sneer, for my opinions on 'the status of European society'. When I finally got him out, he embraced me and thanked me, doubtless with ironic intent, and, as he opened the garden gate, my parting shot was: 'That's the last time you'll be here.' (It was.) With that, he pulled his coat over his head and disappeared into the night.

I wrote him a bitter letter that night. On my way to the post-box the next day, I decided not to post it and turned back; but I changed my mind again and sent it. I next encountered him eight days later in the Captain's Cabin. He didn't mention the letter and neither did I; I discovered later that he somehow hadn't yet received it. (When he did, he treated it as a joke.) I had arranged to meet Dr Eddie Peltenburg – now Professor Emeritus in Archaeology at the University of Edinburgh – who was at the time leading an excavation of the Iron Age hill-fort at Balloch. When I engaged him on the subject of 'bog bodies', Donald must have felt excluded, and interrupted us to deliver a scatological discourse on 'European bogs'. Then the insults began, directed at others in the company as well as me, and I offered to fight him and left the bar. When he finally emerged from the hotel and saw me waiting in readiness for combat, his only response was a comment on my hair 'blowing in a threatening way'. I ended up drinking coffee and listening to Scottish folk music and 'a Ravi Shankar raga' in his rented house in the country. There was little conversation, but he showed me his paintings, and I shook hands with him after accepting his offer of the Earadale watercolour.

My diaries of that period contain pages of analyses of Donald's behaviour. This is all that's worth quoting: 'Needs to impress people. So do I, of course.' By the mid-1970s, I had amassed a big library, which lined two walls of my bedroom, in wooden book-cases which my long-suffering father measured and sawed and assembled in his garden shed. I cannot but believe that these books were for my own pleasure and education, but Donald wasn't the only guest who saw them as evidence of intellectual pretensions: a fisherman who had left school at fifteen and had something more to prove to the world.

The late folk singer Danny Kyle confessed to me, after I'd got to know him a bit, that his first impression of the partying room at 24 Crosshill Avenue was that its occupant was a pseudo-intellectual. None the less, during one of his visits Danny borrowed my copy of Edwin Muir's *Scottish Journey*, which I never saw again and didn't replace until I picked up a copy in a charity shop in 2014, some forty years later. It's odd what one remembers. I hadn't forgotten the loaned book, yet Donald and his painting of Earadale were expunged from memory and only came back to discomfit me in the pages of an old diary.

13 May: Davaar Island

I'd been speaking to Teddy Lafferty in the Co-op two days before, while he waited for a taxi to take him and his shopping bags home, and Davaar Island entered the conversation. I must have mentioned driftwood, because Teddy said there was plenty of it on the island; then he remembered he hadn't been on Davaar Island for many years and added: 'There used to be plenty.' He was right on both counts.

When I collected George McSporran at his house in the early afternoon, a bicycle ride down the Learside, destination unknown, was on the agenda, with Davaar Island an outside option. As we approached the Doirlinn, we saw that the tide was well out and decided we'd cross. Having chained the bicycles to a fence, we set off diagonally over the sand flats towards the ruined cottage on the south side of the island. I timed the short-cut and we were on the island in fifteen minutes.

We decided to sit at the roofless cottage, known as the 'Sheep Hoose', and eat a late lunch before walking round the island. As we passed a bulky foreshore rock close to the ruin, I remarked on its association, in my memory, with Neil McEachran, who was probably the last of the dedicated island-goers. I had an image in mind, a photograph I'd taken of Neil sitting on a wooden fish-box at his camp-fire, stripped to the waist and holding an enamel mug, which he told me had accompanied his father all through the Second World War.

Neil was born on 14 September 1939, the month the war began. On 9 September 2015, while I was leaning on the harbour railings, watching the *Isle of Arran* sailing out of Campbeltown Loch, he appeared on his bike and asked about the hazel crop that year. I told him I'd heard one good report from a lady in Barr Glen, but hadn't myself looked anywhere. He said he was thinking of trying Peninver. Three days later, I saw him again on his bike and he stopped to say that he'd been to Peninver that day, and though there were nuts on the trees, there was next to nothing in them. On the Sunday, he'd mentioned he could cycle all the way to Peninver, and I asked him if he'd managed it. He had, which I thought was good-going for someone of nearly 76 years; I often dismount on High Askomil. His bike, however, with a titanium frame and hydraulic gears, is superior to mine. 'A aye said A'd get a daicent bike afore A snuffed it,' he explained.

George McSporran and I cycled to Peninver on 26 September and, unlike Neil, didn't attempt the braes. We walked the shore south to Stackie and sat there in autumnal sunshine for an hour, after which we visited Frances Hood in the village and enjoyed coffee and cake in her kitchen. As we watched several cyclists pass the window, Frances mentioned a 'test of manhood' to which, about thirty years before, some of the village boys in their early teens would subject themselves: to cycle up the hill without dismounting and then free-wheel down without touching the brakes.

21 July 1991

When I returned home from Davaar Island, I looked out the slide of Neil with his father's mug, found it was dated 21 July 1991 and then looked in my journal for that year. Judy and I had cycled to the Doirlinn with daughters Sarah and Amelia (the latter fell asleep in the bicycle seat and didn't awaken until we were almost across the Doirlinn). We found Neil and his late wife, Mary McKerral, at the camp-site, along with 'a McLean woman', a friend of theirs on holiday. She was explained to me as a sister of 'Sleepy', who had been a projectionist at the Rex Cinema. (Another cinema projectionist would appear from the past on 13 May 2015.)

Neil had a twelve-pint kettle of tea simmering on the fire. He shared it with us and we ate with him, after which he left with his fishing-rod – visible in the photograph, propped against the rock and pointing towards Sarah – to try his luck from Oitir Buidhe, the rock shelf below the lighthouse. His usual catch was 'lythe' (pollack), but, as we heard from him later, his luck was out that day.

Amelia, having seen a large party wading noisily across to the island, wanted to play in the sea, but our plan was to climb to the top, and she had to be dragged with us, resisting all the way. When we reached the trig point on the highest point of the island, I photographed her and Sarah standing on it. We gathered some field mushrooms and puffballs then returned to the McEachran camp for more chat, and probably more tea from the huge kettle.

I had clearly been enquiring about the fauna of Davaar – all islands are interesting for the species which have colonised them, although Davaar with its tidal link to the mainland is hardly a typical island – because my notes from Neil include his having seen a young hedgehog one year, the disappearance of rabbits about eight years previously and the abundance of rats. Mary, when she and Neil were camping on the island one summer, got into the habit of feeding crumbs of crisps and cake to a 'mouse' at its hole, until Neil happened to observe the ritual, and informed Mary that she was feeding a young rat. I turned that anecdote into a poem in Scots, titled 'The Ratton', which was published in *The Song of the Quern* in 1998. (In commercial and critical terms, the 'song' was more of a whisper briefly heard on the outer edge of nowhere.)

10. Neil McEachran with tin mug on Davaar Island, 21 July 1991. Photograph by the author.

Place-names on the island

My notes also record that the big rock below the Sheephoose was named 'Murphy's Rock' by Neil and his friend, the late Donald Blue, 'after Murphy Riddell, who used to pick wilks two tides a day around it'. I noticed at once a remarkable coincidence in that name. The standard name is 'MacVoorie's Rock', which must represent the surname *MacMhuirich*, of which one of the later Anglicised mutations was 'Murphy'. Even more interestingly, the lands of Kildalloig, which probably included, then as now, Davaar Island, were held in 1505 by Johannes McMurthe or McMurchie and in 1541 by Donaldus McMurchy or McMurchie. McMurchy, a surname still found in Kintyre, is another form of *MacMhuirich*, which attached to the distinguished family which served Clan Donald as hereditary bards in Kintyre until the sixteenth century.[42]

As an aside, one night in August 2014, while listening to Late Junction on Radio 3, I heard a name which immediately got my genealogical antennae twitching: Jake McMurchie. He is a notable Bristol-based jazz-rock saxophonist associated with the bands Michelson Morley and Get the Blessing. I contacted him to enquire about his lineage and he told me his grandfather John McMurchie was an engineer from Glasgow who married in England; but beyond that he couldn't go. McMurchie, however spelled, isn't quite a surname of exclusively Kintyre origin, but I've yet to come across anyone of the name who wasn't connected with Kintyre. Jake and I correspond occasionally and I'm hoping that eventually we'll be able to trace his McMurchies back from Glasgow to their cultural homeland. My money is on Kintyre, but I may be proven wrong.

One would assume, from Ordnance Survey maps, that the island was entirely devoid of place-names, but I collected thirteen from oral tradition, most of them admittedly of relatively recent origin. From the end of the Doirlinn, going towards the Lighthouse and around the island back to the Doirlinn, these are: Donald Stott's Broo, The Isle Slip, The

Studdie, Oitir Buidhe, The Riddlings (p 21), Pork Bay, The Cuilleam, Port a' Chapuill/Horse Bay, The Picture Cave, The White Ley, MacVoorie's Rock and The Sheep Hoose.[43]

I'm back with George on 13 May. We'd been discussing the last time we were on the island, and reckoned it was in 2010 and that Murdo MacDonald had been with us. The date was 26 May, and I was there to take photographs for a talk about Davaar I'd agreed to give in Rothesay later that year. I had decided to use slides, rather than have them converted into digital form, as I'd now do, and was assured that a slide-projector would be available. There was a projector, but it didn't work and every photograph looked like it had been taken in dense fog. It was not a happy experience, and I found myself having to deliver an old-fashioned lecture, relying on sparse notes and a fortunately well-stocked memory.

As George and I were sitting near the Sheep Hoose with our flasks, a tall reddish-haired girl walked by. 'Are you going to the Cave?' I asked her. It was an obvious question, as was her affirmative reply. With our usual parochial curiosity, we speculated on who she might be. George had an intuition that his wife Margaret might have the answer. The day before, a visitor to the Heritage Centre, where Margaret worked as a volunteer, was enquiring about family connections with Campbeltown, and George reckoned we had seen her. He 'phoned Margaret at home, but the call rang out. Minutes later, his mobile 'phone rang, and it was Margaret. Descriptions were exchanged and we decided the women were one and the same.

The Crucifixion and Che Guevara

We found her, as expected, in the Picture Cave, looking at Archibald MacKinnon's 1887 painting of the crucifixion, or, at least, its latest restoration, by Campbeltown artist Ronald Togneri, after a lurid image of Che Guevara had been superimposed on the face and torso. The twentieth century revolutionary's face was painted in secret, in

11. The Crucifixion painting on Davaar Island with Che Guevara superimposed, 2006. Photograph by George McSporran.

July 2006, and never publicly admitted to by anyone. MacKinnon's crucifixion was also painted in secret, but he, after its sensational discovery, was pleased to take the credit, though by then, uncertain of its reception, he had 'bolted' to Liverpool and a job in engineering.[44] Indeed, some of his critics suggested that far from being the expression of a religious vision, the painting was calculated to deliver to MacKinnon fame in his own lifetime, which it did. And he is still remembered for that work, though the original has long since disappeared under a succession of restorations.

The cave, in the past decade or so, has turned into a mawkish shrine, with votive objects, messages on stones, and driftwood crosses, large and small, tied together by twine from the shore. Despite my reservations about the motives behind the painting, I concede that it has been an immense asset to the local tourism industry, though, since access is over the rocks at the foot of the cliffs, it is remarkable that no serious injuries appear to have befallen the numerous 'pilgrims'. In a more tourism-orientated economy, a concrete pathway to the Cave Painting would probably have been laid; but I mention this as a reflection and not as a recommendation.

Phillippa Paterson

I asked the girl if she'd been in the Heritage Centre the day before, and she had, so George's hunch had been correct. She wrote her name, Phillippa Rachel Paterson, in my journal, along with her e-mail address and brief particulars of her family, going back to her great-grandparents, who came to Campbeltown from Glasgow, Thomas Baird Paterson, a projectionist in the Picture House, and his wife, Eva McKay. Phillippa had come from Aberdeen to visit Campbeltown for the first time and to pay her respects at the family grave in Kilkerran. After George had taken a few photographs, I said we'd go, as we intended to walk around the island. She asked to accompany us and was rewarded with the sighting of a rare raptor and an otter; we were rewarded with her companionship.

12. *George McSporran and Phillippa Paterson under the cliffs on the south side of Davaar Island, 13 May 2015. Photograph by the author.*

Always at the back of my mind there lurked an anxiety that we might be caught out by tide and stranded on the island. It was illogical, because I knew there would be time enough to get round the island; and, even if 'the worst came to the worst', we could remove our shoes and socks, roll up our trouser legs and wade back across the Doirlinn. ('Health and Safety' warning: the aforementioned last resort is not recommended!)

The Horse Bay

Teddy Lafferty, who preferred to have the island to himself, would cross with the tide closing at his back and so ensure several hours of uninterrupted solitude. To further remove himself from the risk of human intrusion, he'd continue past the Picture Cave and light his fire in a pleasant inlet on the south side of the island which he knew as the 'Horse Bay', and fishermen knew as Gaelic *Port a' Chapuill*, 'Mare's Port', much the same. He liked to be there early in the morning when the sun was shining into the bay. Once, in the 1980s, when he arrived there, he saw something shining on the shore and picked it up. It was a plastic salt-dish with a metal top and he took it home and washed it and still keeps it in his bedroom as a reminder of a summer's day on the island. When we stopped briefly in the bay, while I sawed a branch of seasoned ash into logs, George noticed a raven perched on the cliff top above us, and, on a ledge below the raven, its big twiggy nest.

Quarrying on the island

Between the Sheep Hoose and the Picture Cave, I'd pointed out to George what seems to me to be a passageway cleared in the tidal rocks. These 'ports', as they are called locally, usually extend all the way to the shoreline, so that small boats could be beached and launched conveniently, but this one falls short, which puzzled me when I first noticed it in 1997. Then I remembered that stone had been quarried on

Davaar, and speculated that this 'port' might simply have been a mooring place for boats while they were loaded with stone. The cliffs on that south-facing side of the island are certainly gouged out and the shore is littered with shattered rock. I would later notice two more harbours.

Compared with, for example, the quarrying of granite on Ailsa Craig for curling stones, there is remarkably little documentation on quarrying on Davaar, and nothing about the industrial operation itself, which must have been witnessed by countless visitors to the island, especially after the cave painting became a popular attraction. An article about Davaar in 1851 did, however, extol the merits of the rock: 'There is every kind of porphyry, from the darkest red to a bluish green. The grain of the stone is very close and takes a polish as fine as marble or Aberdeen granite, and presents a more finely-grained and beautiful surface than either.'[45]

I first heard about stone-quarrying on Davaar in 1981, through the late Lawrence Watson, who lived in 'Islestone', High Street. Chrissie McGregor wrote him an account of the origin of the name 'Islestone', which Lawrence showed to me. The house, Chrissie said, was built by her great-grandfather, Alexander Munro, general merchant in Dalintober, who also owned two pairs of fishing skiffs. In 'poor seasons', instead of laying off his crews until the fishing improved, Munro would employ them in shipping stone from Davaar. With that beautiful stone he built his own house, 'Islestone', the adjacent tenement and shop, and the four houses at 44 High Street, in one of which Chrissie herself lived until her death. This construction, Chrissie reckoned, took place in the period 1860-70.

In the 1851 census, Alexander Munro was 43 years old and living in High Street with his wife, Euphemia McMillan, three children and a 15-year-old servant, Elizabeth McMillan. He described himself as a 'Spirit Dealer', adding, significantly, 'formerly Mason'. One of his daughters, Agnes, was the mother of Chrissie's father, Joseph Black, baker in Saddell

Street, and his son Donald, then a year old, would marry my great-grandfather's sister, Elizabeth Martin, in 1882.

These tenements on High Street were built with porphyry, a hard igneous rock, distinctive by its attractive green and red colouration. In 1896, when the island quarry was let to the Wallace brothers, builders in Campbeltown, the stone was described as 'about the best in Kintyre'.[46] It was exploited as a building material long before then, as evidenced by the well-known story of the building of the Longrow – or 'Relief' – Church in 1767.

During that decade, the Established Church was riven on the issue of patronage, and many members left to set up alternative churches in which the choice of minister was decided by the congregation. George Robertson, the minister nominated in 1763 to Castlehill Church by the Duke of Argyll, was ultimately rejected by the vast majority of the Lowland congregation, which broke away and resolved, in 1766, to build its own church. The Duke, naturally enough, took the rejection as a personal affront and barred the rebel congregation from using the town quarry.

The congregation appealed to Campbell of Kildalloig, who agreed that stone could be quarried on Davaar Island and charged £4; but George Robertson and his supporters put the laird under pressure, and, although he refused to go back on his word, he did stipulate that no horses were to be used in transporting the stone. So, the people had to carry the stone themselves, 'on hand-barrows or on their backs', to boats waiting at the shore. Impressed by the tenacity of the congregation, Campbell of Kildalloig later relented and allowed the use of horses, but charged an additional £4 for the concession.[47]

The church, which exacted from its builders such a high cost in physical and mental suffering, and stood as a monument to the democratic imperative, was replaced in 1872 by the present top-heavy edifice, a monument to wealth and ostentation.

Another, later, monument built from Davaar Island stone is still standing. The imposing memorial to the First World War Campbeltown dead, erected by Neil MacArthur and his squad of builders, was unveiled by the Duke of Argyll on 21 October 1923 on Kinloch Green, after much acrimonious public debate about where it should be sited. Fund-raising for the monument began at Christmas 1919 and £3546 was soon gathered from almost 2000 subscribers, individual donations ranging from 2d to £150.[48]

14 May: A return to Davaar

I was back on Davaar the next day for wood, but didn't have to look far. Instead, I looked for a kelp-kiln I'd identified many years before and failed to find in 2010, when I intended to photograph it. I found it higher up the foreshore than I'd expected it to be, and overgrown. It is a narrow rectangular stone enclosure in which dried seaweed would have been burnt for use in the commercial manufacture of soap and glass. Kelp-making was hard and dirty work, from which the island cottars would have earned a few pounds to help pay the rent.

The kiln is next to the wet strip of ground – scarcely a 'stream' – which seeps from an old well. That well, which must have supplied water for the house, and later for 'Coasters' such as Neil McEachran, is now choked and virtually stagnant; but the spring was never constant, and it fails in dry summers, as I have found to my inconvenience.

The archaeology of Davaar Island has never been systematically surveyed. Dr Gary Robinson, who, with Dr Vicki Cummings, led the Southern Kintyre Project team in 2006-10, visited the island once for a leisurely look. That limited exploration revealed several possible cairns, which, if authenticated, would date to the Early Bronze Age (2200-1600 BC), and extensive field walls, also potentially prehistoric. He would have expected to find associated round houses, but vegetation was high at the time of the visit and none was observed. His summary: 'The long and the short of it is, archaeological sites are definitely present on the island, but without further work it is difficult to be certain of date, character, etc.'[49]

Sand tracks

As George and I were crossing the sand flats on the 13th, we noticed tracks which neither of us could readily explain. At first we thought they might have been made by bicycles, but there were too many of them. Then we noticed, at the seaward end of each track, a rock with a stalk of seaweed attached to it. It looked as though the stone had been dragged by the ebbing tide, but could tide pull a stone? There was no alternative explanation we could imagine.

While crossing the flats alone on the following day, I decided to measure one of the longest of the tracks. I paced it out in my size eleven wellies and counted 126 steps, so roughly 42 yards. I still lacked an explanation, but that wasn't long in coming. When I left the island, the tide was flowing in fast over the flats, and, since I was wearing wellies, I decided to wade diagonally towards the end of the Doirlinn, eliminating the longer route over the shingle bar; and that's when the revelation was delivered. I noticed that certain stones were leaving tracks in the opposite direction from before, in other words they were being moved along by the flood tide, and it was clear that the fronds of the seaweed were acting as a kind of 'water sail', catching the force of the incoming tide and propelling the stones over the seabed. These tracks were short, so movement had just begun, and would doubtless continue after I'd reached land.

17 May: Kidney vetch

George and I returned to Davaar Island that evening. On our way along the south shore, I happened to look up at a cliff face and noticed a cluster of yellow flowers. When I pointed them out to George, his immediate response was 'vetch', which startled me because he seldom ventures a botanical identification. When I asked him to photograph the flowers with his zoom lens, he obliged, but he doubted the value of the exercise for identification purposes since the subject was a long way up.

When he forwarded a photograph next day, Judy and I had a look at it and then e-mailed it to Agnes Stewart. Kidney vetch (*Anthyllis vulneraria*) was certainly a possibility. I was familiar with the flower from locations at the bottom of the Inneans Glen, Sròn Gharbh and Dùn Bàn, and associated it with sunny days on the Atlantic coast. After Agnes examined the photograph, she confirmed kidney vetch as the flower. She admitted to having had doubts, until she saw the photograph, because the species is absent from Kildalloig shore, opposite the island, a stretch of coast she knows intimately from her monthly botanical counts.

Days later, I asked George why 'vetch' had come into his head that evening on Davaar, and he explained that Judy years ago had identified as kidney vetch the yellow flowers he'd been seeing on Polliwilline shore. The Castles – three distinctive stacs close to the Glenahervie march – are 'absolutely covered' in the vetch, he recalled.

Geoffrey Grigson had little of interest to say about kidney vetch, other than that it was 'known throughout Europe as a wound herb, or vulnerary'.[50] Its Gaelic names are *cas-an-uain*, 'lamb's foot', and *meòir Moire*, 'Mary's fingers',[51] and Madge Cunningham noted two sub-species in Kintyre, identified by J. Cullen, one of them, *lapponica*, found 'Mull of Kintyre area at least from Keil to Earradale'.[52]

Wondering how extensive kidney vetch was on Davaar Island – had we noticed the only colony or was there more to find? – I decided to look. George and I returned on the 29th, with one main object in mind – to go around the island and check every rock face. Past the colony we already knew about, we saw more, this time at eye-level, shining yellow in the sunlight and outclassing the birdsfoot-trefoil below it; and there was yet more all the way to Horse Bay, where the south shore turns north at the imposing rock face known as the Cuilleam. I found a solitary herb-Robert (*Geranium robertianum*) in flower in that conspicuously grassy bay (the species was still flowering on the island five months later, in October), which, after recent rain, had two little streams running into it from the cliffs. (Neil McEachran used to maintain a water-pipe in the bay for his own convenience.) We sat there for half-an-hour, and then completed the circuit of the island, remarking on the differences in flora on the north side – notably primroses and bluebells – compared to the south. A pair of torn-off wings we found on the shore was identified, by a local ornithologist, Rab Morton, as being from a Manx shearwater, probably killed at sea by a peregrine falcon.

Off Davaar

In November, while looking through the microfilmed issues of the *Campbeltown Courier* for 1930, I came across a little news item I'd never before noticed. It reported that on Hogmanay 1929, the BBC had broadcast from its Glasgow studio a 'dialogue' titled *Off Davaar*. This featured the skipper and crew of the fishing skiff *Willing Lass* (CN 6534) which had 'run into a fog-bank off Davaar Island'. The author was T. P. Maley,[53] whose name was unfamiliar to me. There was, however, a Campbeltown skiff the *Willing Lass* (CN 397), skipper-owner John McLellan, around the turn of the century,[54] but that may have been coincidental. I 'Googled' Maley and the only reference I found was to a 78 r.p.m. Columbia recording of his *A Clachanstoorie Story* by William McCulloch, *c.* 1929. Had Maley some connection with Campbeltown? Perhaps. McCulloch certainly had. In January 1933, the 'noted Scots entertainer' appeared in the Town Hall at the invitation of the Campbeltown branch of the S.W.R.I; his dramatic rendering of Burns's 'Tam o' Shanter' was 'perhaps his best performance'.[55]

18 May: Lewis connections

Back on Davaar Island, I met a brother and sister from Lewis. They had photographed the Lighthouse and were heading to the Picture Cave. Since I had no plans of my own, apart from wood-gathering, I offered to accompany them there. I detected a Gaelic intonation in their speech and asked where they were from. When he said 'Lewis', I set myself the challenge of guessing their surname and was confident of success, since the pool of native names on the island is relatively small, but I could have tried until midnight and failed. It was 'Bailey', which came as a surprise to me. Their father was a Londoner, William Alexander Bailey, who married Mina MacLeod from South Dell, in the Ness district of Lewis, and they were brought up at Back, north of Stornoway. He was Ian Bailey, a retired cable-jointer for Scottish & Southern Energy, and his sister was Patricia, a nurse at the Beatson Oncology Centre in Glasgow, which perpetuates the name of Sir George Beatson, a member of a distinguished Campbeltown family, as, with predictable parochialism, I lost no time in pointing out.

Ian had noticed, while crossing the Doirlinn, a series of wooden stumps which runs the length of the shingle bar. These puzzled me for decades until George McSporran mentioned that, as a boy at Glenramskill in the early 1950s, he'd once seen a Post Office van parked out on the Doirlinn while a telephone engineer worked on the line. After a cable was laid across the sand to the island, the poles were cut down. The cable was certainly in place by 1974, because in that year Charles Macintyre devoted an entire paragraph to a description of it in 'Pilgrimage to Davaar'. His homage to the 'long multistrand wire' concludes impeccably: 'It disappears beneath the surface at the foot of the pole supporting the diamond-shaped red and white marker plaque and runs, entrenched, to the lighthouse.'[56] The pole is now broken at the top, and the 'plaque', which was made of aluminium, is lying in bits on the shore.

I left Ian and Patricia at the cave and carried on until reunited with an ash branch I'd identified for the saw during an earlier visit; but I met them again at the Doirlinn car-park, and showed Ian, himself a dedicated wood-cutter, the log I was shouldering. I asked where they were staying and was told they had rented a flat in Killean Place for the week. After they drove off, I realised they were staying across the road from the house fellow-Lewisman Norman Morrison had occupied for more than thirty years, until his death in 1949. My failure to make an immediate connection irked me slightly, but the chance to pass on the information came a couple of days later when I met them in a local supermarket. As it transpired, they hadn't heard of Morrison, but said they'd enquire about him.

Morrison first came to Campbeltown as a police constable in 1892 and married Elizabeth McKay from Killean five years later, when he was stationed at Port Charlotte, Islay. As a naturalist and writer, he has appeared so frequently in recent books of mine that I shall say no more about him here, except that in the *Campbeltown Courier* of 21 September 1940 I came across a review of his *Adventures of Angus Og and Other Tales*. The reviewer mentioned an article in the book about the Cave Picture on Davaar, and I decided I should read it. I managed to borrow a copy of the book, but the essay was a disappointment. It contained little of substance, a frequent failing of Morrison's, which he explained quite brazenly in his introduction to *Adventures of Angus Og*: '... I have a weakness for inserting "purple passages" or word pictures into my stories. I do this to please myself and not the reader.'

From the essay itself I'll quote only the final paragraph (p 110): 'While the writer was gazing with intent fascination on [the Crucifixion], a large, beautifully-coloured butterfly came sailing majestically into the cave, and alighted on the head of the picture. One could imagine this creature to be a gem in the crown of thorns.'

This anecdote is reminiscent of an experience Morrison claimed to have had in another cave, Saint Kieran's, on the mainland south of Davaar, where he'd gone with a friend to celebrate Christmas Eve. Just before midnight, an oyster-catcher, Saint Bride's 'sacred creature' in Gaelic legend, '... came shooting into the cave, flew right over the well and above our heads, then wheeled about, and with another pensive wail disappeared into the darkness of the outer world'.[57]

A fuller account of Morrison's night in the cave appeared in my *Another Summer in Kintyre*, and the oyster-catcher incident reminded me of an Anglo-Saxon text I'd once seen, but couldn't source, though I remembered the bulk of it. I have since seen it again, in Kevin Crossley-Holland's *Pieces of Land: Journeys to Eight Islands* (p 86), and quote it belatedly. It is from Bede's *A History of the English Church and People*, as translated by Leo Sherley-Price in 1956. I'll skip the historical, and even the religious context, in 7th century Northumbria, and let the passage speak directly to 21st century sensibilities:

> Your Majesty, when we compare the present life of man with that time of which we have no knowledge, it seems to me like the swift flight of a lone sparrow through the banqueting-hall where you sit in the winter months to dine with your thanes and counsellors. Inside there is a comfortable fire to warm the room; outside, the wintry storms of snow and rain are raging. The sparrow flies swiftly in through one door of the hall, and out through another. While he is inside, he is safe from the winter storms; but after a few moments of comfort, he vanishes from sight into the darkness whence he came. Similarly, man appears on earth for a little while, but we know nothing of what went before this life, and what follows.

Kintyre and North Sea oil

Even before oil production in the North Sea commenced in 1975, Kintyre was in the frame for related industrial developments. There were proposals for an oil refinery at Peninver – with a projected output of ten million barrels a year – and concrete platform-building sites at both MacRingan's Point and Davaar Island. Peter Lind & Company – which in 1964 built the Post Office (now BT) Tower in London – was interested in Davaar, and at a packed public meeting in the Victoria Hall, in July 1974, its chairman, Thomas Jaeger, pledged that the company would be 'good neighbours and good employers'. He also promised, ludicrously, '... to return the site to its original condition when we have finished'.

The Davaar Island and Peninver projects came to nothing, but the third – MacRingan's Point – was approved by the Secretary of State for Scotland, William Ross, in January 1975, along with Portavadie, on the east shore of Loch Fyne, opposite Tarbert. That one went ahead, but was already obsolete when completed, steel having replaced concrete in platform construction, and it is now a holiday village.

The MacRingan's Point development would probably have met the same fate as Portavadie, but it failed to advance beyond the planning stage. There was opposition to it from the start, but high unemployment in Campbeltown ensured its acceptance. In April 1975, Campbeltown councillors were expressing 'frustration and annoyance' at the 'prolonged silence' surrounding the project, and at the council's final meeting, before it disappeared in the reorganisation of local government on 6 May, ex-Provost George McMillan's motion to send a telegram to the Scottish Under-Secretary of State for Offshore Oil Development, John Smith, was accepted. The telegram read: 'Request an early favourable decision on the McCringan's Point Project – Signed Campbeltown Town Council.'

The project appears to have died in July, after rejection of the contractor's application to extract 340,000 cubic meters of sand and gravel from Kildalloig Bay. The round-the-clock dredging was expected to take three months, and 'numerous geological and ocean research studies' warned of 'tidal changes and beach movements' and possible damage to the Doirlinn, the 'natural breakwater' for Campbeltown harbour.[58]

19 May: A grave in the hills at Killean
Since 2013, Duncan Macdougall in Glenbarr has taken me somewhere I'd never been before. That year, it was the island of Cara, the following year the ruins of Stockadale in Barr Glen, and in 2015 a glen, in the hills above Killean, where a local laird was buried in 1922. I'd passed that glen during walks with family and friends in recent years and considered it inviting, but didn't think I'd ever explore it. There is no name for it on any map I've ever seen and Duncan had no name for it, yet it's so distinctive it must have been named. On the day after our visit, I went into Campbeltown Library to search for a newspaper report of the unusual burial and found not only the burial, but the name of the glen. It was 'Glencaol', which is Gaelic *Gleann Caol*, 'Narrow Valley', and I recognised at once the perfection of the description. But delight was mingled with regret, because I had already published my compilation *Place-Names of the Parish of Killean and Kilchenzie*, and that name was missing from it. I'd probably come across the report several times over the years and failed to read it closely enough to have picked out the name.

Duncan was first taken to the grave about thirty-five years earlier by an uncle, the late Ian MacDonald, whose father Malcolm had attended the burial. Duncan promised a short but steep ascent through the glen and said that it could be done in an evening. Since Judy and I have no car and the bus service was unsuitable, I asked George McSporran if he would come along with his car. He collected me from Saddell Street at 6.45, and fifteen minutes later, having met Duncan at Glenbarr village hall, we were driving north to Killean in Duncan's car. He drove up the estate road, which also gives access to the wind-farm at Deuchran and is part of the

Kintyre Way walking trail. We passed the ruins of Braids, which, in 1922, would have been as far as a road went, and parked at the upper end of a side-road which leads back down to Braids. The glen, and our destination, lay on the north side of the estate road.

A little burn runs through the glen, and the gravestone is on the left-hand side of the burn under a rock face, where, on Duncan's first visit, peregrine falcons had built a nest. Since then, conifers have been planted on both sides of the glen, to the detriment, I think, of the natural beauty which must have been part of its original appeal as an interment spot. The gravestone itself appears to be of schist and to have come from the immediate area, perhaps from one of the rock faces on the north side of the glen. It may have been hewn out of the rock, or may have been found already detached. When, on the way back down, I searched underneath the faces for a piece of rock for proper identification, I couldn't find even a fragment.

13. Angus Martin and Duncan Macdougall at the grave of James Macalister Hall, 19 May 2015. Photograph by George McSporran.

The gravestone, at just a couple of feet high and undressed, certainly isn't ostentatious. There is a border of stones around the grave, but the enclosure is now overgrown and wet, from the overflow from the well opposite the grave. Duncan was told by Ian MacDonald of a silver cup in a recess at the head of the well, but when they looked for it they couldn't find it. The recess is above a flat stone, and when George probed it with his walking-pole, the pole went in almost three feet and could probably have been pushed further. There was general agreement that the cup could still be there. Duncan donned a pair of waterproof gloves and scooped out a channel to direct water clear of the grave, and with a wire brush swept the face of the lichened headstone to clarify the inscription.

James Macalister Hall

Carved in italics, the inscription reads: 'James Macalister Hall of Killean & Tangy August 1 1922.' He had been walking around his estate at Killean that day, and in the evening called at Kilmory to see his shepherd, Robert Robertson, and died suddenly in Robertson's house. The cause of death, as detailed in his death certificate, may be summarised as heart failure caused by an asthma attack.

The news of Macalister Hall's unexpected death, at the age of 49, came as a shock not just to his tenants, for he was a public figure. An enthusiastic breeder of black-faced sheep and Highland cattle, he took an active interest in the Kintyre Agricultural Society, of which he was several times president, 'his years of office being characterised by personal attention to the shows and open-handedness in the social courtesies associated with these occasions'. Though described as 'invariably displaying some diffidence in letting his voice be heard either in conference or debate', he was active on Argyll County Council and Killean and Kilchenzie Parish Council. His last public appearances were at the weekly market in Campbeltown and at the unveiling of the Killean and Kilchenzie war memorial at Glenbarr.

Macalister Hall's early life was spent on Degnish farm in Lorne, which his father rented. As a young man, he emigrated to Australia and farmed in Queensland until 1904, when he returned to Kintyre on the death of his wealthy uncle and namesake, James Macalister Hall of Killean and Tangy, donor of Campbeltown Public Library and Museum. On the death of another uncle, Stuart Hall, in 1912, he inherited Killean Estate, and two years later, with the death of his father, Allan Hall, Tangy also became his.

An obituary described 'A man in the very prime of life, of commanding physique, apparently in the enjoyment of excellent health ...'[59] Nothing was written then about his cultural background, but he seems to have been a Gaelic speaker. A subsequent report on his burial described 'a Highland funeral ... not inappropriate for one, who, in life, was notably loyal to the traditions, the language, the literature and the music of the race from which he was proud to have sprung'.[60] In 1947, his sister, Grace Macalister Hall, who inherited Tangy Estate in 1940 on the death of James's widow, was described by Neil Shaw as 'a native Gaelic speaker'.[61] Shaw would have known: he was general secretary and later president of the society for the promotion of Gaelic culture, *An Comunn Gàidhealach*, and in 1935 married Lizzie Taylor from High Crubasdale, up the road from Tangy.[62] It appears likely that Grace and her siblings acquired the language in Lorne, though there was plenty of Gaelic spoken in the Largieside when she and James later settled there.

Burial of James Macalister Hall

On 4 August 1922, three days after his death, the body of James Macalister Hall was carried into the hills in a cart from Killean House. The 'mountain well' in Glencaol had been a 'favourite place for the mid-day halt' when Macalister Hall 'went out on the moor with the guns', and it was his wish to lie there, 'in the very bosom of the hills he loved, far from the haunts of men'.

Ten years earlier, on 12 August 1912 – the so-called 'Glorious Twelfth' – Macalister Hall had been on the Killean moors with three companions, and perhaps stopped at that very well for lunch. Eighty brace of grouse were bagged that day, and, on his Tangy Estate the following day, with the same three companions, 65 more brace were shot. That – not including unspecified 'various' – is a total of 290 birds, which were described as 'strong and healthy' ... until shot, that is! His companions all belonged to Kintyre:[63] D. Mactaggart, presumably Daniel, Procurator Fiscal in Campbeltown; Duncan Colville Jnr., a founder-member of the Kintyre Antiquarian Society in 1921 and later a prominent amateur archaeologist; and Dr John Gilchrist, a leading ophthalmic specialist from Corran, Clachan, who would be a pall-bearer at Macalister Hall's funeral.

The funeral service itself was conducted outside Killean House by the Rev D. J. Macdonald, Killean Parish Church, and the Rev John Stuart, Killean United Free Church. Macalister Hall's coffin was covered with a plaid of his 'clan tartan' – Macalister, presumably – and his shepherd's crook was laid on top. The mourners, who numbered hundreds, some of them octogenarians, were faced with a climb to over a thousand feet, on a windless day and under a scorching sun, 'a severe test for many', as the *Campbeltown Courier* correspondent noted.

At Braids steading, the road ended, and the coffin was shouldered for half-a-mile 'over the trackless heather'. The sixteen pall-bearers, a democratic social mix, were: Admiral H. S. F. Niblett, brother-in-law; Alan S. Niblett, nephew; Hugh Phillips, brother-in-law; Major W. Macalister Hall of Torrisdale, cousin; Robert Robertson, shepherd, Kilmory; Neil Thomson, gamekeeper, Killean; Angus Livingstone, chauffeur; Dr John Gilchrist, Glasgow; Colonel Charles Mactaggart, Campbeltown; G. Black, Killean Home Farm; Charles McNiven, gamekeeper, Tangy; Neil McAlister, Drumnamucklach; John McKinven, gardener; Archibald McIntyre, chauffeur; Archibald McMurchy, Drumnamucklach, and William MacKinnon, gardener, Killean.

Duncan Macdougall heard that the coffin was lowered by ropes over the rock face and into the glen, but if that strategy was resorted to, the *Courier* report didn't mention it. The committal prayer was delivered by the Rev Stuart and the benediction by the Rev Macdonald. The dead man's plaid and crook were buried with him.[64]

J. M. Hall was the third prominent Largieside laird to die within a year. John Ronald Moreton Macdonald of Largie went in September 1921 and Major Matthew Charles Brodie Macalister of Glenbarr and Crubasdale followed him in December.

Enid Macalister Hall

James Macalister Hall married Enid Morgan Phillips, elder daughter of Frederick William Phillips of High Elms, Hitchin, on 29 April 1913 in London. On both Killean and Tangy estates, a bonfire was lit. The Killean blaze, atop Drumnamucklach hill, was followed by the firing of rockets, whose 'beautiful illuminations could be seen many miles distant'. At the Killean celebratory dinner, the estate manager, Neil McFater, remarked of the bride that the tenantry had, as yet, no acquaintance with her, 'but the fact that she was Mr Hall's choice was enough to ensure (*sic*) them that she was possessed of all the qualities befitting the future lady of Killean'.[65] They had one child, who died in infancy, and when Enid Macalister Hall herself died in 1940 there was no heir to the estates.

Little is known about Enid in her early years as the 'lady of Killean', but she would later emerge as a keen member of the Kintyre Antiquarian Society and an assiduous recorder of ancient monuments in Kintyre. She recorded and photographed more than 40 standing stones and stone circles, but her special interest was cup-and-ring markings, enigmatic prehistoric rock art forms. Of the 93 she identified, 66 were new to the record, either discovered by herself or reported to her by the 'many observers in the countryside' whom she recruited to the cause. Mrs Frances Hood, of the Kintyre Antiquarian and Natural History Society, was told that she paid five shillings to shepherds and gamekeepers who led her to promising sites. Her rubbings, photographs and notes were ultimately donated to the Antiquarian Society, but she died before she could complete her work.

In December 1939, she informed the convenor of the Society's catalogue committee that she expected to finish in the spring of 1940,[66] but she died in March of that year in Edinburgh. Her obituary in the *Campbeltown Courier* was insubstantial, describing merely 'an enthusiastic member of the Kintyre Antiquarian Society', a Justice of the Peace for Argyll, with 'a keen interest in the affairs of the district', and 'a model landlord',[67] but, at the annual general meeting of the Kintyre Antiquarian Society, a month later, her full worth was recognised:

> … It is an irreparable loss to the Society that Mrs Macalister Hall was not spared to complete the work and to carry into other branches of research her zeal and her distinguished abilities.
> The loss of Mrs Macalister Hall will be felt not only for the cessation of her endeavours in the department which she had made her own. She will be missed in every branch of the Society's work. Her interest in their researches was a stimulus to other workers; and she did much to bring our neglected district to the notice of Antiquarians in the larger world.
> It was owing to her that we obtained the services of Mr [Horace] Fairhurst for the excavations at Kildonan [1936-38]; and on one of her latest visits to Campbeltown she brought with her Dr Adolf Mahr, the Keeper of Irish Antiquities and Director of the National Museum of Ireland, with a view to interesting him in our ancient monuments and bringing archaeological work in these parts into touch with the work which is now proceeding in Eire and Northern Ireland.[68]

She is mentioned in a series of articles, 'Our Holiday in Kintyre', written by an Edinburgh lady whose family rented Cruachan cottage at Tayinloan in 1930. The lady visited Beachar standing-stone, near Muasdale, and was keen to learn about it, but the 'neighbourhood folk' either dismissed it as unimportant or offered 'vague replies, mostly mythical or legendary traditions'. She was finally advised to go to Killean House and speak to 'Mrs Hall', who received her 'very graciously' and gave her 'interesting data'.[69]

The Kintyre Antiquarian and Natural History Society catalogue number for Enid Macalister Hall's archaeological collections is 224. In 2006, the Society was evicted by Argyll and Bute Council from the Burnet Building, Campbeltown, after almost eighty years' use of upstairs rooms there, and its archive ended up, with neat irony, in the Council's own archive in Lochgilphead. Ironically, too, the 'Burnet Building', as it was renamed in honour of its architect, J. J. Burnet, was built, in 1899, to house a public library and museum, with money donated by the first James Macalister Hall of Killean and Tangy, Enid's uncle by marriage.

Her collection was donated to the Society in March 1945, five years after her death, by W. H. T. Nicholls, Gloucestershire, who had just bought Killean Estate from Enid's brother, Hugh Phillips. Two years later, the 94 rubbings of cup-marked stones, in 15 parcels, were passed on to the Society of Antiquaries, Edinburgh.[70]

Uamh Bealach a' Chaochain

On our way back to Glenbarr from Killean, Duncan Macdougall pulled in and parked past Muasdale village. We were going to visit Uamh Bealach a' Chaochain, a cave I'd heard about, written about and looked at from the road in passing. He reckoned it was time I saw inside it, and he was right. He was taken to the cave, as a boy, about sixty years ago, by an uncle, Lachie Park, but didn't get to see inside it; smoke rising from the cave revealed the presence of a tramp, and they turned back.

The cave mouth is deceptively insignificant, a mere angular crack. As we approached the cave, Duncan, who had a big torch with him, mentioned that the last time he'd gone in, some months earlier, pigeons had shot out over his head, so I was prepared for the possibility of a shock. As I followed him inside, the first of five birds flew out noisily. I ducked in alarm, my nerves jolted, and, after the third bird had passed overhead, was startled anew by a flash of light for which I was entirely unprepared – George, at my back, had just photographed Duncan and me!

The length of the cave was amazing, and I decided to measure it on my way back out. With approximately yard-long paces, I got 180 feet. Not only was the cave roomy, but it was very dry, all the way to the back, apart from a wet area at the very entrance. Close to the end of the cave, there is a big well on the left. I assumed that the stone basin was kept full by water drips from the ceiling, but in 1843, in the *Second Statistical Account*, the parish minister, Rev Donald MacDonald, remarked on the cave's 'spring of excellent water, without any visible outlet'.

This may be a clue to the meaning of the name Bealach a' Chaochain, which is locally interpreted as 'The Windy Gap' (Gaelic *caochan*, 'an eddy of air'). An authority on Gaelic place-names, Ian A. Fraser, suggested instead *caochan*, 'the little blind one', which can apply to 'a bog-stream which is overgrown by moss, but continues to flow a short distance underground'. The Ordnance Survey, which mapped the parish in 1867, interpreted *caochan* as 'spirit or whisky' and linked it to illicit distillation formerly conducted in the cave. Bealach a' Chaochain was also the name of a farm, first recorded in the sixteenth century and later shortened to 'Balloch' or 'Belloch'.[71]

Duncan and I agreed we'd never been in a cave in Kintyre better suited to human occupation. It must have been in use from prehistory up until the mid-twentieth century, but hasn't yet been archaeologically excavated. In fact, only two caves in

Kintyre, Saint Kieran's and Keil, have. Duncan's uncle, Ian MacDonald, who was brought up on Beachmenach farm, told me in 2002 of two old men who once shared the cave at the foot of 'Ballochgoichan', one named MacCorvie – a rare Largieside surname, now locally extinct – and the other a Townsley, which links him with the main Travelling family in Kintyre. Neither of them could walk and they survived on charity.

Duncan Williamson (1928-2007), a luminary of the Scottish Traveller tradition-bearers, records in his autobiography, *The Horsieman*, that his mother, Betsy Townsley, was 'born in a cave at Muasdale'. This is likely to have been the one at Bealach a' Chaochain, though there is a smaller rock shelter, An Uamh Fhliuch, 'The Wet Cave', north of Muasdale, which was also occupied at times.[72] Williamson's father, John, was also born in Kintyre, at Tangy Mill. He and Betsy 'ran away together' when he was 17 years old and she 14, and reared thirteen children at Furnace Wood, on the western shore of Loch Fyne.[73]

Willie Watson, who was reared on North Muasdale farm, often played in the cave, despite being told not to. One of his mother's warnings was, 'Don't be going in there – Charlie Greenwood will get you!' Charlie was a fearsome local tramp, who occupied the cave during his wanderings, and may well have been the individual who pre-empted Duncan Macdougall's first visit. Willie remembers a large population of rock doves in the cave at that time, and a colony of bats. The cave also attracted the South Muasdale cattle, and occasionally an inquisitive cow would stick in the passage on the north side of the cave and have to be pulled out. To prevent these mishaps, the farmer blocked the inner end of the passage with old barrels, which Willie and his pals had to move to allow them to crawl through.

When Duncan, George and I emerged from the cave, after our brief exploration, the sun was already down and the grey sky and the roaring of the sea conveyed a sense of March rather than May; but the floral display around the cave –

primroses, bluebells and some early purple orchids – told the true story of spring.

Charlie Greenwood

I suppose Charlie Greenwood was the last dedicated tramp in Kintyre. I never saw him, but heard him mentioned often enough, so often, in fact, that I didn't bother to record the anecdotes and have forgotten all but a few. With his extravagantly matted hair and beard, his layers of coats with tin cans hung from the waist, his vocal outbursts – 'Mahone! Mahone!' and 'Scrap the boneyard!' – and fanatical individualism, he was a bogeyman, a relic of a social class which extends far back into history and includes itinerant tinsmiths and pedlars, along with social misfits and outcasts, like Charlie, who were lumped together as 'tramps' or 'vagrants'. Some of them were from privileged backgrounds and highly educated, but, whatever their history, they had either been – or perceived themselves to have been – rejected by society, or had rejected the social values and conventions of their time. Impelled by unemployment, personal tragedy or mental instability, they turned their backs on the past and left family and friends behind for a life on the roads. Sometimes, in the hills, I stumble on the fading line of an old track which once linked human settlements, now deserted and ruined, and I imagine those rootless wanderers, plodding along with their packs, and plotting where their next bed and bite of food might materialise.

Interestingly, Charlie's background was documented in 1911, when his father, George, was admitted to the Campbeltown poor roll. The assistance was temporary – three shillings and medicines to relieve his constipation – but his circumstances and personal history were thoroughly investigated to establish his eligibility for relief. He was English, born in Burton-on-Trent in 1847 to William Greenwood, a gun and lock smith, and Hannah Railton. He was a pedlar and his three children were born in locations far apart: Christina in Hawick in 1885, James in Campbeltown (1893) and Charles in Ardnamurchan (1895). George's 'paramour', Hannah, was also English, born in 1845 in Stocksley, Yorkshire, to James Hold, soldier, and Catherine Lowther. Hannah married a labourer in Staffordshire, William Shepherd, and soon after his death in 1881 'took up with Greenwood'. George was living in Longrow when prostrated by constipation in 1911, and died in 1916 in Lady Mary Row; Hannah's death followed in 1918. Daughter Hannah married a carter in Campbeltown, Alex Munro, and son James was a butcher in town; but against Charlie's name, in 1911, when he was 16 years old, no occupation was given.[74]

Campbeltown-born writer Moira Burgess remembers her father pointing out Charlie to her from their kitchen window in Mafeking Place, Campbeltown, 'as he shambled down Burnbank, all hair and beard!' At her father's later suggestion, she called her conspicuously hirsute teddy-bear 'Charlie'![75]

26 May: Spring squill

'Spring squill' is a lovely name, but its Latin name, *Scilla verna*, is even lovelier. My retention rate for Latin nomenclature is very poor, not only in botany but in all branches of natural history. This failing doesn't bother me; in fact, I don't regard it as a failing because I have no pretensions to expertise and muddle along year by year with common or local names, and sometimes with none. *Scilla verna*, however, I have never forgotten, and I puzzled over its persistence in my memory until Agnes Stewart directed me to an article of hers I'd published in the *Kintyre Magazine* in 2005: '*Scilla verna* in Kintyre.'

On 24 May, Agnes reported that she'd been a walk that afternoon at Machrihanish and spotted spring squill on a rock past the bus terminus. George McSporran and I planned an afternoon outing somewhere on the 26th, and I suggested we take the 1 p.m. bus to Machrihanish and combine a search for the flowers with a beachcomb along the

Galdrans. We found the flowers right away on the seaward side of the road and admired and photographed them. It was George's introduction to *Scilla verna* and only my second sighting. My first was on 12 May 2012 near Portan Àluinn, Carskey, with the South Kintyre Botany Group, one of whose members, Veronica Togneri, noticed some on a rock. This was a new and an interesting record, because the species was believed to be confined to the west coast of Kintyre, apart from one eastern colony at Ardnacross, which Agnes Stewart failed to find.[76]

The realisation that I'd never noticed the flower myself in South Kintyre puzzled me slightly. I'd done a lot of scrambling along rocky shores, but probably not the right shores at the right time. *The Flora of Kintyre* (p 44) specified: 'Ronachan to Westport, locally frequent: Ballygroggan reaching at least Cragaig: Ardnacross Bay. It does not seem to occur much further south. It is not at Largiebaan.' Agnes Stewart, who saw spring squill for the first time in the mid-1990s south of A' Chleit, decided in the spring of 2004 to undertake a survey (somewhat proscribed owing to the species' limited flowering season). She found some at Westport, among the dunes at Clochkeil, and from Machrihanish south almost to Craigaig Water.

She had noted colonies on the rocks immediately south of Bun an Uisge ('The Water Foot'), at the south end of the Galdrans, and had telephoned me on the morning of the 26th, before George and I set off to the Galdrans, suggesting we also look there. I didn't hear the message she left until I'd returned home, but we looked there, on our own initiative, and found not only colonies of regular blue-coloured flowers, but also one dense colony which was pink-coloured, a variant she too had observed there.

28 May: Craigaig

Two days later, George and I were ready for another outing. There was strong westerly wind, with the prospect of heavy rain, and even hail showers. George reasoned that the Learside would offer more shelter, but, in the thrall of *Scilla verna*, I proposed Craigaig, so that we could search for it south of Craigaig Water. Agnes had checked the beach at Craigaig in 2004 without success, though, as she acknowledged, 'My search there was in early June and I might have missed it, though I'm sure that I would have recognised the seed heads'.[77]

George and I left the Kintyre Way at the morass where cattle are fed and headed diagonally across moorland to cross Craigaig Water at the big sheep-fank. Then we dropped below the natural terrace and made our way to the township, meandering among the multitudinous tumbled rocks in the hope of meeting with *Scilla verna*. 'Craigaig' is Gaelic *Creagaig*, 'a rocky place', and while many old place-names become obscure – landscapes change and descriptions no longer fit – this one remains true to its origins.

The next stage was to search the shore south from Craigaig Bay towards Sròn Gharbh, which required a descent into the bay. The quickest route was down the scree slope below the township, and we took it. On our way down, a ball of colour on the cliff to our right attracted us; it was a clump of sea pink (*Armeria maritima*) which had taken root in a rock crevice and expanded over years into a thing of singular living beauty.

After we'd admired it and were turning away, I noticed at my feet what appeared to be a lump of quartz, but when I picked it up and examined it, it proved to be tallow. Neither of us could suggest an explanation for its being there. I put it in a pocket and took it home for kindling. While prowling on the beach, George lifted what I assumed to be a length of driftwood. It wasn't, and George already knew that. Back in October, on Glenahervie shore, he'd found an identical piece of flotsam, and, believing it to be wood, had taken it home. When he went to saw it up for burning, he discovered it to be solid bitumen, which he has since been slicing bits off for kindling.

We sat at the south end of the bay, close to a rock shelter and surrounded by fantastic schist formations, tortured at birth. I tried to recall the last time I'd been in the bay and couldn't, but I knew it was many years ago. A cherished watercolour painted by Nona Ruesgen, of my dog Benjie and me together, was based on a photograph George took in Craigaig Bay, and Nona and her partner John Brodie had given me the painting for my fiftieth birthday, which was 6 February 2002. George remembered that his son Sandy had once pitched a new tent in the bay to try it out. I later looked in my journals and found, on 11 April 2004, Sandy 'putting up his new "North Face" tent'. So, my last time there was probably over twelve years ago, which didn't surprise me, because the bay at Craigaig has never been a frequent haunt of mine. In the early 1980s, when I did most of my hiking and camping on that coast, I preferred the Inneans to Craigaig; the latter was fine for short walks or as a mid-way halt going to or returning from the Inneans, but latterly I preferred to stop at the ruined settlement overlooking the bay, saving on both time and effort.

We devoted about half-an-hour to scrambling south over the rocks towards Sròn Gharbh, but found no trace of squill. Since I hadn't expected to find any, there was no sense of disappointment. On the rocks below us, grey wintry-looking seas were crashing and sending little balls of spume into the wind. During our search, we were caught in the only shower of the day, but it was fleeting.

Back at the burn, we poked around the level grassy spot where a wooden hut, named 'Hamilton House', had stood for the use of coasters. We could trace the rough outline of the walls, but the only obvious relic of that shelter is a rusting iron object which looks as though it was salvaged from a shipwreck and converted into a stove. Both the hut and the rock shelter, mentioned earlier, are described in my *Kintyre: The Hidden Past* (pp. 152-53), largely from written accounts provided in 1983 by James McArthur Thomson, a Drumlemble man who died at the age of 93 on 6 March 2016.

He was the last remaining member of the hut-building team, and I quote a fuller version of his account here:

> The hut on the south side of Craigaig was built in the early years of the last war, say 1941-42. Apart from myself, the other members of the building team, which I remember, were Callum Galbraith, Ian Munro, Donnie McShannon and the two youngest Hamilton boys, Stewart and Ian. All the wood was hauled from the shore and sometimes from as far away as Tunvahn [Tòn Bhàn]. Stewart Hamilton was the architect, so we had a door and a window and a solid wooden floor and a roof. During the construction, which possibly took a year, we nearly killed the architect! Stewart completed each of the four sections on the flat and then we had to lift each one up and move it into place. We managed to drop one section on top of Stewart, who was supervising. Fortunately for him, the part that collided with his head and back wasn't securely nailed and the boards sprung loose, giving him more anger than pain. The hut was built well above the high water mark; in fact, it was on the best site at Craigaig, with a running burn beside it and vast views of the Atlantic ... There was a visitors' book in it, as there was in the hut at the Lussa, and many famous names appeared in it, such as Wullie Kerter, Mucka Fee, Joe Stalin, Big Neil Thomson, Wullie Mitchell, Jim Kelly, The Duke of Argyll, Wullie Colville and Ian Hamilton.

On our way back to Ballygroggan, George and I headed for a hillock, inland from Tòn Bhàn, on which we'd noticed from distance a boulder which appeared to have been placed there. When we arrived on the top, we found the rock resting on a smaller rock, to level and stabilise it. Like the rock on the ridge of Sròn Gharbh (p 70), here was a heavy rock which had been manhandled into position, but for what reason? I presume it was either a marker of some kind – perhaps for direction-finding or to delineate a boundary – or had some symbolic significance in the landscape, now forgotten. How many more of these transposed rocks remain to be identified on that coast?

14. Boulder on hillock near Tòn Bhàn, looking south-west, 28 May 2015. The locking rock is bottom right beneath the boulder. Photograph by George McSporran.

As an aside, during the past two or three years I have been seeing on Kintyre beaches – particularly in the Galdrans – what I call 'rock towers'. These are built using sea-smoothed stones laid one on top of another. Some structures are quite modest, but others are ambitious in scale. I suspect it's a tourist 'craze' which only reached Kintyre in recent years.

3 June: Largiebaan

Monday 1st June, with its gales and torrential rain, was like a day in winter; Tuesday saw improvement; and the weather forecast for Wednesday was most encouraging. With my developing interest in botany, I was keen to return to Largiebaan to see what changes a month had brought. George and I set off on our bicycles at 1 p.m., left them at Glenahanty, and reached the cliffs around 5.

The sea was strangely calm-looking, despite a brisk north-westerly breeze, and seabirds were few, as I'd noticed all that year during visits. North around the corner from the

Aignish, there is the rocky amphitheatre called the Gulls' Den, from the nesting gulls which occupied the shore in spring. It was the main colony of gulls on mainland Kintyre targeted in early May for egg-gathering,[78] but we didn't see a gull during the two hours we sat below the cliffs. Where have they gone? The explanation may to some extent lie in Campbeltown, where herring gulls have taken to perching and nesting on roofs and scavenging for food. I picked out with binoculars a few seabirds at the foot of the Aignish, and there were doubtless others there and around the corner, out of sight, but the silence was uncanny.

I overshot the spot I'd decided would be most sheltered from the wind, so we turned back to find it, and dropped below the cliff top to examine the botany. The most exciting discovery was a delicate white-petalled flower growing in grassy spaces among the rocks. I recognised it, but couldn't put a name to it. A name came later, but, as will be explained, it was the wrong one.

Above the little colonies we were photographing, we saw the vivid spears of early purple orchids, and decided, on an impulse, to climb to them. George went first and was up in seconds, but when I went to follow I hesitated. The rock obstacle was just a few feet high, but I suddenly felt helpless to proceed and when I looked below me to find a way back down I saw only a dangerous drop. I'd been in similar predicaments before, usually as a consequence of spontaneous adventuring. All it takes to transform a carefree climb into scary entrapment is a step which can't be taken, and, once momentum is arrested, uncertainty invades the mind. After several minutes of fearful indecision, George suggested I use my knees for purchase, and that's what I finally did, having gripped a secure clump of grass in each hand to haul myself up. I'd later scorn my timidity, because the book I was reading at home that week was Heinrich Harrer's *The White Spider*, an account of the first ascent of the North Face of the Eiger, a '6000-foot bastion of rock and ice', as he described it.

15. George McSporran below cliffs at Largiebaan, 3 June 2015. Photograph by the author.

Having settled ourselves on a sheltered grass-topped crag with a view north towards the Aignish, we ate the last of our sandwiches, chatting, but also listening and watching beyond ourselves. Three raptor species appeared during the hour we spent there, and we heard what sounded like demonic laughter carried up on the wind – the cackling of a fulmar on a cliff, perhaps. We noticed a ewe slumped on a grassy slope hundreds of feet below, and I looked at her through binoculars, wondering if she was dead or alive. When I happened to cough, she got to her feet, startled. My cough also surprised a fox which must have been lurking near the sheep. It loped off north, stopping occasionally to gaze back at us, but afterwards, with distance, appearing to lose interest in our presence, and instead sniffing here and there along the sides of the track, and settling on its haunches, dog-like, to gaze around. We watched it for almost ten minutes until it disappeared into a ravine, to double back, I guessed, on the ailing sheep's last bed; but I may have guessed wrongly, because a week later I looked at the spot and there was no trace of the ewe.

We left the cliffs at 7 p.m. and were heading down the Kintyre Way when I noticed a cluster of bright colours at the swing-gate. A quick look through binoculars confirmed the presence of a group of walkers. Our intended route was to have been diagonally across the open ground between the cliff and forest, but my curiosity was aroused, and, with George following somewhat reluctantly, I headed down towards the group, trying to appear casual. I dare say our direct approach could have been misconstrued, but within a couple of minutes greetings were being exchanged and the Martin inquisition had begun.

There were three women and a man, all of them students from Edinburgh and heavily laden. They had arrived in Campbeltown two days earlier, on that Monday of unseasonal gales and rain, and immediately sought refuge in a pub. When the weather cleared, they took to the Kintyre Way and had had no rain since. They had come from Southend and had booked the 11.30 bus from Campbeltown the following morning, intending to visit Oban. One of the girls asked how far it was to the end of the Way, but there was no simple answer to that. A rough estimate could have been offered, but it's the nature of the terrain that determines progress, with distance 'a psychological condition rather than a measurable issue', as Tobias Wolff put it.[79]

They intended camping that night and asked advice about a suitable place. George and I immediately suggested the Inneans Bay and explained that they'd see it appear before them as they descended from the top of the Aignish, but, with that bus they had to catch in mind, a camping spot nearer to Machrihanish seemed more sensible. I couldn't advise them on the morning bus service from Machrihanish into town;

for once, I didn't have a timetable with me when I could have used it. Ten-thirty, I discovered later, was their deadline for reaching the village.

Photographs were taken, and I got the lone male in the company to write his e-mail address in my journal. The following evening, I sent him one of the group photographs George had taken, but he didn't respond. As George and I neared the forest, we stopped and looked back into the west. We saw two figures, bent under the weight of big rucksacks, silhouetted against the skyline, plodding uphill. We waited and watched until the third and the fourth stooping figure appeared, and then went our own way, speculating on how they would fare in the time remaining to them if they were to catch their bus.

Mossy saxifrage

While George and I were on the cliffs, 'mountain avens' popped into my mind as the name of the flower which had excited me. I knew that the Largiebaan area, with its limestone, is the only location in Kintyre where *Dryas octopetala* is found, and my mental picture of it, from books, was of a flower with white petals and a yellow middle. The image was true, but we hadn't seen mountain avens, which, Agnes Stewart informed me later, is concentrated further south. When I consulted *Scottish Wild Plants* that evening at home, I noticed that mountain avens has eight petals – and may produce more, but never fewer – whereas the flower I'd photographed had merely five. Judy, too, was consulting botanical books, and asked me to describe the leaves I'd seen. When I admitted I hadn't checked them, I was given a severe telling-off. Being me, I offered a robust defence – that I believed I already knew the species from its flower, so why examine its leaves? – but the defence was indefensible! I now concede that the patient examination of an unfamiliar flower isn't just a practical requirement, but might also afford aesthetic satisfaction.

In the end, she identified the flower as mossy saxifrage (*Saxifraga hypnoides*), a relative rarity in Kintyre, which Cunningham and Kenneth (p 22) found at Largiebaan and Johnston's Point on the Learside. Agnes Stewart considers it the rarest of the saxifrages at Largiebaan and told me it can be found near the top of the 'Big Corrie'. Cunningham and Kenneth remark that 'Plants in scree near Largybaan are pink in bud and on outside of petals'.

5 June: Rubha Dùn Bhàin

A couple of days later, I again set off by bike for the Atlantic coast, this time alone. I was late starting, for the morning had been wet; however, the day improved and kept improving, so I decided to go. My sole motivation was the mountain avens colony Agnes Stewart had told me about. Considering my late start, I reckoned the best plan would be to push the bike up the Bruach Dearg to Largiebaan steading and from there cycle out the Kintyre Way to a crossing point which would take me to the cliffs. Jimmy MacDonald had shown me a route through forest several years before, but I cut off the track too early and entered the wrong ride. I was too far north, closer to Largiebaan Glen than I should have been, but by keeping the sun ahead of me I knew I was going in the right direction and finally reached my destination without much loss of time.

I reckoned I should be looking for *Dryas octopetala* in the long scree between Rubha Dùn Bhàin and Innean Gaothach, 'Windy Cove', a ruined Campbell settlement, which I discussed in *Kintyre Places and Place-Names* (p 148). I was there on 14 June 2012 with Jimmy and Judy, looking at places and trying to fit their names to the landscape. I descended a fair bit that day to look into Innean Seilich, north of the scree, and Innean Tioram, south of it. The former should translate as 'Willow Hollow', but the likelihood of willows there, unless of the scrub variety, seemed remote; the latter is 'Dry Hollow'. ('Cove' is generally the interpretation I'd take from an *innean* place-name in Kintyre, but in these cases – of features not quite of the shore – it doesn't really work.)

Apart from an apple, I hadn't eaten since lunch at 1.30, so at 6.15 I found a grassy spot which offered a little shelter from the west wind, and sat there, facing north to the sheer rock wall of Rubha Dùn Bhàin. The botany so far had been unexceptional, but the scree, which was right in front of me, had still to be explored, and I was keen to search there; so, after a brief rest, I set off down to the edge of the jumbled rocks. I hadn't gone far, when I noticed white flowers on a rock face, and inside a minute *D. octopetala* was inches from my face. I scrambled north and was soon surrounded by the flowers, which were thickest on the upper slopes of the scree, where the rocks were less concentrated or had grassed over. I guessed there must be many hundreds of the flowers in sight, making *D. octopetala* the most abundant species there (followed, probably, by birdsfoot-trefoil, *Lotus corniculatus*).

The Flora of Kintyre (p 21) refers to two colonies near Largiebaan: 'One south of Rudha Duin Bhain covers an appreciable area, with the *Dryas* locally dominant.' That, clearly, was the colony I had encountered. The other, for which no specific location is given, is described as smaller and isolated. In the decades since these records were compiled, other colonies may have formed; others, indeed, may have been missed. Could Madge Cunningham and her collaborator on *The Flora of Kintyre*, A. G. Kenneth, have comprehensively searched the whole coast from the Mull to Largiebaan? Some bits of that coastline are not accessible without a degree of risk, but that particular *Dryas* colony is relatively safe to visit. The top falls away in grassy slopes to the scree, and sheep and goat tracks cross the scree itself.

In places where humans are now rarely encountered, it would be easy to assume that it was always so, but for thousands of years people have had their own reasons, which we might not now appreciate, for living in such remoteness.

Hunter-gatherers, farmers and shepherds are only the obvious groups, but within these groups were others with more specialised interests, such as dyers collecting plants and lichens for the colouring of cloth and wool. Innumerable generations of children doubtless played in the rocks and scree, the last of them probably Campbells in the eighteenth century, when the shrill voices echoing from the rocks would have been Gaelic. But that day I evoked the shade of Madge Cunningham, who died in 1979, the year *The Flora of Kintyre* was published, and the image of Agnes Stewart, a living presence whose interest in botany has, if anything, increased with the passage of the years, though her geographical range has diminished.

I could have done with longer on the scree, but time was pressing. I promised myself that next time I came, I would set off earlier, allowing myself three or four hours for exploration, and that I would choose a better day: sunny with a cool breeze. I left the cliffs at 7 and headed directly for the forest ride I'd earlier missed. There was shelter in there and I decided to sit for a while in the sunshine. At 7.55, I was back at my bike and on my way home. The return journey from Largiebaan took just an hour-and-a-half.

Reflecting on my all too brief experiences beneath the cliff top, it seemed as though I had stepped through a door and descended into another world of startling differences, and these differences were botanical: not just in the abundance of flowers, but in the variety of species. I suspect that the flora there is now less subject to grazing, allowing greater proliferation: there were no sheep in sight and merely three goats, which were heading my way, but, having seen me, turned back.

Mountain avens

In *The Englishman's Flora* (p 166), Geoffrey Grigson complains that 'No plant so much needs an apt English name'. He dismisses 'mountain avens' and a couple of folk alternatives, suggesting that 'a name suggestive of gold, whiteness, and open sunlight' is required. Grigson was a poet as well as a botanist, so his musings must carry some weight, but, for me, 'mountain avens' is pleasant-sounding, poetic even, whatever its descriptive failings. The Latin name, *Dryas octopetala*, is, however, more vivid: *dryas* summons up the mythical dryad, which is the wood-nymph of the oaks, from the resemblance of its leaf to that of the oak, and *octopetala* is 'eight-petalled'.

D. octopetala is an ancient member of the flora of the British Isles, remains dating back about 20,000 years having been uncovered in southern England, where, in colder times, it grew in tundra-like vegetation along with other arctic-alpine species. The distribution of *D. octopetala* is now related to particular rock types, including limestone, which accounts for its presence in the Largiebaan area.

A remarkable facility, for warming the flowers and attracting pollinating insects into them, is explained by Philip Lusby and Jenny Wright in *Scottish Wild Plants* (p 41): 'The constant glow of the flowers on a sunny day is not an illusion, but an adaptation known as sun-tracking whereby the dish-shaped flowers constantly turn to face the sun throughout the day.' Might 'gilded sun-tracker' be proposed as a replacement name for 'mountain avens'? From Geoffrey's shade I hear a muffled oath!

6 June: Carradale Glen

For a couple of years, Iain McAlister and I had been discussing visiting old settlements in Carradale Glen, and that day had finally arrived. Iain, who is manager of Glen Scotia Distillery, Campbeltown, was brought up at Carradale and has a keen interest in Kintyre history. His father, Jim, from Grogport, north of Carradale, would be accompanying us. Jim knew the glen intimately, having worked all his life with the Forestry Commission at Carradale; in fact, he had just retired at the age of 71. Iain collected me at mid-day and we drove to Carradale and picked up Jim at Tosh's Park, two rows of wooden houses originally built for forestry workers.

There was one place, Lurgan, I was especially keen to visit. I'd seen it in August 2012, when Judy and I went to Narachan, but from our vantage point that day the way down to it looked difficult. Upper Carradale Glen is densely forested and much of the forest has already been felled and replanted, leaving ground that is littered with debris and studded with tree-stumps, as I was about to rediscover.

Deuchran

There was an old settlement I hadn't expected to visit, but I can say I was there, though I didn't see it, and it will never be seen again by anyone. We were driving slowly along a forestry road when Iain stopped the vehicle and announced we were at Deuchran. We got out and looked around, but there was no sign that a farmhouse had ever been there, though Iain speculated that some of the big stones embedded in the road might have come from the buildings. Jim remembered Deuchran as a substantial steading before it was bulldozed out of existence.

There were two farms named Deuchran, the big one (*Mòr*) and the little one *(Beag)*, which appear in charters in 1502. The name has been interpreted as *Dubhcheathramhan*, 'Black quarterlands'.[80] In the 1851 census, there were 25 persons in the two farms. In 'Duchran More', Angus and Elizabeth MacQuilkan, both born in Kilberry Parish, had nine children, as had Keith and Catherine Campbell, from Skipness Parish, in 'Duchranbeg'. Also at Duchranbeg lived 65-year-old widow and pauper Janet McConachy, born in Killean Parish. In fact, none of the adults in the Deuchrans – there were two others, a lodger and a 'servant' – was born in Saddell Parish, in which the farms lay.

Angus MacQuilkan, who died in 1932, aged 74, at Tangy Place, Dalintober, was born at Deuchran, which the family quit in 1889 for the tenancy of Low Ugadale, where his brother Robert (p 13) would remain. Angus was five years in Ballymeanach and twenty years in Ballochgair, where he established a solid reputation as a sheep- and cattle-breeder: 'The name Angus McQuilkan of Ballochgair was known and honoured over a wide area.' He never married and was survived by his brother Robert and three sisters, one of whom, Eliza, married William Semple in Dippen, Carradale. It was a marriage of differing cultures, native and Lowland Scots, but by then the differences didn't matter, because Gaelic was slipping out the back door with a coat over its head. Six of the eight pall-bearers at his funeral to Brackley were Semple nephews: Duncan and Thomas, Dippen; Angus and James, Rhonadale; Richard, High Ugadale; John, Ballochgair.[81]

Iain told me about a postcard he'd seen for sale on the internet. He collects postcards and was interested in it, but someone was already bidding and he let it go. It was a picture of Clachan village and had been franked at Tayinloan on 10 April 1917. Addressed to 'Neil Sinclair, Deuchran, Carradale, Campbeltown', it said merely: 'With kind regards.'

A photograph of Bella Campbell, 'Deuchran Farm', appeared in the *Scottish Farmer Album* – 'the publication par excellence of the agricultural year' – as one of the buttermakers who gained 98 per cent in the *Scottish Farmer*'s butter tests.[82] That was in 1922, not even a century ago.

At the Skipness Ploughing Match in February 1933 at Arivore – won, for the third successive year by John MacKinnon, Achnasavil, a feat entitling him to keep the Kilchamaig Cup – Archibald Blue, Deuchran, came seventh, and received 12s, to which was added 7s 6d for being 'the ploughman coming the longest distance'.[83]

In 1888, when advertised to let by Carradale Estate, 'Duchrau' was described as 82 acres of 'good arable', with grazing for 1600 black-faced sheep and 25 cattle,[84] hard to believe when one stood on that forestry road, where the steading once stood, and looked around at a landscape of coniferous forest. There is a farm on Deuchran Hill, but it's a wind farm owned by E.ON, a company based in Germany. Later that day, I would stand beneath the stately turbines for the first time.

The late Ian MacDonald, Largieside historian and genealogist, was taken by car to the wind farm in 2002, and recounted his visit in a letter to me dated 17 June. He saw all the turbines turning in north-west wind and noted that there wasn't 'much sound coming from them as we stood below the blades and took some photos'. He mentioned that his first time at Deuchran was with his father Malcolm, farmer in Beachmenach, and his cousin John MacDonald, Culfuar. They walked from 'Bradge', or Braids, to 'Johnny Blue's sale'. He dated that trek over the hills from Killean to 'around 1932', when he'd have been about 13 years old. In fact, it must have been 1934, for in that year Deuchran was advertised to let at Martinmas (11 November). The 'sale' must have been a public auction of Blue's stock and gear, because, as the advertisement bluntly stated: 'John Blue, present occupier ... is not to be an offerer.'[85]

Afforestation at Carradale began three years later, in 1937, with the Forestry Commission's purchase of 13,000 acres there. A statement the following year maintained that 'The policy of the Commission is not to encroach on good agricultural land, but to use to advantage rough hill which is far more suitable for tree-planting than for any other purpose'.[86] Looking around Carradale Glen now, one wonders at the veracity of that claim, and I cannot but reflect that in this fast-changing and volatile world of ours, a time may come when the production of home-grown food will eclipse in importance the cultivation of soft timber. Those multitudinous acres of hill arable, which cost farmers millennia of labour in the clearance of trees and rocks and were violated in a matter of years, won't be available. There were 82 acres of 'good arable' on Deuchran alone in 1888, down to 30 in 1934,[87] and now there is little or nothing.

Lurgan

16. Jim McAlister at Lurgan, 6 June 2015. Photograph by Iain McAlister.

Iain was able to take his vehicle quite close to Lurgan, and we made our way down to the ruin through the expected forest debris. Pre-afforestation, it must have been a beautiful spot, and it retains touches of that beauty. It is a Gaelic name, anatomical in origin, and, like many such names, grafted imaginatively on to the landscape. Simply stated, *lurgann* is a 'shin', and by transference the sloping ridge of a hill. It would be virtually impossible now to identify the feature from which the settlement was named, but it won't be far away. It is the only such place-name in Kintyre and isn't on Ordnance Survey maps, though the ruin itself is marked; but nearby 'Lorgie Hill' preserves the name in a variant form.

The best-known example of the place-name Lurgan is the town in County Armagh, Ireland, where Neil Lennon, who both played for and managed Celtic F.C., was born in 1971.

No one has been born in the Kintyre Lurgan for perhaps two hundred years. The earliest mention of the place I have found dates to just 1736. It was probably a smallholding rather than a farm; when abandoned in 1850, it was certainly a smallholding. The ruins are overgrown and obscured by wind-toppled timber, but from what I could see of the structure it appeared to be more a sheep-pen than a habitation, so perhaps the house – which by 1850 was said to have been falling about its occupants' heads – was converted for the use of shepherds.

These last occupants have intrigued me for years. In the 1841 census of Killean and Kilchenzie, 'Lurgine' was occupied by John 'Martine', who gave his age as 99, his wife Mary, aged 82, Alex McConnachy, aged 60, an 'agricultural labourer', his wife Mary, aged 50 and a daughter of John Martin, and two others whose relationship to John I haven't yet established, Isabella Taylor, 45, and Duncan 'Martine', 10.

In the following census, ten years later, Lurgan is absent from the record, for reasons which can be explained in detail. In April 1851, the inspector of poor for Campbeltown Parish wrote to his counterpart in Killean to report an application for assistance by Alex McConachy and his wife Mary. His 'strength [was] failing him' and his wife was 'in bad health'. 'During his residence in Killean Parish,' the letter explained, McConachy 'occupied a spot of ground called Lurgin which he cultivated by spade labour and by this means supported himself and wife and kept a cow or two and were in tolerable condition.' As disclosed, however, in a subsequent letter, 'their house lately was falling about their heads', but the laird, Moreton Macdonald of Largie, declined to repair the property and urged them to quit, offering an inducement of £4 if they would move to Campbeltown. They rashly accepted his offer, resettled in Campbeltown, presumably ran through the money and then applied for poor relief in that parish.

In October 1851, the Campbeltown inspector of poor despatched a further letter to his Killean and Kilchenzie counterpart, urging him to remonstrate with Moreton Macdonald. Mary McConachy's mother, Mary Martin, 'had nursed some of the Largy family and it was always believed that the applicants would not be removed during their lifetime'. John and Mary Martin had presumably died between 1841, when they appeared in the census, and 1850, but their daughter Mary, Alex McConachy's wife, presumably believed that the promise of lifelong accommodation on Largie Estate should have extended to her.

The letter contained strong criticism of Moreton Macdonald and of Kintyre landowners in general:

'You are quite aware that it is an improper action to put away the poor from a Parish, & if Mr Moreton had this burden he had no right to throw it from his own shoulders upon the shoulders of others. He has enough of other houses on his property of Rhunahorine, & elsewhere, to which they could be sent without casting them forth upon the wide world with his offer of £4.

'In the present state of matters, when so much excitement prevails as to Landlords ejecting the poor, it would not be difficult to draw out a case of hardship & cruelty from the above materials.

'It is not to be permitted that any person in authority should use his influence so as to clear himself from moral and legal responsibilities, & ... I hope that you will take occasion to bring this case to Mr Moreton's notice for his reconsideration, either to grant £4 annually or to give them a house upon his own estate.

'This Parish has been sufficiently inundated with the poor from Killean previously, & as this seems a bad case I beg you will take such steps as may lead to the present matter being satisfactorily settled, & also that no such attempts be made in future to Burden this Parish with the poor from either Mr Moreton or any other proprietor in your parish.'[88]

The outcome of the correspondence is unknown to me, but the two letters illumine a little corner of Kintyre social history. The first contains a list of places where the McConachys had lived prior to their arrival in Campbeltown, information elicited from them in order to assess their entitlement to relief. By April 1851, they had been in Campbeltown for 6 months; they were in 'Lurgie' for 14 years, Skipness for 9 years, 'Auchinhork' (Oatfield) for 13 years, with 'Major McVicar, Pennygown' for a year and with 'Mr D. Breckenridge, Killelan' for 5 years.[89] They had clearly been around in Kintyre during their marriage, and presumably moved to Lurgan *c.*1836, to be with Mary's ageing parents there.

Alex McConachy was born at Ballygroggan near Machrihanish, and there were also McConnachies in all five settlements south of Ballygroggan. In 1686, John buie McGeachy and John McConnachie in Craigaig came to blows and were fined for 'bloodwit and battery' and jailed until they paid up.[90] In 1694, the next two settlements down the coast, Innean Beag and Innean Mòr, were tenanted by John and Donald McConikie and Alexander and Malcolm McConikie respectively, and, further south again, there was a John McConnachie in Largiebaan and another John in Gartnacopaig.[91]

McConnachie, however, is not the surname I am primarily interested in at Lurgan. I am curious about the Martins there, because the several Martin families in Campbeltown, including my own, all originated in the waist of Kintyre, straddling Kilchenzie and Saddell parishes. In 1824 Dugald McConachy, Kilkivan, married Katherine Martin in Lurgan, and in 1830 a 'natural daughter', Effy, was born to a Martin woman in Lurgan. Most unusually, there is a blank where her forename should be, though the father's name, John McCallum, Clachaig Glen, is complete.[92] These two women were presumably daughters of old John Martin at Lurgan in 1841, and there I'll leave that Martin family, in print at least.

A 'serpent ball'

I'm back in June 2015 with Jim and Iain McAlister, sitting on the grassy bank of the burn which flows past Lurgan from Gleann Drochaide ('Bridge Valley'). Several burns meet nearby at the Junction Pool, a recent anglers' place-name. Carradale Water flows thence to the sea, and in the 1960s Jim planted trees on the north side of the stream. While he and his fellow-planters were sitting having lunch – just as we were that day – one of them, who had wandered off, discovered a 'serpent ball' in a heathery bank. By the time Jim reached the spot, the adders – at least half-a-dozen of them – were separating. As Jim remarked, 'There are certain things in life you see only once, and are lucky to see'. Records of this phenomenon aren't exactly bursting out of natural history literature, but there is another local report. Mathew MacMillan, Glasgow, claimed that on 13 February 1895 he shot 'five red adders coiled up in a ball below Cour Graveyard'.[93]

Breaclarach

Our final destination that afternoon was Breaclarach, which we visited on our way back down the glen; but, to be honest, amid the thickly afforested hills I didn't have a clue where I was! Iain parked the car beside the forestry road and we set off downhill, through trees which Jim himself had planted in the early 1990s. There was a belt of sitka spruce on the top side of the plantation and larch on the bottom side, the latter having been planted experimentally inside containers known as 'plug-pots'. The route was overgrown, and Jim had gone ahead, but Iain took me right to the site of Breaclarach.

Gaelic *breac* essentially means 'speckled' or 'spotted', while *làrach* has various meanings. Dwelly's dictionary lists half-a-dozen – to which may be added, from Kintyre, the base of a corn-stack[94] – but the relevant one here is probably, and prophetically, 'ruin', the remains of an old habitation.

Breaclarach, like Lurgan, does not appear on record until the eighteenth century, but it was a once-populous settlement. In 1771, between 17 January and 19 April, there were six baptisms there, involving four families: Blue, Brown, Campbell and McCallum.[95] Three years later, in 1774, John and Archibald McIlchallum in 'Brecklarach' were cited in a legal action, raised by the Duke of Argyll against illegal wood-cutters on his lands, but whether as witnesses or accused is uncertain.[96]

The forest round Breaclarach was clear-felled in the mid-1990s and then replanted, so between new trees and the remains of old trees, exploration of the site is 'no picnic' – and I'm using that cliché in a literal sense, because I couldn't see a patch of clear ground anywhere that two or three visitors could have occupied and enjoyed a picnic. The first feature we looked at, however, was a beauty: a skilfully made and well preserved corn-drying kiln. I'd say the kiln at Craigaig just surpasses it in both construction and preservation, but the Breaclarach kiln has a feature which the Craigaig kiln – and all others I have seen in Kintyre – lacks: a series of stone steps in the wall, leading on to the top of the structure.

Somewhere in the ruins, there was a quern-stone which Iain found and photographed during his first visit to Breaclarach about twenty years before. He described it as a smooth flat stone with, in the middle of it, a hole so finely formed it could almost have been 'laser-cut with surgical precision'. The kiln and quern-stone were linked to each other in the life of the community at Breaclarach. The first enabled grain to be heat-dried and the second enabled that grain to be hand-ground into meal. But we searched in vain for the stone; if it's still there, it's concealed by natural growth or the litter of forest-clearance.

An eccentric-looking chimney-head in the gable of one of the roofless houses was the final interesting feature. It was bulky, square-shaped and faced with thick slabs of stone. I'd never seen a chimney-head like it anywhere else. In design and dimensions it appeared to be a minor architectural 'folly', but I'll let a photograph do my work for me.

17. Chimney-head at Breaclarach, 6 June 2015. Photograph by the author.

Sheila Maclean

The name Breaclarach is also found at Tarbert. It was recorded by the Ordnance Survey in 1867, attached to a little ruin on the hill above Rubha an Sàirdseant, and was later transferred to a house on the Pier Road.[97] The latter was associated with a literary family. Sheila M. P. Maclean's only known work was a novel, *The Coming of Judith*, published in 1939. This book has intrigued me for years, for the simple reason that I have never seen a copy of it. I enquired at Campbeltown Library and discovered to my surprise that the book isn't held even at headquarters in Sandbank.

I mentioned Sheila Maclean to Lisa Tuttle, the American-born writer who lives near Tarbert, and she too became intrigued by the mysterious novel. Lisa discovered that merely three copies appear to exist in public libraries, two in the British Library, London, and one in the National Library of Scotland, Edinburgh. Owing to the rarity of *The Coming of Judith*, the latter wasn't prepared to loan out its copy; so, Judith wouldn't be coming from Edinburgh!

Lisa had the idea of posting a query about Sheila on the Facebook forum 'All Things Tarbert', and one of the respondents remembered working for her in his youth. In her old age, she had eighteen cats, and his job was to feed them and clean out their litter boxes. She had given him a copy of her book, but it was, alas, destroyed in a fire. Miss Maclean took in lodgers at Breaclarach, and when the poet George Campbell Hay returned to his childhood home for the last time in 1983, the year before his death, he stayed in her house. I had two letters from him 'c/o Miss MacLean, Breaclarach, Tarbert', the first dated 18/1/1983, days after his arrival, and the second dated 27/8/1983, before his return to Edinburgh. In the latter, he remarked that he wouldn't 'be coming to Campbeltown just yet' – he never did reach me – and ended gloomily with: 'Am beginning to feel my age.'

Was he aware that his landlady had written a novel? If so, he never mentioned it to me. Coincidentally, just as his father's great Tarbert novel, *Gillespie*, had been published in the year the First World War broke out, and was overshadowed by the cataclysm, Sheila Maclean's novel appeared in 1939, three months before the Second World War was declared. Its publication was noticed in the *Campbeltown Courier* of 15 April 1939, under the heading 'Tarbert Authoress's First Novel'. The publisher was Messrs. Arthur H. Stockwell Ltd.,

London, and the price was six shillings. I quote the review in full, since it's likely to be the closest the reader will ever get to the elusive novel:

> This charming novel, redolent of the countryside, attractively portrays village life.
> The story is an absorbing one, and centres round Judith, who enters the village as organist at the Parish Church, finds romance and love after disappointments, and becomes part of the village life as the wife of one of its most honoured members.
> There is intrigue, romance, disillusionment; and the aspirations of the characters, which are all clearly etched and make a strong and lasting impression upon the reader, are faithfully, indeed graphically, portrayed.
> The characterisation is effective; the dialogue is natural and unforced, convincing and photographic in its presentation of the people; and there is sufficient plot and incident to retain the interest throughout.
> The leisurely, happy life of the countryside, which forms the background, is insinuated surely and provides a restful atmosphere for the story, which, whilst not pulsating with action and excitement, unfolds itself at a tempo well in keeping with its nature.

Sheila Maclean, who died in 1987 at the age of 77, is still remembered in Tarbert, chiefly for her eccentricities.

Hugh Maclean

Sheila Maclean's grandfather, Hugh Maclean, who died in 1902 at Kildalton, Islay, was also a published writer. If he is remembered at all in Kintyre, it'll be for his poems *Stray Leaves*, reissued as *Kintyriana*, and *MacCalien's Raid*. He was an 'esteemed contributor' to the *Argyllshire Herald*, and, less transparently, was 'connected to the *Glasgow Herald* at one time'. I reproduced an article of his in the

Kintyre Magazine, without at the time knowing who he was. He was sent to Canada in 1880 by the Kintyre Agricultural Society to report on the state of agriculture in Manitoba, and an interesting report it was, not least for the number of Kintyre settlers he met and named.[98]

Maclean was born in Campbeltown Parish and spoke Gaelic as well as English, according to the Tarbert census of 1891, when he was in 'Brecklarach Villa' with two daughters. He was predeceased in 1882 by his wife, Catherine MacDonald MacLiver; by a son, John, who was employed by the British India Steam Navigation Company and died at sea returning home from India in 1883; and by a daughter, Catherine, who died in 1893. Son Hugh died in Christchurch, New Zealand, in 1919, and daughter Annie in 1941. A third son, Angus Maclean, Sheila's father, died in 1948 at the age of 84, and his wife, Maud Pagan, in 1953.

Hugh Maclean's background was farming – he was factor of Stonefield and Kintarbert Estate – but he also engaged widely in public life, as a Justice of the Peace, church elder, school board member and lieutenant in the Tarbert Artillery Volunteers, of which forty uniformed members attended his funeral.

A 'noted antiquary', Maclean was instrumental, in 1892, in bringing Dr Robert Munro, author of *Ancient Scottish Lake-Dwellings*, to excavate the crannogs exposed by drainage at Lochan Dùghaill, near Clachan. Maclean was considered one of Tarbert's 'intellectual forces', and an obituarist recounted, evoking a time when education was valued for its own sake and counted also as entertainment, that 'His lectures and scientific addresses will be recalled by those who were privileged to hear them as literary treats'. Of his poetry I'll quote only a verse, from 'The Dirge of Somerled'. It may be compared with the torrent of jingoistic outpourings which would come twelve years later with the Great War: 'O cruel, hateful war – thou demons fell,/ Worst scourge of all the woes this side of hell./ Fools, without thinking, rush to thy embrace/ And lick the horrors of thy bloody face.'[99]

7 June: Largiebaan

On a sunny, breezy day, I returned to Largiebaan with botany again foremost in my thoughts. A few years ago, the notion came to me to one day climb from the shore to the cliff top and photograph every flower species I encountered. I was hoping for rarities, a motivation akin to that which propels me into a charity shop whenever I see one: the chance of finding a book – if a first edition or signed by the author, so much the better – or a CD which suits my taste. I had begun to appreciate what I'd only vaguely known for years, that Largiebaan, owing to its geology and remoteness, is a fascinating botanical hunting ground, and I was still fit enough to reach parts of the coast that other local botany enthusiasts, more knowledgeable than I, would hesitate to venture into.

As I had done two days previously, I took my bike up the Bruach Dearg and left it beyond Largiebaan steading, but this time there was no boggy ground to cross and my feet stayed dry. I angled off the Kintyre Way between the last strip of forest and the cliffs, and descended to the shore along the north flank of the glen. The colony of kidney vetch which Agnes Stewart had noted years before on the rocks at the foot of the glen was still there, and I later saw small colonies on rock faces between there and the caves. It's a common flower on cliffs along that coast.

Rose-root and wild strawberry

Having gained the shore – not without a few anxious moments – I began making my way north and noticed a plant I'd never seen before, growing from a damp, shady overhang. I photographed it and then found a grassy spot in which to sit and eat. I was surrounded by fading sea pinks and had for company a fading peacock, the only butterfly I saw all afternoon below the cliffs. I was about to move on, when I said to myself, 'Damn it, you're still not observing carefully', and returned to the plant for a closer look. It was then I noticed that, under the foliage, several of the thick roots had been exposed by erosion.

When Judy examined my photographs that night, she identified rose-root (*Sedum rosea*), a member of the stonecrop family which grows on sea cliffs and mountain rocks. Grigson described it as 'rather a dull plant' with 'mean yellow' flowers, but said that if the stock is cut it gives out a lovely fragrance, 'like the damask Rose', as John Gerard observed, going on four centuries ago.[100] On Largiebaan shore, I wasn't yet aware of that tip, but even had I been, I wouldn't have taken a knife to the plant, which was the only one I saw there.

Judy forwarded the photographs to Agnes Stewart, who confirmed the identification and described *Sedum rosea* as 'another of the Largiebaan specialities', which she herself had seen once 'up Largiebaan Burn'. *The Flora of Kintyre* (p 22) describes its distribution as 'from near Ballygroggan to east of Signal Station', in other words Atlantic coast. So, I hadn't yet discovered a rarity; but I'd discovered a flower that was new to me, enjoyed meeting it, as it were, and will recognise it next time I meet it.

Before I got the length of the caves, I decided to cut straight up the 800-foot slope to the top of the cliff. This route ends in a tight grassy gully which I believe is the map feature Bealach Ghillean Duibh. Gaelic *bealach* is aptly a 'pass' or 'gap' and the remainder of the name commemorates a mythical 'Black Lad' who was killed there while trying to entice the fort-dweller's beautiful wife to elope with him.[101] That has been my exit route of choice for the past thirty-odd years. It is steep, fairly safe, and no rock-climbing is required. The ascent took me just over an hour, including frequent stops to photograph flowers; but there would have been frequent stops for rest, anyway.

There was one species I was delighted to find, and that was wild strawberry (*Fragaria vesca*). The late Willie Colville, Machrihanish, told me many years ago that he had found strawberries on Rubha Dùn Bhàin. I never doubted his word, but until then simply hadn't noticed the plant, which, since it thrives on limestone, should be an obvious member of the Largiebaan flora. I was too early for the tiny, delicious fruits, which I have sampled infrequently elsewhere in Kintyre.[102] Richard Mabey, in *Food for Free*, rightly dismisses the commercial monsters as 'freaks, so dogmatically grown to astonish by their colour and size that their insides taste like snow'.

Snails also require lime – for shell formation – and from the bottom to the top of the slope I encountered small colourfully banded snails all the way. It seemed impossible that I should manage to avoid crushing at least one of them, but I was spared that sickening crunch, for although quite numerous, they were also visible in the sparse vegetation.

Air Training Corps

I have seen only one pre-1970 photograph, published or otherwise, of people at Largiebaan, and while lunching on the shore there I remembered it. It appeared in the *Campbeltown Courier* in May 1957 and captured members of the 1405 (Campbeltown) Squadron of the Air Training Corps 'hav[ing] a breather during a hiking and climbing expedition at Largiebaan'. There were fifteen boys in the group, their ages ranging from early to late teens, accompanied by two adults, their Commanding Officer, Flight Lieutenant John Galbraith, and their past C.O., Flight Lieutenant Archie McGougan. Some of the boys are wearing outdoor gear and others are quite casually dressed, and from the clarity of the background cliffs, they seem to have had a day of fine weather for their outing. The boys include, as far as I can determine, John Smith, Archie McGown, John McCormick, George Durnan, John McKinlay, Angus Gillespie, Ronnie Murray, Duncan McIsaac, Leslie Bywaters, Campbell McGeachy and George McMillan.

18. Campbeltown ATC at Largiebaan, May 1957. John Galbraith is in the back row, wearing beret, with Archie McGougan at his left. Campbeltown Courier, *30/5/1957.*

The ATC, which was established in 1941 as a recruitment organisation for the Royal Air Force, is still flourishing, but not in Campbeltown. In the year of the Largiebaan 'expedition', two other adventures were reported in the *Courier*. In August, sixteen cadets and one officer of the Campbeltown Squadron spent their 'annual camp' at RAF Topcliffe in England, where they flew 'an average of 2½ hours' in Marathon and Chipmunk aircraft,[103] and in September an Anson aircraft came to Machrihanish airport from RAF Leuchars to give cadets further flying time. Some were taken around the Mull of Kintyre and saw ships of the NATO fleet 'manoeuvring off Southend', while others, accompanied by Flight Lieutenant Galbraith, were flown to Prestwick airport for lunch.[104] Fundraising that year consisted of a 'Grand Bazaar and Fun Fair' at Rieclachan on 3 July, followed by an evening dance, and, later in the month, a dance in the Victoria Hall.

Squadron-Leader John McLaren Galbraith, D.F.C., G.M.

The word 'hero' is so freely employed in tabloid newspapers as to be virtually worthless, but John Galbraith, commanding officer of the ATC in Campbeltown, unarguably merits the description at its pre-tabloid value. A son of John Galbraith, farmer in Polliwilline, he was a student at Glasgow University when the Second World War broke out. He was conscripted into the Royal Army Service Corps and served in France until evacuated at Dunkirk in 1941. Soon after his return to Britain, he applied successfully for a transfer to the Royal Air Force and, having trained as a pilot in the United States, at the end of that year he was posted to an RAF Coastal Command station in the south of England.

He was awarded the Distinguished Flying Cross for an attack, during a reconnaissance operation, on seven enemy minesweepers in the Bay of Biscay. From a supplement to the *London Gazette*: 'In the face of intense heavy and light anti-aircraft fire, Flying Officer Galbraith pressed home a most determined attack, setting one of the ships on fire. This officer has set a fine example of skill, bravery and devotion to duty.' His George Cross followed, when he and a fellow crewmember 'strove to pull three colleagues from their burning aircraft'. Towards the end of the war, he was promoted to Wing-Commander and served as personal assistant to Air Vice-Marshal Sir Hugh Lloyd in Malta, and later held a command in Greece, whence he returned to Britain to be demobilised.

He helped on Polliwilline Farm and involved himself as a volunteer in local organisations – the ATC, the church and Dunaverty Players drama club, as both actor and stage manager – but his wartime service, not least the wounds he suffered, took its inexorable toll and he died in a hospital in Dumfries on 14 May 1961, at the age of 42.[105]

John's nephew and namesake, John Galbraith, who farms Polliwilline, inherited his RAF logbook, and also inherited the trees and daffodils which he planted on the coast of the farm while home on leave before his departure for pilot training in the US.

10 June: Below the Aignish

I was at Largiebaan yet again, and yet again the motivation was botany. Without a strong motivation, I certainly wouldn't have gone so often that summer. I am always thrilled to be there, but the journey out had become increasingly tiresome. It was probably a touch of fatigue, mental as much as physical, which companionship would have alleviated, but again I was alone. The day was one of the warmest of that summer, which admittedly isn't saying much. As well as a large flask of tea, I had six small cartons of pineapple juice with me, and emptied them all.

For the first time that year, I was looking for somewhere to sit that would catch rather than shield me from the wind, and chose a grassy spur above the spot where Jimmy MacDonald was bitten by a spider (p 19). I was facing north to the Aignish and contemplating what route to take to reach the foot of the cliff and the *Oxytropis campestris* I hoped to find. Off to my right, I noticed a lovely little clump of primroses looking 'freakishly fresh', as I noted in my journal, but when I scanned the Aignish with binoculars for remnants of the myriad primrose colonies I had seen clothing the cliff on 17 April, there was no sign of any flowers. On that day, I had traversed the Big Corrie almost to the foot of the Aignish, and then climbed up and out. This time, I decided I'd retrace my steps and regain the cliff top at a lower point, sparing myself time and effort.

I soon found myself on a well-defined sheep and goat track which led right to the boulder field under the cliffs. The Aignish has shed thousands of tons of rock over millennia, but the track took me – or I allowed it to take me – to a spot beneath the bared face of a fall which could only have happened a year or two ago. When I got under it, I reckoned the area of the collapse at roughly 40 by 10 feet, and speculated on the density and species of the plants which had gradually colonised its cracks and ledges and then plunged to oblivion with the rock. The fresh-faced fallen slabs were all around me, contrasting with earlier debris which had weathered and welcomed colonising flowers and lichens. On and beneath the cliffs, the predominant colour was yellow – kidney vetch, birdsfoot-trefoil and tormentil – but I noticed, on arrival, clumps of light-coloured flowers resembling clover ... but growing on the cliff. A couple of these clumps were low enough to be accessible, and on my backside I slid down the scree of small stones at the very base of the cliff to examine and photograph them.

Yellow oxytropis

I had found Largiebaan's yellow oxytropis (*Oxytropis campestris*), but didn't at the time realise that's what it was. Somehow it didn't much resemble the photographs I'd examined in a book the previous evening; yet, when I looked again at the same photographs, on my return home, the resemblance was plain. I realised, of course, that I had encountered an unusual flower, but didn't realise what it was. The 'yellow' in the name probably deceived me, but when I later consulted *The Flora of Kintyre* (p 19), I read that at Largiebaan 'flower colour ranges from parchment, parchment tinted palest mauve, parchment tinted palest violet, to – exceptionally – pale purple'. I suppose I had seen 'parchment'. *The Flora*: 'The plant is in fair quantity in each of its stations and although it grows best on south and west facing cliffs, it seeds freely in the steep grassland below the cliff and is capable of reaching flowering size in such conditions. The plants flower and fruit freely despite the numerous wild goats, which seldom seem to touch it. On the more accessible ground it is however grazed by sheep.'

When I returned home and showed Judy my photographs of the 'mystery' flower, she at once recognised *Oxytropis campestris*, and then so did I. But that was all right: ignorance is remediable. I would recognise it at once if I saw it again, and quite probably be able to put a name to it, perhaps even two names, the Latin one as well. It's called 'education', and I'll pursue its joys until the day I die, if my mind holds out.

There are two *Oxytropis* species in Britain, *O. campestris* and *halleri*, both rare alpines and both regarded as climatic relics. In the whole of Britain, *O. campestris* occurs only in Angus, Perthshire and Kintyre. *Scottish Wild Plants* (p 74) remarks, without specifying location, that the flower 'descends to near sea-level in Kintyre, where it grows on the face of an exposed limestone sea-cliff together with other alpines such as mountain avens (*Dryas octopetala*) and hoary whitlowgrass (*Draba incana*)'.

O. campestris is known in North America as 'yellow locoweed' and is poisonous to grazing livestock – *loco* is Spanish for 'crazy' – but there is no record or tradition of its toxicity in Kintyre, where, as Cunningham and Kenneth noted, it is grazed by sheep. Perhaps its relative sparseness on accessible grazing minimises ill effects, but I am merely guessing.

Andrew Young (1885-1971) – Scottish clergyman, poet, and lover of wild flowers – was led to what he called 'Yellow Mountain Oxytropis' by a mysterious footprint in a Scottish glen. The anecdote is so strange, it could have been written as fiction. Young was 'wandering in an Angus glen', when, to his surprise, he came on a footprint in a patch of sand. The print 'pointed up the mountain' and 'looked so meaningless' he 'felt it had a meaning', so he started climbing. He almost turned back several times, thinking his impulse foolish, 'but each time went on, as though kicked by that footprint on the sand', and finally found *O. campestris* on a rock which, with startling exaggeration, he described as 'perhaps the only rock in Great Britain where it grows'. He concluded: 'That the footprint had been left by a botanist, I did not doubt, yet in that lonely glen, so lonely that I felt no one had been there before, it looked like the footprint of a ghost. I wanted to think it was, encouraging the hope that I too might revisit the earth as a ghost.'[106]

I had seen a flower – not an especially beautiful one, in my estimation – which probably only a few dozen folk in Kintyre have knowingly seen, and I consider myself privileged, even if the satisfaction is retrospective. (Three days later, Judy and I were at Largiebaan and identified small clumps of *O. campestris* on the walls of a deep cleft in the cliff opposite the Kintyre Way swing-gate.)

I'll return to the sloping, sliding foot of the Aignish, and not necessarily with botany foremost in my mind. Like all special places, wherever in the world, it has to be experienced to be appreciated, and preferably on such a beautiful day. Words must fail in their description, but here goes. The Aignish is a towering cliff at the north end of a great amphitheatre – of grassy slopes, scree and boulders – which resounds to the rhythmic crash of Atlantic swells and plaintive bird cries, and, on a warm day, gathers heat and shimmers in haze. In the south-west, across a sea sparkling in the sun as though the shards of a thousand broken mirrors were scattered on it, Rathlin Island and the north coast of Ireland lie, otherworldly behind a diaphanous blue screen. It's kind of poetic, but you're not there; not even a rock the size of your brain has bounced into life.

13 June: Largiebaan

I was back at Largiebaan, this time with Judy and a visitor, David Martin, whose paternal great-great grandparents, Donald Martin and Rachel MacIlhatton, emigrated from Kintyre to Upper Canada around 1835. David is 71 years old, but could pass, I imagine, for one of his sons, of which he has three. He e-mailed me at the end of May to say he would be attending a conference in Blackpool in mid-June and could arrange a visit to Campbeltown. I failed at first to 'place' him, but realised I must have had genealogical dealings with him in the past. I assumed the contact had been many years in the past, but in fact it was just over a year ago! Anyway, I said I'd be pleased to show him around, and added: 'Are you fit and active enough for a hike of some description (only if you enjoy walking)?' He replied in the affirmative.

David arrived on 11 June and I met him for lunch the following day. We spent a couple of hours that afternoon wandering around Kilkerran, looking randomly at gravestones and discussing surnames and our family histories. There is no obvious connection between our Martin families, but he later resolved to add his DNA to the database which holds mine.

I proposed a hike to Largiebaan next day, and he agreed; being dependent on my local knowledge, and presumably confident in my judgement, he was unlikely to have disagreed! I had 'swithered', however, over my choice of destination, because I'd been to Largiebaan so often that year there were grounds for a change of scene. Yet, I consider it scenically the most spectacular place in all Kintyre, and the one obvious place I'd want to take a visitor who was both fit and keen. I must also admit to having been tempted selfishly by the prospect of getting half-way there without recourse to bike or bus; and the fact that Judy was also enthusiastic about Largiebaan settled the matter.

So, on the Sunday we met David at 11 a.m. and proceeded out the Homestone road in the car he'd hired in Manchester. He parked it at the end of the Glenahanty road and we proceeded to the cliffs on foot. The day was cloudy and dull, but as soon as we'd settled ourselves on the grassy spur overlooking the caves, the sun, as though by magic, broke through and shone unhindered into the evening. David therefore experienced Largiebaan at its very best and was duly impressed, not least by the clear view across to the north coast of Antrim and Rathlin, and beyond to the Donegal hills in the distant west.

Colin Martin

The evening before we went to Largiebaan, I'd told David about Colin Campbell Martin, an uncle of my father's, who had died in 1912 at Lewiston, where David now lives. Colin was one of ten sons born to John Martin and Sarah Campbell in Dalintober. All of them, except Donald, a ship's carpenter, became fishermen, but Colin gave up fishing, joined the merchant navy, and ended up plying the fresh waters of Lake Ontario.

Before setting out that morning, I'd looked through a family history file, found a copy of Colin's obituary from the *Campbeltown Courier*, and tucked it into my 'hiking journal'. When I opened the journal on the cliff top, to enter a few notes on the outing, the obituary fell out and, remembering why it was there, I handed it to David. He was immediately fascinated, for many of the references were familiar to him.

I'd never given much thought to Colin Martin. He'd died overseas forty years before I was born, had never married and had no known descendants. Yet, there on the sunny cliffs of Largiebaan, my Canadian companion of two days had brought him – or a ghostly imagined version of him – a little nearer to me. David remembered having seen the very steamship on which Colin had last sailed – the last survivor of her kind – and knows the very quay she'd moored at on the night Colin died in his cabin. These were slender links at the end of a chain of circumstances extending from Kintyre across the Atlantic to the very country which lay under the horizon, west of our cliff perch.

Colin Martin was doubtless already buried when word of his death reached Dalintober on 27 July 1912. His was a strange departure which nowadays would require a post-mortem examination. He was second mate on the Lake Ontario steamer *Chippewa*, which moored at Lewiston – on the American side – on Sunday 14 July. Her captain talked to Colin minutes before he retired to his bunk at about 11.30 p.m. and found him 'in the very best of health and spirits';

but, when the steamer's watchman went to wake him at 4.40 a.m., he found him dead. Family tradition attributed his death to asphyxiation.

Colin's body was taken to the Canadian side, and the funeral was conducted from the house of a cousin of his, a Mrs MacDonald in Argyll Street, Toronto, about whom I know nothing. He was buried in Humbervale Cemetery – since renamed 'Park Lawn' – described then as 'a pretty burial ground about three miles outside of the city'. Several Campbeltonians attended the service, including Donald, John and Dugald McLellan, Alex McLean, Archie Fisher, and John Harvie, an ex-Alderman of Toronto, and some were pall-bearers. The floral tributes covering the coffin included those from the captain and crew of the *Chippewa* and from the crew of the *Cayuga*, his previous ship, of which he was 'wheelman' for three years.

Through the late Neil Short, whose mother Flora was a sister of Dugald McLellan's, I was able to contact a grand-daughter of Dugald's, June Wigmore, in Peterborough, Ontario. Dugald, who emigrated to Canada in 1907, had kept a list of Campbeltonians who visited him and his wife in Toronto. There were 24 names, including couples, on the list. Colin's was one of them, and he was a regular visitor.[107]

I have developed, over the years, a robust scepticism about obituaries, for character assessments often appear over-generous, if not downright idealistic. Doubtless such excesses may be attributed to shock-induced sentiment, as with the expressions of eternal love and inconsolable loss which appear on the gravestone of a dead spouse, and which are later rather negated when another partner comes along. Such, however, is the capacity of the human spirit to transcend grief and despair, and a good thing too.

Colin's obituary in the *Campbeltown Courier* included the following anonymous tribute, which seems sincere enough to quote: 'To all who knew him in his native town his sudden and untimely death will cause the deepest regret. Colin

Martin was a quiet and unassuming fellow, and a man of exemplary character and conduct, and it is not surprising to learn that the high esteem and regard in which he was held at home he also won for himself among the people with whom he came into contact on the other side of the Atlantic.'[108]

The *Argyllshire Herald* obituary, despite its relative brevity, contained more errors, but I'll quote from it too: 'The deceased was well known and very highly respected in shipping circles in Toronto, and [by] his employers he was looked upon as a man who would rapidly rise in his profession, being likely to be promoted to a ship of his own in the near future.'[109]

In a diary I kept in 1974 there is a page containing a list of the children of John Martin and Sarah Campbell, with notes on spouses and offspring. My father was the source, and some of the information is muddled or wrong, which isn't surprising since it all came from his memory alone. Against Colin's name I noted: 'Skipper in passenger boat on Great Lakes. Gassed in his cabin. Engaged to Martin girl in U.S.A.' He wasn't the skipper, but the remainder of that first sentence is true. What of the other claims? True or false? I simply don't know.

A photograph of Colin was preserved in the family. I acquired it when my father and I cleared my Aunt Sarah Martin's house at 38 Saddell Street after her death in 1970. Sarah, a kind and gentle soul, had cared for her parents in their old age and never married. Many surviving family documents and photographs were in that musty old house. The photograph was taken in Aylett's Studio, 1118 Queen Street W., Toronto, probably about 1910. Colin wears the smart uniform of the Canada Steamship Lines, whose vessels' names all began with 'C-' and ended with '-a'. He is sharp-nosed and clean-shaven, but for a full moustache; his right hand is tucked in his jacket pocket, his left arm held at his side. The jacket has eight brass buttons – doubtless polished for the occasion – paired in two vertical rows, and a watch-

19. *Colin Martin in Toronto, c. 1910. Author's collection.*

chain below the left lapel catches the eye. Doubtless the photograph was admired by his siblings back home. It can still be admired, and it's all that remains of Colin Campbell Martin in his prime.

23 June: Johnston's Point

Mossy saxifrage, in *The Flora of Kintyre* (p 23), was said to grow 'near Johnston's Point' as well as at Largiebaan. I'd seen it at Largiebaan and wondered if I might also see it 'near Johnston's Point'. How near is 'near'? I can't answer that, in this case, because I didn't find any of the flowers, though there may be a colony there or thereabouts, near or not so near, maybe even far.

The botany on the stretch of coast I walked, Johnston's Point to Ru Stafnish, offered other species to admire, and one which confused me until I satisfied myself that I was seeing a plant with which I was entirely familiar, but in a habitat I hadn't previously noticed it. The plant was honeysuckle, also known as woodbine (*Lonicera periclymenum*), and it was growing up through shingle on the shore, but when I began tracking its presence, I was led off the beach and on to the foreshore. These beach flowers were presumably originally of the foreshore and were covered by storm shingle but continued to thrive. Another species which caught my eye was the tall yellow-flowered sea radish (*Raphanus raphanistrum ssp. maritimus*), a rampant colonist within the past several years. I see it on the coasts of South Kintyre everywhere I go, but have yet to notice it on any beach between the Galdrans and Largiebaan and between New Orleans and the Second Water. It is hardly a newcomer – *The Flora of Kintyre* (p 13) in 1979 deemed it 'probably widespread' – but it appears to be gaining ground rapidly.

Three curachs and two canoes

I had stopped at the bridge at the Second Water, where I drank a cup of tea and ate a lump of cake. The burn was flowing very gently and weaving a delicate song among the stones. Near the seventh milestone – which enigmatically declares itself to be the eighth milestone – I stopped again for refreshment, at the Winny Corner spring. While standing in the road with a cup of water in hand, to my surprise I saw three little black boats in Feochaig Bay. They looked out of their time and rather sinister. When I examined them through binoculars, I could see a crew of rowers in each. They were heading north on the flood tide and close inshore. Had I been twenty minutes earlier, I'd have been on the shore and able to see the boats close up and probably even to communicate with the crews. Then again, I reflected, had I been even five minutes later, the boats would have passed without my seeing them at all. I parked my bike near Feochaig and hurried down to the shore, hoping I might glimpse the boats before they rounded Ru Stafnish, but by the time I got there they were out of sight.

Two canoes, however, were in sight between me and the Ru. One of the canoeists had gone ashore and the other was sitting in his vessel close to the rocks. I was heading in their direction and reckoned I might reach them before they pushed off, but after my disappointment with the little black flotilla I wasn't pushing myself. I looked at flowers on my way north, occasionally glancing ahead to see what the canoeists were up to. Half-way towards them, I saw them begin paddling south, against the tide. When they came abreast of me, I took a quick photograph of them and then trained my binoculars on them. I was looking at a nephew, Malcolm Docherty, and his son Lewis (p 16). Had I been more alert, I might have guessed their identities, because they had driven down to Polliwilline the day before with my sister Barbara and two canoes for a couple of nights' stay at her caravan.

I shouted 'Malcolm!' and waited, but they hadn't noticed my approach and, at sea-level, couldn't see me among the rocks, so I called again and began rock-hopping to the water's edge. Having identified me, they turned towards the shore, and I learned from Malcolm that the black boats were 'curachs' from the north of Ireland; he and one of the helmsmen had spoken briefly in passing. Malcolm and Lewis had paddled north to Saint Kieran's Cave and were now returning to Polliwilline. Malcolm said he'd 'felt in his waters' that he might meet me that day, but had expected the meeting to take place at the cave. I photographed them side by side in their canoes, and we parted.

I found out later in the week that the little boats I'd seen were of a type called a *naomhóg*, a 'sub-species' of *curach* associated with Kerry on the west of Ireland, where they were used for trade and fishing. The vessels, which are made of tarred canvas stretched over a wooden frame, were crewed by a total of 14 rowers, of mixed nationalities, who had left Cushendun, on the Antrim coast, at 4.20 a.m. and arrived in Campbeltown at 4.20 p.m., a distance of almost 37 miles covered in exactly 12 hours. I had assumed they had crossed the North Channel to attend a conference on Saint Columba which was held in Campbeltown that week-end, but in fact the crews returned to Ireland two days later, before the event took place.[110]

Two fantasies

At 2.15 p.m., as I am pushing my bicycle up Corphin brae, a car stops, and a woman, seated next to the driver, pokes her head out of the window. 'Excuse me,' she says, 'but we're looking for an old farm that was around here.' I know at once there's a genealogical avalanche about to descend on me. 'Do you have a name for the family that was there?' – 'MacIsaac,' she replies hesitantly, mispronouncing the name. 'It's just down there,' I say, pointing across the fence. Then I point back along the road I've come: 'There's a gate back there and a track that goes right to the ruins.' – 'That's wonderful. I guessed you might know,' she replies, gratitude enriching her tone. I'm interested now in her and her companion, so

I hear myself saying: 'I'll take you there. Just follow me.' She protests at the inconvenience I'm putting myself to, but I assure her: 'The ruins aren't far away and I can spare half-an-hour.' During our stroll to Corphin, I tell her I have written about the MacIsaac family in a book just published. She's the one with the Kintyre blood, and the revelation amazes her. She and her husband are booked into the Ardshiel Hotel for that night, and I promise her I'll deliver a signed copy there that evening. As she dips into her purse for money, she asks if I have written any other books about Kintyre, and when I reply 'A lot', she declares that she would like to buy as many as I can supply her with. A glow of satisfaction suffuses my being: I feel valued and rich.

Walking back along the shore to Johnston's Point, having failed to find *Saxifraga hypnoides,* I see a figure standing on a rock ahead of me, gazing at the hillside. After a quick look through my binoculars, I establish that the person is female and that I don't recognise her. The binoculars are no sooner back inside my shirt when she turns and sees me. She is still on the rock when I reach her. Pleasantries are exchanged and I ask her the question I most wish to ask: 'What brings you here?' She tells me she is a student of botany at an English university, and I enquire at once if she has seen *Saxifraga hypnoides.* Her eyes widen in surprise. 'I haven't. Is it here?'

Four dolphins

I wasn't back in Feochaig Bay until 16 October, towards the end of that remarkable 'Indian summer', but again I experienced a 'right place' moment there. After I'd gathered a few driftwood branches from the shore, I sat on top of a grassy rock near where Duncan McLachlan had his caravan in the 1980s.[111] I was merely minutes there when I noticed splashing offshore where no rock should have been advertising itself at high tide. Then I saw Risso's dolphins, powering north and close inshore. Cetaceans, especially in large numbers, are difficult to count, because they appear and disappear at different times and in altering formations, but I reckoned I was seeing four. Now and again one or other would leap from the water and twist in mid-air, entertaining stuff for me and doubtless exhilarating for them.

My first response was to grab my little digital camera from the rucksack, but I thought again, put the camera down and reached for my binoculars. I'd succumbed to the modern phenomenon of photographing an event at the expense of enjoying and learning from it in the actual moment. I see this trend manifest at social events. Young guests, particularly, are often reluctant to join in the fun, preferring to photograph or film it, so that it can be 'posted' on 'social media' for the world to view. I'd go so far as to say that, for some people, an event – even if they were there! – has little or no reality unless there is a visual record of it.

Two Scottish poets

Old poet friends keep turning up in this book, and here are two more. Robin Fulton Macpherson arrives in a very round-about way, by a back door that shouldn't have been open. He was preceded through that door by an older poet, Andrew Young (p 140). I wrote to Young in 1969, two years before his death, asking for a poem to publish in a magazine I was editing, *form*, and received a brief reply explaining that he was old and no longer wrote poetry. That letter would have accidentally gone to the town dump with hundreds of others (p 49).

If I never got to publish Young, I was published with him, in *The Faber Book of Twentieth-Century Scottish Poetry*, a greater honour; and Robin Fulton (Macpherson) was also in that anthology, edited by Douglas Dunn. Martin Seymour-Smith, a critic whose erudition I admire, described Young as 'a tough, precise, even dour poet who says almost all that he has to say through a rapt contemplation of nature. Watching birds through binoculars, he feels his shoulders prick as though he himself were sprouting wings'.[112]

I like to think that Young reached Kintyre in his solitary travels, and perhaps he did. Since he climbed the Paps of Jura and left a poem to mark the occasion, I presume he sailed first to Islay – the poem opens with the line, 'Before I crossed the sound' – and passed through Tarbert to his ferry at the West Loch.

Young was cycling one day on the west coast of Arran and from the corner of an eye noticed on the beach a blue flower which he somehow assumed to be brooklime. A mile or so along the road, troubled by his hasty judgement, he jumped off his bike in a state of indecision. 'Don't be a fool; it was only brooklime', he scolded himself, and continued his journey. But two or three miles further on, he changed his mind again and decided to turn, and on cycling back to the beach he found not brooklime, but oyster-plant. He was late arriving at Blackwaterfoot – which he calls 'Broadwaterfoot' – where the minister had been expecting him for tea. In explaining the delay, Young – himself a cleric: he left the Church of Scotland for the Anglican Church – told his host that wild flowers were his hobby, to which the minister replied: 'What a disgusting habit!' [113]

Reading that anecdote, I remembered that Robin Fulton Macpherson's father had been Church of Scotland minister in Shiskine, near Blackwaterfoot, and I had to wonder if he might have been Young's irascible clergyman. I should now explain that Robin's father was the Rev J. S. Fulton and that Robin recently assumed the surname Macpherson. He is a poet in his own right and a distinguished translator of Scandinavian poetry into English; indeed, he has lived in Norway since 1973. I have never met him, and probably never will, but have corresponded with him intermittently for the past forty-five years, and had the benefit of his critical expertise in the preparation of my first poetry collection, *The Larch Plantation*.

I recall a piece of advice he gave me regarding the back cover blurb for that book, that it should not mention my being a postman, for that would give some reviewers a 'handle' with which they could put me into 'some meaningless category'. He had dealt with that very matter in his review in 1974 of Alasdair Maclean's poetry collection *From the Wilderness*. Maclean was described in the blurb as living 'on a croft near Ardnamurchan', which led some English reviewers into ignorant assumptions about 'the hard crofting life'. Maclean, in fact, as Fulton pointed out, had lived only intermittently in Ardnamurchan and had 'probably seen more of the world than most of his reviewers'.[114] A decade later, Maclean wrote *Night Falls on Ardnamurchan*, an elegiac memoir as dark as its title.

I e-mailed Robin in May with my questions and was informed that his parents moved in 1935 to the manse at Shiskine, where Robin was born two years later and lived until his father moved again, in 1943, to Clarkston, south of Glasgow. There is no suggestion of a year or even a decade in Young's story, but, in any case, Robin convincingly disposed of the implied calumny: 'Since the Rev. J. S. Fulton was a very knowledgeable gardener, he would never have said that about plants!'

Robin's parents kept in touch with several Arran families, but never returned to the island. Robin himself went back around 1978, when he experienced the usual phenomenon of finding that every feature he remembered now seemed diminished in size. The church had become 'a kind of village hall' and the manse was being let as a holiday home.[115]

'Shiskine', where Robin spent the first seven years of his life, has the same Gaelic origin as the two places in Kintyre, one near Stewarton and the other in Southend, called 'Chiskan': *seasgan*, a marshy place. I have my own memory of Shiskine, but it amounts only to this: on 12 October 1999, my three daughters and I had a plate of chips in Shiskine Golf Club![116] Almost sixteen years later, in October 2015, Amelia and Bella spent a week-end on Arran, and on the 9th, as Bella told me, 'From outside the hotel in Blackwaterfoot, where we had dinner, we could see the lights of Campbeltown'.

McBrides in Pirnmill

Before Bella's trip to Arran, I'd told her that she had relatives named McBride buried at Lochranza. She said that she and Amelia would look for the gravestone, but they failed to find it. I discovered that connection in a rather curious way. In the early 1970s, with a Campbeltown friend, David Mewse, I crossed to Arran to camp for a boozy week-end at the Fairy Dell, north of Lochranza. Having disembarked from the Claonaig ferry, my first stop – naturally enough for me – was Lochranza graveyard. One of the first stones I looked at commemorated 'Angus Martin McBride', and the sight of my own name on the stone intrigued me so much that, when I returned home, I asked my father about it and learned of the marriage of Isabella Martin, his aunt and my daughter Bella's namesake, to a Pirnmill fisherman, Willie McBride.

Isabella, I was told by her niece in Carradale, Ellen Oman, was an outstanding beauty, but she died at the age of 39, in 1909, and Willie took their surviving children from Dalintober to Pirnmill, where they were brought up and where he eventually remarried, as recounted in *Kilkerran Graveyard Revisited*. The McBride boys – Jackie, Lawrence and Angus – followed their father to the fishing, and I regret that, while researching *The Ring-Net Fishermen*, I didn't make that short crossing from Kintyre to Arran to tape-record the last of them; but, to be truthful, my knowledge of the family, and its fishing history, was scant at the time. In 2003, however, the diaries of Angus, the youngest of the brothers, were loaned to me and I was then able to publish a belated tribute to the family's fishing history.[117]

Two of Bella's children, a son and a daughter, predeceased her in Dalintober, William Wilson in 1896, aged three, and Sarah Campbell in 1908, aged 13. The raw tribute to Sarah, published with her death notice, cuts me emotionally every time I read it: 'A gentle, loving child, deeply mourned.'[118]

The link between the Martins and McBrides was maintained even beyond the death of the last of the brothers, but was earlier – and naturally – stronger. My aunt 'Tory' used to spend school summer holidays on Arran, taking the steamer from Campbeltown and disembarking into the ferry-boat that came out from Pirnmill,[119] and my father's cousin, Angus Martin, was close to Jackie McBride, both in years and friendship. Angus's daughter Jean often took holidays at Pirnmill and her daughter, Marilyn Crowther, had her first birthday and 'walked her first step' there.[120]

Oyster-plant

Young's encounter with the oyster-plant (*Mertensia maritima*) on Arran at once stimulated an interest in it, and I wanted to see one. John Lightfoot, the author of *Flora Scotica*, published in 1777, considered it one of the loveliest of British plants: '... its undulated glaucous leaves contrasted with red and blue flowers, are extremely ornamental to the barren shores where it grows, and readily discover the plant to any curious observer.'[121]

When Judy and I looked at photographs of it, we both thought we'd already seen it, but couldn't recollect when or where, and agreed we could be mistaken. *The Flora of Kintyre* (p 30) recorded colonies at Keil and Carskey Bay, Southend, and on the east coast of Kintyre, across the Kilbrannan Sound from where Young saw his plant.

I knew there had been a colony on the shore at Keil, and that it had been effectively destroyed ten years earlier. Agnes Stewart saw it in 2005, when it looked as though it had been whacked with a stick, and again, as a tiny growth, the following year, but thereafter there was no trace. Veronica Togneri, who lives in Southend and often walks that stretch of shore, confirmed that the former site of the oyster-plant had been overgrown by marram grass and lime grass.[122] Around the time the plant was vandalised, Keil shore was frequented by youths from the caravan site who lit bonfires and clowned around until the early hours of the morning, and the demise of the Keil oyster-plant colony – singled out in the *Flora* as 'very fine' – may date to that period.

Rare plants which grow on beaches at popular picnic places are inevitably at risk, but it's also true that one arm of nature may take away what another arm has bestowed, and a storm which throws rocks around might well sweep away a bank of shingle and its community of plants. No surviving colony of *Mertensia maritima* is known in Kintyre. A couple of years ago, a local botany enthusiast collected seeds in Orkney, where the plant is widespread, and tried to grow them in Kintyre, but without success. So, if I am to see the oyster-plant, it looks as though I'll have to find it elsewhere ... perhaps in Arran, where this began.

Cuckoos

Andrew Young was plainly fascinated by cuckoos. In his *Collected Poems*[123] there are four poems about the bird: 'Cuckoo', 'The Cuckoo', 'Cuckoo in May', and 'Cuckoos'. Of these I prefer 'The Cuckoo', in which he sees a cuckoo in a tree and waits for its call after it flies: '... so faint and faraway/ It sounded out of yesterday,/ Making me start with sudden fear/ Lest spring that had seemed new and near/ Was gone already ...' Perhaps the most poignant line on the cuckoo I have ever read appears in an Old English poem, 'The Husband's Message'; in Kevin Crossley-Holland's translation: '... that mournful sound in the mountain woods'.

Here, however, is the point. In *Another Summer in Kintyre* (p 38), I commented on the superstitious concern to hear the cuckoo after its arrival, but wondered had anyone ever noted a date for the calls' cessation. Agnes Stewart reckoned 'before the Summer Solstice' and gave the date 18 June for the last call she heard in 2014. In 2015, however, I heard one half-hearted call on 23 June, as I pushed my bicycle up Corphin Brae, and around the same time, on the same day, Allister Stewart heard a call from New Orleans. So, 'around the Summer Solstice' is probably about right.

29 June: Southend

As I set off for Largiebaan by bike in the early afternoon, rain was coming on and kept coming as I cycled out the Southend road, so I decided it wasn't a day for the remote west and carried on to Southend. The decision turned out to have been the right one, but I wasn't too bothered about foregoing Largiebaan: the place had been good to me so far that year and I had accumulated a store of beautiful memories.

Passing through the village, I stopped to look at a roadside plaque which refers to the massacre at Dunaverty in 1647. The text explains that in 2009 the 'Scottish Cultural and Fraternal group', *Siol nan Gaidheal*, 'carried out some restorations to the memorial tablet' on the rectangular stone monument, erected in the field by Rev. Douglas Macdonald, 12th Laird of Sanda, in 1846. The original wording at the monument is quoted in its entirety, but *Siol nan Gaidheal* should have revised the text, because it contains inaccuracies exposed by later research.

The claim that the memorial marks the spot where the Rev Macdonald's ancestors Archibald Mòr and his son Archibald Òg were 'shot and buried after the battle of Dunaverty' is wrong. There was no 'battle', in any meaningful sense of the word, but a siege followed by a massacre, and its context, in a barbarous civil war, is unexplained. Further, Archibald the son was not at Dunaverty, but had earlier fled with Alasdair 'MacColla' Macdonald, his leader, and died with him at the battle of Cnoc na nDos in Ireland in November of that same year.[124]

Eight years after that battle, in 1655, Marie McNeill petitioned the Presbytery of Kintyre to be allowed to remarry, since it was 'generally reported and asserted' that her husband, Obrian McNeill, 'was killed in Ireland with Alester Macdonald, so that these eight years bygone there is no word heard of him being alive, it being also notoriously known that at that battle few obtained quarter'.[125]

Something more is needed in Southend to commemorate the Dunaverty massacre. As I have opined before, had the castle not been demolished in the late seventeenth century, it would have provided Kintyre with the big, unique tourist attraction it lacks: a visitor centre with the 'Massacre Tearoom' attached to it, and guided tours of the rebuilt stronghold, which, when the dimensions had been worked out, would turn out to have been smaller than the tearoom!

I sat for lunch at one of the picnic tables near the public toilets at Dunaverty Bay and noticed that the sewage-pipe into the sea had been removed. I felt a strange pang of nostalgia, because in the summer of 2002 I'd watched my daughters play on the rocks around the pipe, while I sat with David and Katie McNaughton in their caravan overlooking the beach. We had all gone to Southend by bus and, during the journey, David, who was a herring fisherman in his younger years, told me a strange story which I published in *Herring Fishermen of Kintyre and Ayrshire* (p 125).

He was alone at the wheel of the *Nobles* of Campbeltown, taking her across the Irish Sea from Ardglass to the Isle of Man fishing grounds in July 1946. He was fatigued and drowsy, and in that state 'saw' a uniformed English policeman, complete with helmet, emerge from the forecastle and walk aft, glancing into the wheelhouse at him before disappearing into the nothingness whence he had come.

Dunaverty beach was surprisingly quiet. A young boy sitting under the dunes throwing sand with one hand was the sole human presence. Above and along from him, a man was washing his car beside a caravan. A few cars came and went, but no one got out unless to visit the toilets. Many folk in the countryside seem content to sit in their cars, either reading or looking out a window, which might or might not be open, and it's common enough at play parks as well as beaches to see adults watching listlessly from cars as their children amuse themselves outside.

The beach was popular for picnics before mass ownership of cars changed the recreational habits of the public, and a journey became more important than a destination. I can't remember being at Dunaverty as a child, but have photographs to prove that I was. In one of them, I'm aged about five and sitting in the sand with my parents and sister Carol. My parents are eating from plates, there is a blackened tea-kettle in the foreground, and not one, but two, primus stoves visible.

20. The Martin family at Dunaverty beach, c. 1957. L-R: Carol, Amelia, Angus Jnr. and Angus Snr. From Carol Martin.

I wheeled my bicycle from the end of Dunaverty Bay to the start of Carskey Bay, looking at flowers. Sea sandwort (*Honckenya peploides*), with its fleshy leaves and tiny greenish-white flowers, was in dense mats on sandy patches, sea kale (*Crambe maritima*) was in full flower and looking vigorous, there were colonies of fading kidney vetch on the sea-wall below Keil cliffs, and a profusion of sea radish (p 147) the whole way along the road. Agnes Stewart had mentioned to me its attractiveness to bees and butterflies, recalling that the greatest concentration of dark green fritillaries she ever saw was on a patch of the flowers near Clochkeil; and I can say that I saw more bees on the sea radish along Keil shore than I had seen in total all that spring and summer. I was back at Keil on 13 July with Don O'Driscoll – p 166 – who decided the flora of Southend could lose one radish. He pulled up one beside the road, skinned the root with his knife and sampled a bit of it; as might have been expected, it was very peppery, and he spat it out. Early in November, Catherine Barbour in Keil Farm reported that the seed-heads of the sea radish along the roadside were attracting numerous small birds, doubtless a welcome late food resource for them.

2 July: The Galdrans

My sister Carol came over from Louisiana on 1 July with two of her grandsons, Andrew and David, for a three-week holiday which would take in my other sister Barbara's eightieth birthday celebration. On the day after Carol's arrival, we took the boys to the Galdrans for a couple of hours' exposure to the outdoors. During our walk to Fionnphort, we stopped, with sentimental intent, at a spot on the flat grassy foreshore where my father had camped as a boy. I mightn't ever have identified the spot, but for a distinctive rock formation in one of the photographs: a pillar with a big 'sugar-lump' on top.

In the series of photographs taken there, my Irish Granny, Caroline Stewart, is wearing one of the ostentatious wide-brimmed hats she favoured. The photographs at first puzzled me. My father is present, and there are large tents in the background. I assumed, by his uniform, that the occasion was a Boy Scout camp, which a report in the *Campbeltown Courier* for 26 August 1922 confirmed: Scouts from Campbeltown had camped for a week's training in the Galdrans. Granny and my aunts Sarah and Bella, who are also pictured, presumably travelled out west by the 'Wee Train' to visit the youngest of the family on what might well have been, at the age of twelve, his first unaccompanied absence from home. As the photographs of Granny in middle-age show, she kept her looks and dressed with style. Her granddaughter, Carol McAulay, who remembered her as 'a bonny wee wumman', once asked her how she had managed to keep such a trim figure. 'Well,' she replied, alluding to her four daughters, 'if ye look at all the bits that came off me!'

21. Campbeltown Boy Scouts' camp in the Galdrans, August 1922. L-R: Sarah, Isabella, Caroline and Angus Martin. Author's collection.

4 July: Crosshill Reservoir

My sister Barbara's eightieth birthday party had been organised for that evening, and family members were gathering for the event. Chomsky (p 2) was lodging with us for the week-end, and I was keen to give him a decent outing since he'd be on his own for about five hours. I took him, as usual, on to Ben Gullion, but, owing to midge hordes in the forest, I waited until we reached Crosshill Reservoir before sitting to eat. There had been a thunderstorm that morning, and the accompanying rain had obviously been much heavier than I'd realised. The lifeboat gala day went ahead, but a golf competition at Machrihanish, scheduled for an earlier start, was cancelled. I discovered on the walk that all the burns were in spate and that a sheet of hissing water was pouring down the dam overflow. As I sat at the south end of the dam, I watched three teenaged boys descending Crosshill to the opposite end of the dam. When they reached my position, they took one look at the water depth on the overflow and decided to turn back. 'This is the footwear you should have on,' I remarked to them, lifting one of my legs to show them a wellington boot.

The construction of Crosshill Reservoir was completed in 1852. In May 1851, the *Campbeltown Journal* – the first local newspaper, founded in that year – reported that 'one of the miners, engaged in operations connected with the Crosshill water works, was very severely injured by a very large quantity of earth falling upon him. Medical assistance was speedily procured ... and he is recovering from the injury'. A fortnight later, an identical accident was reported. Another workman had been 'severely injured', prompting the *Journal*'s reporter to comment unnecessarily that this further accident 'should act as a warning to the men employed at the works'.[126] This tunnelling operation must have been for the piping of water from the reservoir under the hill to the water-house, since demolished, near Barley Bannocks Hill. The tunnel entrance, below the dam, is now closed by a metal cage, but in my boyhood it was open and the tunnel itself could be explored, a fearsome adventure which I never attempted all the way.

10 July: Davaar Island

Carol wanted to take her grandsons to the island, and the tide that day suited, so I accompanied them across the Doirlinn. We were one of six parties, which confirmed for me that the cave painting is one of the main tourist attractions in South Kintyre.

In mid-May, George McSporran and I had seen a few clumps of sea radish (pp. 147 & 159); now there were hundreds of them on the cliffs. English stonecrop (*Sedum anglicum*) formed lovely pink carpets; there was a colony of honeysuckle (*Lonicera periclymenum*) on top of a shore rock; I saw my first harebells (*Campanula rotundifolia*) of the year on a cliff face, a solitary blue clump; kidney vetch was seeding ...

Navelwort

And there was navelwort or wall pennywort (*Umbilicus rupestris*) in abundance, a tidy sum's worth, if every plant could have been counted and its pennies converted into pounds! The flowers were all over the cliffs and even growing up through the rocks of the shore, without visible leaves. I described, in *Another Summer in Kintyre* (p 156), coming across navelwort – a member of the stonecrop family – flowering from the walls of Corphin ruins, and failing at first to identify it, even thinking I'd spotted a rarity.

A friend in Southend, Catherine Barbour, shared a similar experience with me. While she and her husband, Cameron, were covering their silage-pit at Keil farm, on 16 July, she noticed the flowers. She had often seen the flat, low-growing leaves on walls at Keil, but hadn't realised until that day that they produced a tall spiked flower. This was exactly my own experience a year earlier, and with a similar explanation behind it – a developing interest in botany, and, with it, a greater environmental awareness. The flower-spikes are remarkable, relative to the base of leaves from which they emerge, as though a humble cottage had suddenly sprouted a cathedral spire or a field mouse grown a roe deer horn!

I hadn't known until March 2016 that navelwort is edible. When Judy and I visited Rob and Jennifer Lee at Torrisdale for lunch on the 1st of that month, the leaves were sitting on top of a bowl of salad, and I sampled a few. Jennifer told me that she finds the plants on damp and sheltered cliff faces all the way from Torrisdale Bay to Saddell. 'The leaves,' she said, 'are best eaten in late winter and early spring and make a lovely addition to salads and sandwiches, having a mild taste but interesting texture. They can be cooked lightly in butter as well.' In folk medicine, the juice was used for treating epilepsy and liver and spleen problems, and the leaves for piles, gout, chilblains and skin conditions.

Chris Wood

My explorations of side-roads into twentieth century music history bring me to Christopher Gordon Blandford Wood, who was born in Quinton, a suburb of Birmingham, on 24 June 1944, and died on 12 July 1983, a casualty of the alcohol and drug addictions which ruined his later career. So, how does Chris Wood fit into this book? Very tenuously indeed – to my knowledge, he was never near Kintyre – but, by means of cumulative tangential connections, I'll attempt to justify his inclusion.

He first came to prominence as a member of Traffic, described in 1997 as purveyors of 'musically accomplished, thinking man's psychedelia'.[127] The band – Stevie Winwood, Dave Mason, Jim Capaldi and Wood – was formed in April 1967 and released its first single, 'Paper Sun', in May. In September of that same year, as the 'Summer of Love' cooled into history, I camped for the first time at the Inneans, with my friend Iain Campbell, an adventure described in *A Summer in Kintyre* (pp. 25-29). We had taken a transistor radio with us, and among the repeatedly played 'singles' which most excited me was Traffic's 'Hole in My Shoe', which reached number 2 in the music chart. Chris Wood was therefore, in a sense, with me in the Inneans on 23 and 24 September 1967, though his name was doubtless unknown to me at the time.

In December 1971, a mutation of the band released an album, *The Low Spark of the High-Heeled Boys*, the title track of which entranced me, and still does, despite the absurd title, and, indeed, lyrics. If I were allowed only one piece of music to listen to in my remaining time in the world, my choice would be the title track of *The Low Spark*; and Chris Wood's atmospheric saxophone solo and fade-out are intrinsic to the appeal. There are doubtless factors other than musical which intensify the nostalgic charge which that composition carries for me, but I cannot identify them now, apart from a lost love.

Another local connection: Wood featured on John Martyn's album *Inside Out,* issued in 1973. Martyn's real name was Iain David McGeachy and he was a great-grandson of Edward 'Iver' McGeachy, a notable boat-owner and herring fisherman in Dalintober. Martyn, like Wood – like most rock and jazz musicians, it would be safe to say – had his own demons of addiction to contend with and died in 2009. Yet his creative energy, unlike Wood's, hardly faltered throughout a long career as composer and guitarist, and his musical legacy encompasses a range of genres – folk, rock and jazz – which met and merged.

During one of my weekly chats over coffee with local guitarist and music historian, Les Oman, in Amelia's Café Bistro in Longrow, I mentioned my growing interest in the musical legacy of Chris Wood. I had just acquired a copy of the CD *Vulcan*, largely a collection of Wood's late recordings, which was released in 2008, twenty-five years after his death. Les recalled that when the Linda McCartney Memorial Garden was being created in Campbeltown – it opened in 2002 – he was enlisted to help with research, thus the panel documenting her career as a photographer observed that she 'initially made her name chronicling the musical revolution of the Sixties', and included Traffic in the list of bands she photographed. So, there was another slender link with Wood.

I'd had an idea to mark his death in some way. Why his death, and not his birth, I can't fully explain. Prior to sending *Another Summer in Kintyre* to the publisher, I hastily added to the Introduction the following appeal for readers' participation: 'On 12 July 2015, given favourable weather, I hope to celebrate the 32nd anniversary of the death of Chris Wood, saxophonist and flautist, with a hike ...' The phrasing wasn't quite what I intended, but the death anniversary happened to be a Sunday, when I'd be more likely to have company, whereas his birthday, 24 June, would be a Wednesday. But who would come, anyway, and where would we go?

I'd already missed obvious anniversaries because the idea hadn't yet emerged. Does any of this matter to anyone but me? Probably not, and I'll skip the tedious track to its end, in the Inneans Bay, which I looked down into on 12 July 2013, and where Iain Campbell and I camped in September 1967, and I heard Traffic and became a follower.

12 July: The Inneans and Don O' Driscoll

My sole companion on 'The Chris Wood Memorial Walk' was Don O'Driscoll, who had never heard of Wood. Lachie Paterson was enthusiastic about the walk and planned to come, but was unavoidably detained in Carradale. A couple of weeks after the trip, I found in a diary of August 1972 an entry which revealed that I had been introduced to the *Low Spark* album by Michael McGeachy, who then lived two doors from me in Crosshill Avenue and now lives around the corner from me, in Benmore Street. I'd invited him along, well in advance of the walk, but hadn't seen him for several weeks and omitted to renew the invitation.

Don and I and his Labrador Charlie walked out by the Kintyre Way from Ballygroggan. Don, who is the John Muir Trust conservation manager at Sandwood and Quinag, had come from Kinlochbervie, near Cape Wrath, for a camping trip with me. I hadn't camped on that coast for almost thirty years and didn't welcome the prospect, because I have difficulty enough sleeping in comfortable beds. As it transpired, Don doesn't sleep well in tents either, and had suggested the trip because he assumed from *A Summer in Kintyre,* which he had read, that I was still a dedicated camper. It was just as well we didn't camp, because Monday was very wet and by then I was going down with a head cold.

When we arrived in the Inneans Bay, Don immediately fetched water from the piped spring on the south side of the burn and prepared to light a fire. I'd noticed, on our way down the glen, that he was collecting dead heather stalks and bog cotton heads, and after he'd arranged this kindling in a fire-place improvised with stones, he said he would light the fire with sparks struck from flint. This, he explained, was 'for the craic', but there was no 'craic', because the fire took with the first strike, and, since I was looking elsewhere at that instant, I missed the demonstration.

While we ate and supped Lapsang Souchong tea, which was even smokier in flavour, from the driftwood fire, I brought out the little MP3 player with its single speaker which Les Oman had loaded with two Traffic songs, 'The Low Spark of the High-Heeled Boys' and a Chris Wood composition, 'Tragic Magic', and an obscure Spencer Davis Group single, 'Strong Love', which featured a young Stevie Winwood. The song, which I happened to mention to Les, is tied in my memory to a winter's day aboard a trawler in the Kilbrannan Sound, probably during the Christmas school holiday in 1965. I remember a flat blue sea, a clear blue sky, the mountains of Arran white with snow and 'Strong Love' playing and replaying in my head. I heard it only a few times on the radio that year, but I never forgot it.

Les had shown me several times how to operate the equipment, but I was struggling to recall the sequence of actions and finally handed it to Don and invited him to try. 'Strong Love' appeared and kept reappearing and then he managed to nail 'The Low Spark ...', which I listened to as attentively as I could through the crashing of the surf and Don's occasional conversation. It wasn't the experience I'd imagined I might have, but I'd got there and heard music. 'Tragic Magic' eluded Don's search, but he accidentally activated a Rory Gallagher album, *Tattoo*, which Les had loaded to test the equipment when he bought it.

It occurred to me later that white blues maestro Gallagher had as much claim to my attention in the Inneans as Wood, having been born in Donegal, which was visible in the west from where Don and I were seated, and brought up in Cork, where Don attended school with Rory's cousin Frank, who later became a priest. We heard out the first Rory Gallagher track and then I switched off the machine, my possession of which, in any case, had been an aberration – when I am out walking, the only sounds I care to hear belong to nature.

Don told me he was inexplicably drawn to Kintyre when he saw it for the first time from Donegal about thirty years ago, and that the 'grip' on him is stronger than ever. He has a more tangible connection with the place in his wife, Maureen McPhee, who was brought up in Campbeltown, where her father Norman was stationed with the Argyll constabulary.

We walked over to the Sailor's Grave, and while we were standing there Don pointed to the Pinnacle Rock, at the north end of the bay, and asked me, 'Are these starlings?' He had left his binoculars at the camp-site, but I had mine with me and looked at the top of the rock and indeed saw starlings, six of them, the first I'd ever noticed in the bay.

The Sailor's Grave

The cross on the grave, as reported in *Another Summer in Kintyre* (p 176), is in poor shape: the top had broken off and been tied on with twine. My suggestion, in that book, that a more durable memorial should be erected for the centenary of the interment, May 2017, had already elicited responses. An old school friend in Canada, Alastair Thompson, sent me £200, suggesting I buy myself a bottle of ten-year-old 'Ardbeg' malt whisky and put the balance towards the memorial, a generous and inspiring gesture, and John MacDonald (p 235) later donated £100.

I favour a stone cross, lodged in a cement base, but all the previous crosses have been wooden. At least six of them have succumbed to natural decay, weathering and the rubbing of animals; in other words, a wooden structure in that exposed spot can't be expected to last longer than about fifteen years on average. As the last of the grave's caretakers die out, has the time come to erect a lasting monument there? Since I have no authority to end the tradition of wood, as the centenary of the burial approaches I'll arrange a public discussion on the question of a replacement memorial. I hope, however, that considerations of longevity will prevail over those of custom.

I referred to 'caretakers', and I'll introduce some of them now. They were assembled, as it were, in an article in the *Campbeltown Courier* in 1964. I didn't know the article existed until I found it in 2014 while checking the newspaper files for something else. I was 12 when it was published and don't remember seeing it; even if I had seen it, it wouldn't have meant much to me because I'd probably never heard of the Inneans, let alone the Sailor's Grave. But when I read 'For 50 Years They Have Tended Unknown Sailor's Grave', its poignancy hit me. Fifty years further on, I was familiar with the story and with the men and boys mentioned in it, but, of course, most of them are now dead.

The article contains a few errors, and I'll offer corrections, but in a spirit of humility, since my later researches enabled me to pick away the embroidered edges of a story which had been preserved in oral tradition alone. The burial was not reported in either of the local newspapers at the time; in 1917, the pages of the *Argyllshire Herald* and the *Campbeltown Courier* were packed with news of the war and with obituaries and photographs of the Kintyre soldiers and sailors who had been killed, wounded or captured on the battlefields of Europe. Information on skeletal remains washed ashore on a remote beach either didn't reach the newspaper offices or was disregarded.

The *Courier* article opens with the statement that 'For almost 50 years a few Kintyre men have tended the grave of an unknown sailor whose body was washed ashore near Machrihanish during the First World War'. There was no evidence on the corpse to suggest that the man – if a man and not a woman – had been a sailor. When a police report turned up in the Argyll and Bute Archive in Lochgilphead in 1985, the remains were described as skeletal and unidentifiable. However, the assumption that the remains belonged to a sailor was entirely reasonable, and that the grave became known as 'The Sailor's Grave' was almost inevitable. On other coasts, bodies washed ashore were generally assumed to be sailors, and the graves named accordingly.

The article continues:

> The story began on one sunny morning in May 1917, when three young men from Drumlemble Village, out camping, came across the sailor's body on the shore south of Machrihanish. They were Donald Munro, John Lambie and Duncan McPhail. After reporting their find to the Receiver of Wreck, a coffin was obtained and the body was buried in a field overlooking the sea.
> There was no fuss and no funeral service. Since the body was partly decomposed and there was no means of identifying it, the civil and military authorities did not come into the picture.

Of the three men named as the finders, in 1964 only Donald Munro, aged 66 and living at 14 Rhudal Cottages, Drumlemble, was 'still alive and resident in the district'.

While researching the Sailor's Grave for *Kintyre: The Hidden Past* (1984), I encountered two conflicting stories about the finding of the corpse: the one above and one which credited Duncan Sinclair as the finder. Donald Munro was by then dead, but Duncan Sinclair, who had been head shepherd at Ballygroggan, was still alive, living in retirement in Machrihanish. He supplied me with a written account of his role in the corpse's discovery and I judged that to be the 'strongest evidence'. As I remarked in the book: 'It is quite possible, of course, that the body could have been "discovered" several times over, but it certainly could not have been buried several times over.' The counter-claim therefore remains a puzzle.

The police report, by P.C. John MacDonald in Machrihanish, is dated 12 May 1917 and records that the body was found by Duncan Sinclair, shepherd at Largiebaan, on Sunday 6 May, and that the 'bones' were buried on 11 May 'above high water mark at the place where they were found'. Duncan Sinclair gave the following statement:

> On Sunday 6th May 1917 I was going through the hill attending to my Sheep Stock, and when about two miles from Largiebaan nearer Machrihanish I went along the shore I noticed that my dogs observed something on the shore amongst the rocks on the shore. I went to the place where I found a Skeleton lying below a rock, the skull & feet was amissing. And as I was sure it was a Skeleton of a human being I went to Machrihanish and reported the matter to the Constable.

In the account Duncan later gave me, he identified the burial party on 11 May as Machrihanish lobster fisherman Robert Rae, in whose boat the party sailed to the bay, Robert's daughter Nellie, Duncan's sister Annie, and P.C. MacDonald. Duncan was preoccupied with lambing that day and missed the burial.[128]

The 'sailor' wasn't forgotten, though, and the tending of his grave was the focus of the 1964 *Courier* article. As the anonymous writer observed: 'There is no special organisation, no committee behind this remarkable example of parochial humanity. It has been done so quietly and spontaneously that only a handful of people in Kintyre know where the grave is.' The outline of the grave was described as being 'covered with pebbles, sea shells and glass bottles'. (The latter were doubtless glass flotation-balls which were lost from fishing gear and drifted ashore. These were collectable, until replaced by plastic floats, and could be seen as decorative features on pathways and in gardens.) The cross bore the 'roughly cut out' date 16 May 1917 and the words 'God Knows'. The specificity of the date is misleading, and 'May 1917', which would cover both the date of the body's discovery and of its burial, might now be preferred.

Malcolm Hamilton (p 68) was interviewed for the article. His father, Robert, had tended the grave before him, and Malcolm occasionally took his sons Robert (13) and Leslie (7) with him to the Inneans. In the following week's issue of the *Courier*, a photograph of the grave was published with two young boys – Robert and Leslie, presumably – flanking the cross. 'As long as I am here,' Malcolm is quoted as saying, 'I will continue to go round. My two boys are very keen on those trips to Eanon and I am trying to encourage them.'

Willie McArthur was also interviewed. When asked why he and the other 'volunteers' gave 'their time and effort to caring for the grave of a man they did not know', Willie replied: 'One or two of us are old soldiers and I suppose it is a feeling of comradeship.'[129] Willie McArthur was the only one of all the adults mentioned in the article – the others were Willie Colville, Willie Brown, and Duncan McLachlan – I ever met in the Inneans, and that was in 1980, as recalled in *A Summer in Kintyre* (pp. 22-25).

A mystery verse

Several days after my walk to the Inneans with Don O'Driscoll, Agnes Stewart mentioned to me that Robert Brown had asked her about a 'poem' he'd seen, as a young boy, on the Inneans cross. He recited a couple of lines of it, but she didn't recognise them and didn't remember seeing them there. I did remember lines connected with the Sailor's Grave, but they were out of reach in memory and I abandoned the struggle and fetched my file of Inneans material. I wasn't optimistic of success there either, but the information was in that file and I'd forgotten I had it.

When I tape-recorded Duncan McLachlan in February 1981, he had plenty to say about the Sailor's Grave. He had acquired, from Kilkerran Cemetery, a wheel-headed teak cross, of 'Celtic' design, which had marked the grave of an English sailor who drowned during the Second World War and was buried in Kilkerran. The sailor's family had erected a new memorial and the cross was redundant. Duncan, a skilled sign-writer, added the customary lettering to the cross, John Kelly took it to the Inneans in his motor-boat, and it was set up on the grave by the Hamilton brothers and stood there until replaced in 1981.[130]

But Duncan told me he had added something extra to the cross, a verse from a poem. He quoted the couplet, 'Borne ashore by tidal hearse/ created a mystery time cannot pierce', adding: 'Well, it's taken from the *Ancient Mariner*, isn't it?' These were indeed the lines I had struggled to recall, but I didn't remember them from Samuel Taylor Coleridge's famous ballad, and they didn't, to my ear, sound as though they could belong there, even had Duncan misquoted them slightly. His own uncertainty about the source of the quotation is obvious from his quizzical remark. The question was easily solved, of course. I read the entire Coleridge poem and failed to find the lines, but a further question took its place: what was the source of the couplet?

When I contacted Robert Brown to hear the lines he had recited to Agnes Stewart, they transpired to be substantially the same as those I had heard from Duncan. As Judy and I had done, Robert and his wife Margaret tried internet searches to establish a literary source, likewise without success. I asked him when he had seen the lines on the cross, and he reckoned his first time at the Inneans was with his father, John, around 1955, when he would have been about eight years old.

Alan Spence

The Sailor's Grave has been written about many times in the past half-century, not least by myself, but I'd forgotten until recently that it appeared in a work of fiction by the Scottish author, Alan Spence. I was led to the short story by a memory which surfaced when George McSporran and I were descending the scree slope into Craigaig Bay on 28 May. I suddenly found myself back on the same scree with Alan Spence and Maggie, his girlfriend, about forty-five years ago, when they came to Campbeltown and spent a few days with me at 24 Crosshill Avenue. Maggie, I recall, lived in Drumchapel at the time, not far from my sister Barbara in Southdeen Avenue.

I remember very little of their visit and my erratic diaries contain no record of it, but Alan Spence's short story collection, *Its Colours They are Fine*, published in 1977, contains many impressions of Kintyre, including, in 'Auld Lang Syne', an account of a visit to the Inneans: 'And back a little from the water's edge was the simple grave of some foreign sailor, whose body had been washed up here, far from home. And over the grave was a marker in the shape of a Celtic cross, and the inscription read simply GOD KNOWS. And the ocean rumbled and crashed, endless.'

My first contact with Alan Spence was inauspicious. I'd included two poems of his, 'On the Last Morning' and 'Introvert', in a poetry magazine, *Spindrift*, which I edited and published in 1968. The poems had been submitted by a friend of his, but without his knowledge, let alone his permission, and, following the magazine's publication, I received an irate letter from Spence, which I no longer have, but which contained a line I haven't forgotten: 'I'll never darken your letter-box again.'

The misunderstanding was sorted out and I met him and his friend on Saturday 7 December 1968 at the 'Information Kiosk in George Square', as arranged in an exchange of letters; there was no telephone in my house and probably not in his either. A week afterwards, I met him by chance in Glasgow and later wrote to him, inviting him to Campbeltown 'for a few days'. I suppose, therefore, that his visit took place early in the following year, 1969.

I'd visit him in Glasgow several more times before contact lapsed and his name disappeared from my diaries. Hoping to restore communication, I wrote him a letter, care of his publisher, in 1990, and wrote again in 2015, care of Aberdeen University, where he holds the post of 'Professor of Creative Writing', but there was no response to either letter. I had hoped he might contribute something to this book – in particular on his Spence family connections with Campbeltown – but the account ends here.

Meditations on botany

A lot of botany, like a lot of genealogy, could spoil a book of this kind for the general reader, but there may be a factor in my favour here. Since I am a recent convert to serious botany, my approach to the subject probably tends towards naivety. The discovery and identification of the rarer flowers in Kintyre is exciting to me, and perhaps that excitement, and the passion for knowledge stimulated by it, will carry even ambivalent readers along without undue suffering.

My outing with Don O'Driscoll exposed to me the limitations of my botanical knowledge. I lack the patience to search for and – more to the point – identify the minutiae of moorland and grassland, which doubtless explains my gravitation to cliff and scree, where the plant life is plain to the eye and can be examined and photographed with ease.

On our way down the Inneans Glen, I pointed out to Don a little colony of common butterwort (*Pinguicula vulgaris*), a carnivorous plant which traps insects on its sticky leaves. He looked at the butterwort and immediately noticed a further carnivorous species growing with it, round-leaved sundew (*Drosera rotundifolia*). I looked again, and there it was, tiny but beautiful. I couldn't recall noticing it anywhere before, though I must have passed it, and trampled it, many times.

Curiously enough, Robert Brown mentioned the sundew to me on 8 April. His first acquaintance with the flower was about ten years earlier in a forest ride near Rubha Dùn

Bhàin, when he saw its leaf tentacles actually close over an insect. I was curious as to how he, a dedicated birder, had happened to see the sundew in action, and he explained that there was a roe deer ahead of him and he had been checking the ground for its tracks. He admitted that it was unusual for him to be looking down rather than up!

The sundew was a medicinal plant – in Ireland, the leaves were boiled in asses' milk and swallowed by children to combat whooping cough – and was also an ingredient in 'the once celebrated liqueur, the French *rossalis* [and] the Italian *rosoglio* ...'[131]

Not far from these insectivorous plants in the glen, we admired a bright splash of yellow saxifrage, the last of the three saxifrages I was keen to see on that coast and which I'd later find at Largiebaan. The colony is established at a little stony stream which runs off Cnoc Moy, and I reckon it is expanding. It was certainly, at the time, the most colourful feature of the entire glen. It also grows on the wet slopes above the shore south of the Inneans Burn, and I picked out a patch through binoculars.

On our way up the coast to Craigaig, botany provided the main talking points, apart from a couple of ant-hills near Earadale. The first of them we noticed had been partially excavated, but the second had been entirely tunnelled through. Whatever foraging mammal was responsible – a fox, presumably, since Don had detected no signs of badgers on the coast – had broken open the ant-hill on its south side and dug through to the north side.

I mentioned to Don the little holly bush beside the burn that runs down to the south end of Craigaig Bay (p 71), and hoped we'd meet with it at our crossing point. As we approached the burn, I didn't at first see the holly and thought we might be in a different place, but I did see a solitary pink flower, which turned out to be a dog-rose (*Rosa canina*) sapling growing up through the holly. When Don asked me if there was dog-rose anywhere near, I replied that the nearest bush could be miles away; but when I looked up the course of the burn, I was forced to concede: 'It could be up there; just about anything could be up there.'

I have assumed for years that I know that coast well, but here was a mere stream I'd probably crossed at just three or four points along its entire length. The rest of it was unknown to me. My familiarity with the topography was actually scant, certainly compared with that of the old-style shepherds who walked that coast daily. Like most recreational walkers, I have certain routes which I follow for their convenience and from which I seldom deviate, though time and again I have found that a new route, taken for whatever reason, often yields a new discovery.

The folly of assumption was reinforced about an hour later, when we were heading back towards the Kintyre Way from Craigaig sheep-fank. On a rock face to our left, I noticed clumps of bushes which had eluded, by their inaccessibility, the attentions of foraging sheep and goats. That little elevated thicket contained not only dog-rose, but also burnet rose, plus honeysuckle, bell heather, wood sage and bluebells gone to seed. I'd never noticed it before, though I'd probably passed it half-a-dozen times in the previous two years. All remaining visible rock faces were checked in passing, but none evinced such profusion. There are, however, hundreds more rock faces on the coast between the Inneans and the Galdrans ... and that one, 'as the crow flies', was less than a mile from the dog-rose and holly together!

In 1935, Dugald Macintyre, in an article on the Mull-Machrihanish coast, mentioned a raptor's nest at Tòn Bhàn, 'on a ledge, the sole ornament of which is a solitary stunted dog-rose bush'.[132] Roses and lilies are the two most frequently mentioned flowers in Shakespeare, and the dog-rose appears, in the guise of 'eglantine', in Ophelia's well-known speech in *Hamlet*, in which she lists the flowers to strew in memory of her father.[133]

19 July: Ben Gullion

George McSporran and I were on the hill in the evening, our first outing together for more than six weeks. I was to travel to Glasgow the following morning to meet my sister Carol for a farewell meal on the eve of her return to America, and fancied taking with me some blaeberries for my grandson, Lachlan Gillies, in Glasgow. His mother, Sarah, couldn't get enough of the berries when she was a child. As I anticipated, however, this year's crop was relatively meagre, owing to the wet and windy spring and the scarcity of pollinating bees. Between the two of us, we managed to collect a few dozen berries, despite the prevalence of midges. While we were gathering, I reminisced to George about a hike Judy and I had to the Inneans when Sarah wasn't yet a year old. I remembered that day with unusual clarity because on our way back across the moors, we spent so long feeding her with berries that darkness was almost down by the time we reached Machrihanish. George, too, was reminiscing about blaeberry-gathering and brought up his annual August expedition to the Slate with the late John Kelly in Machrihanish.[134] When I checked my journal for my Inneans hike with Judy and Sarah, I discovered, to my surprise, that we had seen George and John that day, a detail I had entirely forgotten.

7 August 1988: The Inneans

Sarah was fifteen days short of her first birthday, and it was her third time at the Inneans. The morning was clear and sunny and Judy suggested cycling to Machrihanish and heading south from there. We left the bikes in the cattle shed at Uisaed – demolished when the Marine Environmental Research Laboratory was built in 1991 – and walked into the Galdrans. We met a Glasgow family engaged in cowrie-hunting and at the south end of the bay stopped to release Sarah from the baby-carrier for a break. I wandered off to gather sea-coal, and 'while I was prowling, Judy shouted and I looked up at the cliffs and saw two figures – George McSporran and John Kelly. They must have been returning from the hill, because after busying themselves looking at something in the burn, they passed on north to Machrihanish'.

Above Craigaig Waterfall, we stopped again, for coffee and biscuits, and then ascended to the moorland and finally dropped down into the Inneans Bay and cooked a meal over a driftwood fire. There was a huge bull grey seal washed up and decomposing: 'The hair is off it & the guts are beginning to swell out of the carcass.' It was the biggest seal I'd seen since David Mewse (p 154) and I encountered a living bull asleep on a rock on the shore near the Mull. It was just a few feet from us, hauled out and snoring, when we passed it, and it didn't waken. Neither of us had a camera with us at the time – the early 1970s – which was probably just as well: the click of the shutter might have wakened the beast from its slumber and cost us a soaking as he crashed into the sea.

On our way back to Machrihanish by the moors, we saw eight red grouse rise ahead of us, the first I'd ever seen on that coast; doubtless they, like us, were feasting on berries. We lost track of time that evening, and, unlike the grouse with which we shared nature's wild fruits, we had far to go before we reached the place we knew as 'home'. By the time we reached our bikes, it was almost dark, and our journey back to town, though not much further than five miles, turned what had been a wonderful day into a nightmarish ending. The Machrihanish road is a fast one, and the headlights of the cars whizzing by were so distressful to Sarah that we were forced to complete the last two miles on foot, Judy with Sarah in her arms and I pushing both bikes. We weren't home until 11 p.m., by which time Judy's daughter Doreen was frantic with worry and about to telephone Teddy Lafferty for advice.

24 July: Liberator AM915

This was the bomber that crashed into a hill near Auchenhoan in 1941, killing crew and passengers, ten men in all. I'd thought I'd written my last on it in *Kilkerran Graveyard Revisited*, published in 2011, but in 2015 relatives of two of the dead men came to Kintyre to visit the location of the crash and I met them. I should declare at the outset that I have no special interest in aviation wrecks in Kintyre and am not an expert in the subject, but these crashes assuredly belong within the broader frame of 'local history' and are impossible to ignore, particularly since, in some locations, their wreckage still litters the landscape.

With the exception of the Chinook helicopter crash at the Mull on 24 June 1994, which killed all 29 people on board – the vast majority of them Ulster counter-terrorism experts – this was the most controversial aircraft accident in Kintyre history, and one that was shrouded in secrecy owing to a link with atomic bomb research in the U.S., and UK research into radio-operated proximity fuses, 'which went on to have a devastating effect in the Battle of the Atlantic against U-boats'.[135]

I first visited the supposed Liberator crash site on 31 January 1993 as a member of Campbeltown Auxiliary Coastguard. We were engaged in a map-reading exercise and divided into three teams with the task of converging on the site from different departure points. We all succeeded in reaching the general location – a hilltop at the head of Balnabraid Glen – but it was left to George McSporran, who had been there as a teenager, to find the memorial, a metal plaque, attached to a post and bearing the inscription: 'The Liberator, 1 Sep 1941.' I wrote up that expedition in the *Kintyre Magazine*, but mistranscribed the date, which I gave as '7 Sep'. The grid reference which we agreed upon – this, of course, was pre-GPS – was also wrong:[136] it should be NR 733 157.

George remembered Alastair Thompson – a mutual friend whose Learside exploits enliven *Another Summer in Kintyre* – being there on that day, c. 1967, but could remember nothing more about the outing, except that someone in the group killed an adder. I e-mailed Alastair, a retired engineer in Canada, and asked him what he remembered, and his reply was surprisingly informative. He was a member of the Air Training Corps in Campbeltown at that time, which may, along with his engineering interests, explain his greater recall. The group headed up Balnabraid Glen from the Second Water to reach the hill-face. Alastair saw fragments of aluminium and Perspex scattered around the site, and a plaque, which he described as 'a rectangle of carbon steel plate c/w the word LIBERATOR & the date weld-beaded on the surface'.

On 15 December 1995, almost three years after my first visit, I was back at the marker with George, his son Sandy and brother John, and two Coastguards, Kenny McLellan and Robert Houston. We set off along the track to Balnabraid ruins and from there headed up the north side of the glen, on a track which eventually disappeared into rough ground. This was the route along which, in 1941, the human and aircraft remains were brought down, and on our way up John McSporran found two bits of metal wreckage. The plate on the marker, I noted on that day, 'has become loose and wants fixing'.[137] George took a group photograph at the marker, which stood in what appears to be a slightly elevated piece of ground, covered with grass and a few heather clumps. The spruce trees in the background are small, no more than six feet high.

George, Alastair, Alastair's Canadian wife Liz, and I, went looking for the Liberator marker on 17 October 1999. My account of that day in *By Hill and Shore in South Kintyre* (p 132) conveys the impression that we reached the site, but we didn't; in my defence, I was more taken by a string of long-tailed tits which undulated by us as we sat with our flasks near the head of the glen. I checked my journal and found the entry, 'Couldn't find Liberator site', and at the foot of the page, in Alastair's hand, the following: 'A climb up memory lane – & if George & Angus had a better memory the Liberator would have been found! Next time.'

22. At the Liberator marker, 15 December 1995. L-R: John McSporran, Robert Houston, Sandy McSporran, Kenny McLellan and Angus Martin. Photograph by George McSporran.

On 24 July 2015, George and I had one of the interested parties with us, a retired journalist from Jerusalem, Jon Immanuel. That journey began with a letter published in the *Campbeltown Courier* on 10 July, in which Jon explained that his maternal uncle, Dr Mark Benjamin, a physicist at GEC Wembley, had been killed in an air crash in Kintyre in 1941. George has a sound knowledge of the ground around the head of Balnabraid Glen, and when he suggested an approach to the crash site from Glenramskill, I concurred with his judgement.

Jon had arrived in town by the previous evening's ferry, and we met him in Amelia's Café Bistro at mid-day on 24

July to discuss the hike. Jon was concerned about the suitability of his footwear, and George, sharing his concern, suggested he buy a pair of inexpensive boots in the Factory Shop before we set off. But I'd noticed a pair of hiking boots, of a reputable make and priced at £7.50, in the Red Cross shop the day before and asked Jon what size he took. The second-hand boots – broken in, but hardly worn – promised to fit, so we decided to go straight to the charity shop.

As we rose to leave, I noticed two local men, Jimmy Hall and John Bannatyne, sitting at the table opposite us. John's father, Calum, was a shepherd in Auchenhoan at the time of the Liberator crash and had discovered the wreck. John's presence in the café that day seemed, like the boots, to be somehow fated, and after we'd gone outside I mentioned him to Jon. He was intrigued, but first we had to secure boots. Those I'd seen in the Red Cross Shop were still on the shelf, Jon tried them on, was delighted with the fit and bought them. In fact, since there was a woman ahead of us whose many purchases were being scanned, in the interest of a quick departure he handed over the price-tag and a £10 note and left without waiting for the change.

Back at Amelia's, we found Jimmy Hall and John Bannatyne still there. I introduced Jon to John, left them together and hurried home to pack my rucksack. As I later discovered, the noise in the café was not conducive to conversation, so a visit to John at his home in Ralston Road was agreed.

Jon was 65 years old – the same age as George and two years older than I – but is lightly-built and fit. I was still weak from a cold I'd caught a fortnight before, and the climb up Glenramskill to around 1000 feet was a trial to me, but we took our time. At High Glenramskill cottage, we were greeted by two sheepdogs and knew that the Low Glenramskill shepherd, Dugald McKendrick, must be around. As George and I suspected, 'Dougie' was clipping in the fank, and Jon witnessed, and photographed, a rare sight indeed in the twenty-first century: a shepherd seated on an old-fashioned wooden clipping-stool, shearing a ewe with hand-clippers.

Once we'd reached the head of the glen and begun to descend on to the moorland, we halted for a late lunch at an isolated straining-post overlooking Arinarach Hill and the Meal Kist Glen. From there, we crossed a stretch of moorland to the belt of coniferous forest which we'd follow to the crash site.

23. *Angus Martin and Jon Immanuel in hills above Glenramskill, 24 July 2015. Photograph by George McSporran.*

En route, we came on intriguing remains, which, given the nature of our presence there, assumed an almost symbolic significance: a dead peregrine falcon, part-plucked and part-eaten. As I remarked to my companions: 'The killer killed.' A peregrine falcon is not only a top killing-machine, but is reckoned to be the fastest animal on the planet, capable of attaining speeds of more than 200 miles an hour in its hunting 'stoop', or dive. What could have killed it? I guessed a golden eagle, and Rab Morton, a local ornithologist to whom I sent a copy of a photo, was inclined to agree. He speculated that it may have been killed as an 'interloper', and afterwards become food. The photograph lacked certain information he'd have preferred to have, but, from the bird's small size he supposed it could be a young male. Each of us lifted a barred feather from the ground as a souvenir; I stuck mine in my cap, but lost it that same day.

Earlier in the month, at Polliwilline, George had seen a golden eagle attack a hen harrier, and he suspected this might be the work of the same bird. He was with his wife at the time, and when he saw the big raptor he remarked to her: 'I'm quite sure that's an eagle, Margaret.' Then he exclaimed: 'Look at that, Margaret – it's heading down!' It was dropping out of the sky to hit a hen harrier, but the harrier presented its talons to the eagle, and there was a brief tussle. When the two birds separated, the harrier zig-zagged east and the eagle alighted. The whole drama, George said, lasted no more than three minutes.

As we approached the crash site, I decided not to venture down to it. I'd been there before and preferred to rest, so I sat in the shelter of trees and let George and Jon complete the search. In fact, they weren't much more than a five-minute walk from where I sat. After an hour had passed, I decided to look for them, and saw them climbing towards me. They had, with difficulty, found a post marked 'LIB' beside the fence (grid reference: 73381 15848) but when they entered the forest to look for the metal plate, they failed to find it. In the twenty years since George and I were last there, the spruce plantation has grown dense. The marker may still be there, standing or fallen, but, if so, it'll be difficult to find. Jon can be satisfied, however, that he stood on the hillside where the huge aircraft broke up, and where his uncle, and nine others, lost their lives.

There is probably no way of knowing how many relatives have visited the crash area in the past seventy years. Aviation historian Ian Davies, who contributed two technical articles on Liberator AM915 to *The Kintyre Magazine*, mentioned in one of them that Simon Mair, nephew of the aircraft's First Officer, Geoffrey Panes, reached the marker on 1 September 2001, the sixtieth anniversary of the crash. The RAF accident report, Mr Davies points out, gave the crash site as 'Achinhoan Hill',[138] but that is doubtful. Duncan Pursell, who visited the site the following year, said that he found a crater on Arinarach Hill. One of the shepherds at Auchenhoan told a reporter from *The Scotsman*, three days after the crash: 'The 'plane struck the hillside 20 feet from the summit and plunged over the top and down the other side, travelling over a mile before eventually coming to rest. Parts of the 'plane were thrown in all directions and the propeller landed in a gully. One of the bodies also landed in the gully.'[139]

Jon Immanuel and I visited John Bannatyne on the day after our hike and spent a couple of hours with him and his daughter Shirley. He was born in 1933 at Strone, a remote sheep-farm in a glen near the Mull of Kintyre. When he was three years old, the family left there and moved to Achnaglach; afterwards came a spell in Largiebaan, and from there they moved to Auchenhoan, where, in 1941, John's father Calum – or Malcolm – was a shepherd. John's mother, Helen McSporran, belonged to Killervan, and appears in a photograph I published in *Kintyre Country Life* (p 34). The caption is 'Women in corn field, Southend, *c.* 1925', and Helen – on the left, holding a pitchfork – is the one woman I failed to identify.

John said right away that I should have spoken to his father about the crash. I had tape-recorded Calum, who had an exceptional store of folklore (p 57), several times in 1977, but to my recollection he never mentioned the Liberator, and, even had he mentioned it, I doubt if I would have shown much interest. I should also have spoken to John when I last researched the Liberator crash five years before for *Kilkerran Graveyard Revisited*, but it didn't occur to me. Perhaps I assumed he wasn't born then or was only a baby;

but he was eight years old in September 1941 and at school in Campbeltown, with his sisters Mary and Betty, when the drama erupted.

Liberator AM915 was on a flight from Canada to Scotland and was due to land at RAF Heathfield, near Ayr. When she arrived over Ayrshire at 8 a.m. on 1 September, the cloud base was at 2000 feet, with a visibility of 12 miles. Her captain, Kenneth Garden, could apparently have landed using standard bad weather procedure, but decided to divert to Squires Gate, Blackpool. That airport, however, was already closing, on account of the weather. Unable to land there, Captain Garden opted to return to Ayr, on a navigational track which took him towards Kintyre. Shortly after 9.36, radio communication with AM915 was lost and at 10.10 she crashed.[140]

The above sequence of events is known from the official accident investigation and may be accepted as factual, but the immediate aftermath of the crash – and, in particular, the circumstances in which the wreck was located – remains obscure and may never be clarified. For those who witnessed the destruction and carnage, the experience must have been traumatic; indeed, John Bannatyne attests that his father 'took a long time to get over it'.

The crash was not reported in the *Campbeltown Courier*, but appeared in newspapers all over the world. John Bannatyne inherited from his father a yellowed page from a Glasgow daily newspaper, *The Bulletin*, which – now laminated for preservation – he showed to Jon and me. The item consists of a photograph of Calum Bannatyne with one of his dogs, Roy, and the following caption: 'The shepherd who, while tending his flocks on a hillside in the West of Britain, discovered the wreckage of the Transatlantic Ferry 'plane which crashed on the hillside this week. The bodies of the last three victims were brought down by a party of naval ratings to the home of the shepherd yesterday.' The newspaper is dated September 4, 1941 – three days after the crash – and the caption is so brief and devoid of detail that no reader could possibly guess the location.

The Scotsman report, of the same date, was subject to the same security constraints, and no place or person is named, but it does contain an interview with 'a shepherd', whose cottage was described as being 'the nearest habitation to the spot where the crash occurred' – that is, Auchenhoan. Who was the shepherd? There were two shepherds at Auchenhoan, and if Calum Bannatyne was the one who found the wreck, then the shepherd who was interviewed must have been the other. The following statement, given two days after the accident, must be considered the definitive account of the sequence of events at Auchenhoan:

'I heard the drone of a 'plane on Monday morning but I could not see it. I next heard a loud bang and felt certain that the 'plane had crashed. As soon as dawn came next day I sent another shepherd out on the hills while I remained working at the hay and told him to search for a crashed 'plane.

'He came across the 'plane about three miles from our house and hurried back to tell me the news without even waiting to examine the wreckage. Word was sent to the nearest house with a telephone, and the occupant instructed his wife to inform the police. When the police arrived at mid-day on Tuesday I took them to the wrecked machine.'

I doubt if these were entirely words spoken by the anonymous shepherd – could a working man in Kintyre really have come out with '... and the occupant instructed his wife to inform the police'? Regardless of that quibble, the statement itself contains a curious claim. The shepherd heard the drone of the aircraft, followed by a bang, 'on Monday morning', but didn't act until dawn of the 'next day'. Since the crash happened just after 10 a.m. on 1 September, which was indeed a Monday, I had assumed the shepherd had mixed up the days. Further on, however, he confirms the day – 'When the police arrived at mid-day on Tuesday I took them to the wrecked machine' – which suggests, indeed, that no action was taken until the day after the suspected crash. Shortly after the wreckage was found by the shepherd who had been despatched to search for it, 'a party of naval officers who were out on the hills shooting grouse came on the wreckage and at once communicated with the naval authorities …'[141]

John Bannatyne remembers the aftermath of the Liberator accident differently. The crash was heard at Auchenhoan, but there was a war on, and distant explosions, such as from military exercises, weren't so exceptional as to cause alarm. His father and the other Auchenhoan shepherd had intended to bring in the hay and stack it, but the day was too wet – and misty with it – and decided instead to whitewash the byre. Around mid-day, they stopped work and had lunch. While listening to the wireless, they heard a report that an aircraft was missing. Calum fetched his dogs and went into the hills to look for signs of a 'plane crash. As he approached the head of Balnabraid Glen, he saw an unusual object on the top of the hill which he knew as 'Glenmurril Hill', from an old ruin of that name on the south side of the glen. Glenmurril Hill formed part of his beat, and he knew it well; in fact, John said that the sheep stock was generally gathered on that hill before being herded down for clipping and dipping. At first Calum thought he was seeing a horse on the skyline, but as he approached closer he realised that the object was the tail of an aircraft. He returned to Auchenhoan at once. ('Glenmurril Hill' was also the name used by a later shepherd at Auchenhoan, Gilbert Muir.)[142]

John believes it was his mother who was despatched to find a telephone, since Auchenhoan at that time had no such link with the outside world. She would have walked, or run, about two-and-a-half miles, before she found a telephone at Davaar House. The school car in which John Bannatyne and his sisters were travelling back to Auchenhoan, about 4 p.m., was caught up in the emergency traffic, but they got home all right. 'Home', however, was a scene of chaos for long afterwards, John remembered. Once the ten corpses had been recovered, the work of removing the wreckage began. John wasn't allowed near the hill for several days, but when he did get there, he was amazed not only by the extent of the wreckage, but also by the incongruity of some of the other stuff lying about. He particularly recalls seeing packs of playing cards strewn around, and big hams; the civilians on board had been in America, and may have seized on the opportunity of taking home commodities which were scarce in wartime Britain, which was subject to strict rationing.

John remembered that the military presence at Auchenhoan continued for months, as the wreckage was transported off the hill by a 'Caterpillar' tractor towing a sledge. The wreckage was removed in 'low-loaders', which were sometimes parked overnight at the farm steadings, and he remembers plunderers being chased away by his father. (Perspex was, at that time, a novelty and highly collectable, rings and brooches being fashioned from it.) Calum himself found a clothes-brush which bore a coat-of-arms, that of Count Guy de Baillet-Latour – Economic Counsellor in London to the Belgian Ministry of Colonies – who was one of the fatalities and a probable link with the earlier export of Congolese uranium oxide ore to the United States, in a quantity theoretically sufficient to supply the uranium for the three atomic bombs exploded in 1945. The souvenir remained in the Bannatyne family in Campbeltown until Mrs Bannatyne gave it to one of her daughters in England. When the removal work was finished and the military finally left Auchenhoan, the Bannatyne family was presented with a box of chocolate bars, which, as a rationed product, was compensation of sorts for the upheaval.

Duncan Pursell, a mining engineer in Australia, was brought up at Davaar House and remembers episodes of the story differently, but that's in the nature of oral tradition. Like John Bannatyne, he was just eight years old at the time of the crash. One morning before he set off for school, he answered the front door and saw a 'short, dark-haired man', whom he recognised as one of the Auchenhoan shepherds. Duncan led the 'visibly shaking' shepherd into the kitchen, and heard him mention an 'explosion' and a 'flash'. Duncan also recalls hearing that the shepherds had 'sat up all night with their shotguns', a detail with which his sister, Iona MacNeill, agreed. One of Duncan's parents telephoned the commanding officer of HMS *Nimrod*, Captain Farquhar, who was actually billeted at Davaar House and for whose use the phone had been installed (Iona MacNeill still has the four-digit wartime number).

Soon afterwards, Duncan recalled, Naval personnel and 'flatbed lorries' were passing Davaar House. His older brother Bill, in Canada, recalled that the road at Davaar Cottage had to be 'modified' to allow these large vehicles around the corner. They were loaded with the wreckage in a quarry on the hill before Auchenhoan farmhouse, and Bill remembered that for months afterwards the lorries would pass Davaar House with 'cut-up plane parts'. Since the boys' father, Edward Pursell, who was headmaster of Kinloch School, was entitled to 'a few petrol coupons' – petrol, like most other commodities, was rationed – he drove the family to the bridge at the Second Water, whence, Duncan recalled, the crash site was visible as 'a brown scar on the hillside'.

Bill Pursell, with 'the curiosity of a young teenager', visited Arinarach Hill in early summer of 1942 and found 'a large, fairly shallow hole about 10 to 15 feet from the heather-covered top of the hill, with long scars down the slope beyond, presumably from the main structure of the plane as it slid downwards'. He understood that 'the cockpit flew across the top of Balnabraid Glen and became the "official" site of the crash'. He brought back two 'beautifully made' pulley wheels, which lay in the workshop at Davaar House for decades. Duncan revisited the crash site in later years and remembered 'parts of the plane scattered over the hill'. One of the flight crew, he was told, had silk stockings – in great demand owing to wartime austerity – wrapped around his body. 'Let us be charitable and assume that they were there for warmth!'[143]

There remains the question of where the Liberator struck. I may be wrong, but from the evidence so far available the initial impact appears to have been on Arinarach Hill, with the final resting place across the head of Balnabraid Glen, on the hill which shepherds called 'Glenmurril Hill', where the memorial was placed. There is, however, a great deal more information still to emerge about Liberator AM915 and the nature of her passengers' business in the US.

30 July: The Black Loch

Including the Gaelic form, there are quite a few little lochs in Kintyre called the Black Loch/*Dubh Loch*, but the one I was at is the only one I've ever seen, as far as I remember. It's at the back of Ben Gullion and its darkness isn't at all apparent until you get close to it and look at its peaty bottom and peat-tinged waters. It is one of the few natural bodies of water in South Kintyre – there are dozens of them nestling in the hills in the northern part of the peninsula, as any energetic angler will attest – and all the more precious for that.

It had an earlier and more interesting name, however, which preserved an Old Norse place-name, itself probably dating back more than a thousand years: 'Loch Grunidale.' Its last appearance was on an Argyll Estate map of Dalrioch drawn in 1836. The Norse elements probably comprise *groena,* 'green spot', and *dal-r,* 'valley', with Gaelic *loch* added. In *Kintyre Places and Place-Names* (p 200), I speculated inconclusively on the location of the forgotten valley, but, sitting above the loch itself that day, looking south, I had a strong feeling that the glen which runs up from Uigle could be the feature in question.

My approach to the loch was by Tomaig Glen in sunshine, which brought me my greatest tally of butterflies of the summer – ringlets predominated, followed by meadow browns, and my first few common blues of the summer. Within fifteen minutes of my settling for lunch, however, the sun disappeared behind cloud for the day. Butterflies also disappeared, but memories swarmed in their place, and the landscape round the loch was alive with family and friends.

Landscapes and imagination

I could see, from where I sat, Lochorodale farmhouse and the road winding uphill from there. As I scanned its length with binoculars, I recalled days in spring when I had pushed my bike up it; in a sense, I was back there.

My route to the Black Loch had taken me across a stone dyke where it meets the western edge of Ben Gullion forest. I always cross at that point, which I have come to associate with an outing with my daughters Sarah and Amelia. The date was 10 June 1992 and we were going to a peat-bank near the Black Loch, but by the time we reached the bank, it was almost time to go home. I remember a sweltering day and the girls wearing lime-green sun-hats. In *By Hill and Shore in South Kintyre* (p 24), there is a photograph of them sitting on Killeonan Hill, surrounded by bog cotton. Why I connect that day with the stone wall, I can't say.

I can see the wall from various parts of town, particularly Lochend Street, and it always registers as a visible link with the past. I wrote a subdued poem about it one evening on Ben Gullion, in September 2008, and published it in *Paper Archipelagos*. The family dog Benjie's health was failing at the time, so Judy would drive us to Narrowfield to start us on our way to the hill. The wall was visible on the way to Crosshill Reservoir, and from time to time I'd stop and study it through binoculars, returning in memory to that summer's day sixteen years before. The poem is titled 'Crossing Point' and ends: 'That clever wall has led me to the past/ drawn me uphill to the crossing place/ a neglected gap of tumbled stone/ I see my daughters cross again.'

The poem 'Looking from Point to Baraskomel', which was published in *The Larch Plantation*, also attempts to express the notion of past and present intertwined. It was written, on 31 March 1990, at Point, a ruined cottage at the far side of the field opposite the Doirlinn car-park. Around that time, I had taken to cycling to Point for the sole purpose of writing poetry, for the atmosphere was conducive to thought. The place is close to town and close to the road, yet obscure enough that I was seldom bothered by human intrusion, though, on that particular day, the farm manager's daughter and her boyfriend arrived to feed ten ewes, he shouldering a bag of fodder and she calling 'Come and get it!' I got a poem, 'At Point', out of that unexpected event, and it too appeared in *The Larch Plantation*, along with a third, 'I Have Remarkable Faith in the Dead'. In fact, I wrote eight poems that day, a facility I reflect on now with wonder.

LOOKING FROM POINT TO BARASKOMEL

Now I look on places that I gave
days to, days that have blown
behind me like leaves from the rootless
tree of my life.

No longer there, I am no longer there,
but here, and what has become
of those selves that had belonging
in the time it took to cross

hill, shore, moor, anywhere?
I bear those times as growth-rings
in this mind that hangs above
the moving feet, a moon of white wood.

After Benjie's death, on 22 December 2008, I turned to poetry to help me through my grief. The poems in *Haunted Landscapes* are probably too intensely personal to mean much to anyone else, but they meant a lot to me. The last poem was written, on 20 September 2009, in a clearing on Ben Gullion where I often sat with Benjie, patiently casting hooks into my subconscious to try to catch a poem. That spot – which mostly drew me in autumnal evenings – looks on to Crosshill, another place Benjie and I used to sit, sometimes with my daughter Bella; and as I sat, looking over the reservoir to the hill, I imagined the three of us there, in a gathering which could never happen again.

LAST ILLUSION

I have been watching myself on Crosshill
intent beneath the telegraph pole
twisting the lid of a gleaming flask –
I wonder what it might contain?
It's another mundane evening on the hill
but you are there and Bella too;
I see you clearly though a hint of shadow
has crept into the hollow where we sit.

Then nothing at all is happening
and I seem to see a photograph
which the magic dust of time
transforms into a sacred marvel
except I can't possess it;
but if I wait here long enough
till dark engulfs the last illusion
then may I say: *They've all gone home.*

The clearing where I wrote the poem has since been blocked by fallen trees and I seldom go there. When I left the Black Loch, I decided to take an old route through the western edge of Ben Gullion forest, but it too was blocked by wind-blown timber, and several frustrating detours were necessary. The ageing forest is falling.

3 August: New Orleans and a skua

George McSporran and I had an afternoon cycle to New Orleans and a very short walk to the grassy stack just before the Wee Man's Cove. If I had to design a rock for sitting on, a rock combining easy accessibility, safe elevation, and comfortable turf, I'd base my design on that one. We sat on the top of it, drank our tea and looked around. There were hundreds of Manx shearwaters flying south over the wave-tops, some of them quite close in, but we'd already seen the most remarkable seabird sighting of the day.

It looked almost gannet-sized and was flying south towards Auchenhoan Head with a small flock of gannets, but it was dark-coloured, and I at once thought – a young gannet. It couldn't have been, as I would rationalise later with the help of Rab Morton, but in any case it did what I'd never noticed a gannet do, which was make a strike at another gannet over the sea. My next assumption was – a skua. Now, I'd never knowingly seen a skua of any kind before, nor had George. While sitting on the stack and looking seaward, we saw the dark-coloured bird again pass south, this time keeping up with a larger flock of gannets. I stood and trained my binoculars on it and, once again, off Auchenhoan Head, I saw it 'launch itself at a solitary gannet'. The evidence seemed conclusive, but which species of skua could it have been? Rab Morton, on the basis of the descriptions I gave him, and on the bird's assaults on gannets, considered the great skua (*Stercorarius skua*) the likeliest.

Skuas are commonly likened to 'pirates', from their habit of chasing and harassing other seabirds to force them to disgorge their crop's contents, which the raider then catches in the air. Fishermen observed these tactics, and Hugh MacFarlane, the best of my oral history informants in Tarbert, gave me a Gaelic name for 'skua' (itself of Norse origin). It was *fasgadair*. When I visited Hugh on 20 April 1978, he couldn't remember the name, but it came to him after I'd gone and he conscientiously wrote it down and gave it to me when I returned on 13 May. He described the *fasgadair* as a 'grey bird' which 'chases the gulls', so his skua may more likely have been the smaller and commoner Arctic (*Stercorarius parasiticus*). The 'latter-day boys' at the fishing, when Gaelic was going out of use, called the bird a 'squeezer', he recalled. This establishes the root of the Gaelic name: *fasgadh* means 'wringing, squeezing, pressing', therefore *fasgadair* is a bird that squeezes or pressurises other birds into feeding it.

4 August: A Scotch Argus

On my way across Kinloch Green to do some shopping in town, I met Sue Holland and Steve Walker outside Aqualibrium and engaged them in conversation; in fact, the conversation lasted so long – about an hour and ten minutes – that the shops closed before my mouth did. Flowers and butterflies were high on the agenda. Sue remarked that Scotch Argus were much less common south of Campbeltown than north; I had no opinion on that, since my knowledge of the subject is limited, but I did mention that the most Scotch Argus I'd ever seen together was in a field near Auchalochy in the summer of 2013. Minutes after the Scotch Argus discussion, I saw a dark-coloured butterfly flutter into sight over the grass and set off after it, Steve behind me. Yes, it was a Scotch Argus, my only one of the year, and not quite where I'd have expected to see it.

7 August: The Kintyre Agricultural Show

I hadn't been at Largiebaan for nearly two months, owing to a head cold and poor weather combined. I took the 12 o' clock Southend bus, which stopped at Anderston to let a family off at the venue of the Kintyre Agricultural Show. The field looked busy, and would be busier still, because the event was blessed with a fine sunny day. The night before, while waiting for Judy to arrive on the ferry from Ardrossan, I'd been talking on the Quarry Green to an acquaintance who bemoaned the present location of the show and reminisced fondly on the years when it was held in upper Kintyre Park.

He recalled money-hunting in the field when the tents had been removed. The site of the beer-tent was especially lucrative, and half-crowns, even, could be found in the grass there. In the 1960s, a half-crown – two shillings and sixpence – was big money. The practice of converting old money into straightforward decimal equivalents – in this case, 12½p – is meaningless.

This comparison should demonstrate the true value of two shillings and sixpence: my weekly pocket-money in the early 1960s was one shilling, which paid my way into the Saturday afternoon matinee in one of the local cinemas and left me with threepence for sweets. When the allowance was increased by threepence, that extra sum enabled me to buy a bottle of chilled 'Coca Cola'. Tommy Duff, manager of the Rex, was often on the chiller. At the pull of a handle, a bottle, with beads of condensation on it, would emerge from a slot at the bottom, and Tommy, a smug expression on his face, would twirl it aloft and catch it, before handing it over. To my knowledge, the trick never failed. A fizzy drink in those days was a treat, and, before refrigerators became standard household equipment, a chilled drink was the ultimate joy.

I don't remember ever finding money at the show-field, but I do remember returning home with my pockets full of cattle cake, lifted from the sample bins at stalls. I wasn't eating the little nuts, so I must have played with them until, in all probability, my Mother threw them out. And I also remember a drunk man following a balloon-seller and jabbing the lit end of his cigarette into balloons and exploding them. The victim, who was carrying a huge plume of coloured balloons, was understandably furious with the fool who was destroying his assets, but I forget how the outrage ended.

Nothing like that would have appeared in newspaper reports, of course, but I had an idea to combine the agricultural show and the cinemas in a piece of quick research. I decided on 1962, when I'd have been ten years old. That happened to be the last year the show was held at upper Kintyre Park (which is to become the site of the new Campbeltown Grammar School). The show at that time was held on the first Friday of June and was known as 'The June Show' (it still is by some people). More than 2,500 people attended the event on 1 June 1962. Duncan Smith, Barrmains, took the supreme award for Ayrshire cattle, David Smith (formerly High Knockrioch) won the top Clydesdale horse prize, A.G. Black, Tangy, 'swept the boards' with his black-faced sheep, and in the white-faced section the champion sheep belonged to A.F. Binnie, Low Ballevain, the same farm which had produced the previous year's champion for the late John Gilchrist. During the prize-giving ceremony, the Royal and Highland Agricultural Society's long service medal was presented to Alex McKinven for thirty years of shepherding on the Argyll Estates.[144]

On the Friday of the show, and on the Saturday after it, the films shown at the Rex Cinema were *Teacher's Pet* (Clark Gable, Doris Day and Gig Young) and *The Baited Trap* (Richard Widmark, Tina Louise and Lee J. Cobb), and at the Picture House *Springfield Rifle* (Gary Cooper, Phyllis Thaxter and David Brian) and *Laughter in Paradise* (Alistair Sim, Fay Compton and Joyce Grenfell),[145] none of which I remember seeing, though doubtless I was in the Rex – which I preferred for its modernity and more up-to-date films – on the afternoon of 2 June.

Walking to Largiebaan

I got off the bus at Auchencorvie and began walking to Largiebaan. Butterflies were numerous and the roadside botany interesting. On the brae past Lochorodale bridge, I noticed a small colony of Grass-of-Parnassus (*Parnassia palustris*) in full flower in the ditch. A bit further on, the ditch held the fading yellow spikes of bog asphodel (*Narthecium ossifragum*), and, still further on, two garden escapes, tutsan and montbretia (the latter probably from the garden at Lochorodale steading). I was also noticing the big daisy-like flowers of mayweed, not because they are unusual, but because all of them, along that road, were growing next to piles of salty sand deposited at the foot of braes for the use of motorists in icy conditions, a nice illustration of the opportunism of seeds when offered an artificial, accidental habitat.

Butterflies

I decided to stop for lunch at the top of the hill past Lochorodale, where the road disappears down towards Clachan Ùr bridge. I'd parted from Judy at the lay-by there on 17 April, a small event which somehow expanded in my mind, so that, on my way home that evening, I memorialised the separation with a ribbon tied to a roadside heather clump.

Before I reached my resting place, I noticed a green-veined white butterfly at rest beside the road, and paused to look at it. In past summers, I wouldn't have given it a second glance, because the species was by far the commonest of all, so common, in fact, that it is routinely omitted from butterfly counts. That summer, however, I reckon it lagged behind meadow browns and ringlets in numbers, at least where I'd been counting. But here's the point. Close to the white, I saw what I thought was a common blue on a bracken frond, but when I looked closer I saw two. They were mating, and so preoccupied I could have lifted them off the frond. Instead, I photographed them, over and over again, trying to capture the exquisite colour patterns on their underwings, but my little digital camera let me down, and I found myself wishing I had an SLR camera with me, loaded with slide-film and with an X4 magnifier on the lens. (Four days later, I would see a pair of meadow browns mating in the grassy slope of Leac a' Chreachainn and record my first small tortoiseshells of the year and my first fritillary, a dark-green.)

I was reading, that week, a biography of Agatha Christie, and recalled a strange anecdote from that book. During a family holiday in France in 1896, a guide, thinking to please the young Agatha, caught a butterfly and pinned it to her straw hat. She could feel the insect's wings fluttering against the hat and felt 'sick and miserable'. Her father, noticing her distress, asked her what was the matter, but, not wishing to hurt the guide's feelings, she could only shake her head. Finally, she 'gazed dumbly, agonisingly' at her mother, who at once divined the problem: 'I believe she doesn't like that butterfly in her hat. Who pinned it there?'[146]

I have always espoused the purity of butterflies, so I was surprised to read that dog excrement is frequently a 'delicacy' preferred to nectar. Butterflies taste with their feet,[147] which I suppose makes the shit-eating less of a jolt to the imagination.

As I sat eating lunch on the roadside opposite the lay-by, the sun disappeared behind cloud. Largiebaan suddenly seemed a long way off, for I hadn't slept well the night before and the corn on my left foot was troubling me. I must have looked dispirited, because a local woman stopped in her car and asked me if I was 'all right'. Having my reassurance that I was fine, she pointed to the darkening sky and remarked: 'It was too much to expect ...' She didn't finish the sentence. Now I was contemplating cutting the walk short by heading down Glen Breackerie and catching the 6 o' clock bus at Southend, but the allure of Largiebaan was too strong and when I came to the turn-off to Glenahanty, I took it without hesitation.

As I approached the cliffs, the sun reappeared, as if on cue, and I congratulated myself on a sound decision. I found a grassy hollow overlooking both the Largiebaan and the Aignish cliffs and settled in there. The time was 4.30 and I reckoned I'd have to leave at around 6 to catch the 9.45 bus at Keil, so I'd be getting an hour and a half at Largiebaan for about eight hours' walking, which didn't seem a great return for the effort. Close to my resting place there were several narrow splits in the cliff, in one of which I'd noticed flowers I didn't recognise from distance, and I decided I'd go down for a closer look. I entered this resolution in my journal, noting that the old boots I was wearing, for the sake of my corn, had 'worn treads', and, in a flash of dramatic imagining, these scribbled words became the last record of my life, to be discovered before my corpse was hauled up from the foot of the gully. But when I looked again at the gully, it appeared too steep to attempt, and, without regret, I abandoned the idea.

Wood vetch

I decided to check the other gullies before I left the cliffs, and on the upper edge of one of them, I noticed a cluster of unfamiliar flowers, which I noted as 'bluey-white' and 'vetchy'. They were close enough to touch, and I examined and then photographed them. When I got home, I showed the photographs to Judy, who went to work with books and identified the species as wood vetch. In the location I'd seen them, there wasn't a native tree within miles, and I remarked: 'Wood vetch is a silly name.' – 'That's why Agnes [Stewart] is right – it's better to use the Latin,' Judy replied. 'What is the Latin?' I asked. There was a pause as she checked the book: '*Vicia silvatica* – it's just the same!'

The photographs were duly e-mailed to Agnes, who confirmed the identification and remarked that the species is found in several locations in Kintyre. She had seen it along Craigaig Water and at Putechan Burn, and the South Kintyre Botany Group found it near Bellochantuy. She hadn't herself seen it at Largiebaan, but recalled that, *circa* 2003, another keen local botanist, Ian Teesdale, had searched the gorge of Largiebaan burn and 'found the plant on a spur of land where a tributary joins to make the burn (596 144)'.[148] *The Flora of Kintyre* (p 19) described *Vicia silvatica* as 'Especially fine near Largybaan where it occurs in two colour forms, with blue striae and with mauve striae'. I'd seen the blue. I was fortunate, because there was just one clump of it in that particular spot. Once again, and unfailingly, Largiebaan had given me a new flower to admire.

Glen Breackerie

I reached the end of the Glenahanty road at 7.45, so had exactly two hours to catch the bus at Keil. I was going to stop at Dalsmirren bridge and drink a cup of tea and recall my times there with the crew of the 'bin lorry' (p 11) – ah, sweet memories! – but the air was very still down in the glen and midges were out, so I supped the tea as I walked. It was probably just as well I hadn't lingered, because the longer I walked through Glen Breackerie, the more I began to worry that I'd miss the bus. It appeared as I was approaching Keil Gate, and I slowed my pace, but my anxiety wasn't over yet. It turned quickly and seemed about to head back to town. I broke into a run and waved to attract the driver's attention, but my alarm was unnecessary. The bus pulled up beside the lodge and when the driver handed me my ticket I noticed that the time on it was 21.39. I'd got there with six minutes to spare, but I took so much out myself in the final few miles that muscular strain in my left leg caused me to hobble for days afterwards.

I hadn't walked the length of Glen Breackerie for many years, so the journey was almost like a foreign holiday to me. It's a beautiful glen and was all the more beautiful in the peace of that evening. Clips of nostalgia were playing in memory all the way, and I indulged them. I walked that road quite often in the spring of 1968, while tree-planting in Strone and later in Glen Breackerie itself.[149]

One evening, on my way down the glen, I found in a ditch a thick copper coin, which I placed in a jewellery-box which an uncle, Archie McCallum, had made. He made and gave away many of these boxes, which were in the shape of little houses, covered in sea-shells; the roof opened on hinges and there were compartments inside. Years later, I decided to try to have the coin identified, but when I looked in the box, it was gone.

And I fished out from the river at Low Glenadale bridge a belt of bullets, which I stupidly took home. When I finally decided to dispose of the useless cache, I threw it – fool that I was – into the rubbish-bin at the back of the house. A day or two afterwards, my father decided to burn the rubbish in the bin, triggering a series of deafening bangs and clangs, as the bullets one after another exploded. As the first detonations resounded, he dashed out, at risk to himself, I now realise, and slammed on the lid, which contained the danger. A succession of alarmed neighbours emerged from their back doors, and the bin ended up with multiple dents in it. Few families at the time – around 1970 – would have had telephones, otherwise the police would doubtless have been called, and I'd have had some serious explaining to do.

Eating an adder

Before I set off for the Southend bus, I had a visitor who had read *Another Summer in Kintyre* and had an adder story to add to those in the book. It was a remarkable story – illustrating, I think, the irrational responses that sudden encounters with our only native venomous snake can trigger, especially in the young – and I asked him write it out for me. I met him by chance on the Ardrossan-Campbeltown ferry on 20 August and he handed me the hand-written account. This is it:

> It must have been in '71 or '72. Iain and I were going through a knife phase. At that time you could get exotic versions easily through the post. We had graduated from simple lock knives on to Bowie knives, then heavy-duty diver's knives with serrated edges. For a time we stalked the hills tooled up like a pair of Corsican bandits.
> Climbing over the lip at the side of Dun Bhan, I nearly put my hand on an adder and in my confusion managed to stand on it. I cried out and Iain who was slightly ahead of me despatched it (with the previously mentioned diver's knife) using a degree of skill that I can still recall.

We both felt immediately ashamed at killing this beautiful creature and decided not to waste the animal. It was taken home and carefully skinned. The flesh was grilled with butter – it flaked like fish but tasted more like chicken. The skin was made into a watch strap, which served its purpose for a year or two. My parents did not partake but watched on, I think aware that a lesson was being learnt.

We never came across adders at Largiebaan for many years after this and, needless to say, we never killed an adder again.

He remarked that 'snakes are still uncommon at Largiebaan', and I can vouch for that, never having seen one there. The 'snakiest area' in Kintyre, in his experience, is 'the scree hollows that dot the ground above and below The Goings at the Mull', though the greatest number of adders he ever discovered together was in wet ground at a drystone dyke below High Glenadale steading. He reckoned there were six or seven of them, but he 'couldn't count them accurately, they moved so fast'.

11 August: Largiebaan

I returned to Largiebaan four days later, this time by bicycle, an altogether more relaxing journey. By then, with rest, the muscular pain in my left leg had eased. The ploy that day was to look for the wood vetch Ian Teesdale had reported about twelve years before (p 202).

Exceptionally on the Homestone road, I encountered another cyclist, but our conversation could hardly have been briefer. I was pushing my bike up the long hill past Lochorodale, lost in thought, when I heard a sudden voice: 'Hello, mate!' This was a middle-aged man, on his bike and in full cycling attire, whom I hadn't heard coming up behind me. I was startled and exclaimed: 'The fright I got!' He mumbled an apology, which wasn't necessary – had he passed me without speaking, I'd have condemned him for that! – and then enquired, in a Northern English accent: 'Is this the way to the Lighthouse?' – 'In a round-about way,' I called after him. Cycling to the Mull? Well, that made me feel a lot better about cycling to Largiebaan.

I kept going until I'd passed Gartnacopaig, then stopped at the side of the track for a late lunch and a smoke. The day by then was perfect, the breeze cool and the sun emerging from fluffy white clouds, which were exposing in the west an inviting expanse of blue sky. After twenty minutes, I was ready to resume pushing my bike, but I checked the impulse and decided, 'No, this is precious, just sitting doing nothing', so I stayed longer.

Leac a' Chreachainn

I chained my bike to a fence beside the Kintyre Way and headed out towards the cliffs on foot. Past the last strip of forest, I began angling down towards the burn and 596 144, the co-ordinates for Ian Teesdale's wood vetch record. I was diagonally crossing Leac a' Chreachainn, which I recalled examining in *Kintyre Places and Place-Names* (p 193). I quoted two interpretations of the place-name, 'Declivity of the hard rocky surface' (1866) and 'Hill face of the bare rocky height' (1938), noting that the only shared descriptive term was 'rocky'. These interpretations seemed cumbersome and I wondered if I might improve on them by considering the nature of the feature as I traversed it. Gaelic *leac*, in this context, is basically 'cheek', and by extension a sloping surface, and that's straightforward: the *leac* is the northern flank of the glen. The second element, *creachann*, is the bothersome one: 'rocky' is certainly implicit, but the slope itself is relatively rock-free, so the simplest interpretation would be 'mountain'. It's too simple, however, and doesn't ring true for Kintyre. 'Hill face of the bare rocky height', quoted above, is perfectly apt if the 'bare rocky height' is taken to mean the cliffs at the western extremity of Leac a' Chreachainn.

Yellow saxifrage and wood vetch

When I reached the foot of the glen, I found myself in a half-ravine – cliffs on the north side of the burn and sloping ground to the south – which I couldn't remember having visited before. It was a magical spot, and botanically luxuriant, though I didn't attempt to list the species there, noting only a few which stood out for me – cuckoo flower, harebell, honeysuckle – with one other, which, though I couldn't find wood vetch, justified the descent. It was yellow saxifrage, which was growing from wet rock faces and overhanging the peat-dark waters of the burn, turbulent after the previous day's heavy rain. I'd already left the ravine when I realised that that must have been the very spot where Agnes Stewart once told me she had noted yellow saxifrage years before. When I later showed Judy the photographs I'd taken there, she at once remarked: 'It's like a garden!'

I followed the burn towards the sea until I came to the grassy spur above the waterfall, and then decided to head up towards the top of the cliffs. I noticed a path which ran above the rock wall I was facing, and decided to try that. Much of it was bare rock, eroded by the passage of generations of goats and sheep, and I made good progress along it until I reached a point at which it narrowed and disappeared round a corner. At that point, my nerve failed and I instantly decided to climb straight up, so I quickly hauled myself over a heathery bulge, without once looking back, and found myself viewing a familiar prospect: the cliff-edge ridge which would take me to where I now wanted to be.

I hadn't found Ian Teesdale's wood vetch in the ravine, but I was to see plenty of it on my ascent. The first clump was on top of a crag below the cliff line. I was certain it was the vetch, but decided to go down to it to confirm that I was correct. That's what it was, and I took a photograph with the flowers in the foreground and the cliff face and caves in the background. I also broke one of my own rules by taking a sprig of the flower away with me. The blue striations on the petals were so delicate yet vivid that I felt I'd want to admire them after I'd left Largiebaan. (By the time I arrived home, three hours later, the flowers had wilted and I rather regretted having removed them from their home, but after a night in water they revived.) By the time I arrived at my usual resting place opposite the Kintyre Way swing-gate, I had counted nine more substantial colonies of *Vicia silvatica* under the top, and was wondering how many more there might be between me and the Aignish.

I sat for an hour, facing south, before leaving for home. For ten or fifteen minutes, Largiebaan was 'idyllic in sunshine and silence', but then the sky began to cloud over, the sea turned pewter-dull, and Rathlin and Ireland darkened. It was, however, a strange darkening, because, if anything, the land assumed greater definition than before; I could even see, with the naked eye, the houses of Ballycastle, in behind Fair Head. In truth, as I noted in my journal, I felt the day had turned 'a little sinister', which I attributed to sea sounds. Under the rhythmic breaking of waves there was a near-continuous tone, like the muted roar of distant aircraft. It was probably the seas' echoing on the cliffs, but I couldn't be sure, and, from where I was sitting, no part of the shore was visible to me, which contributed, I suppose, to my sense of disconnectedness.

13 August: Largiebaan

If the contents of this book had been more of a consideration, I'd have varied my destinations more, but the allure of Largiebaan was unrelenting. That day, in George McSporran, I had welcome company. We set off from his house in Argyll Street just minutes ahead of the 12 o' clock Southend bus and kept going until we got to the top of the hill past Lochorodale, where I'd stopped for lunch on the 7th. A place-name, 'Parting Lay-by', had by now emerged for it. It was where, on 17 April, Judy and I had separated on a cycle ride to Largiebaan, which she couldn't complete. I had a feeling, as George and I settled ourselves at the roadside, that this would become a customary lunch spot. The place had another, earlier association which I'd somehow until then overlooked. Robert McInnes's peat-bank lay in the moorland hollow south of the road, and that lay-by was where, in the 1980s, his wife Isobel would drop him, and occasionally me, when I was able to give him a day's enjoyable labour.

A bicycle accident recalled

George was wearing, for the first time, a bicycle helmet he'd bought after our trip to Largiebaan on 3 June, and, as we drank tea and chewed on out-of-date coconut buns, he proceeded to explain why. He didn't, he said, 'want injured like that again'. I assumed he meant his fall on Ben Cruachan in April 2010, which hospitalised him and permanently damaged his health, but he was referring to a bicycle accident I didn't know about. It happened when he was seven or eight years old, and I couldn't resist commenting: 'You took your time getting round to the helmet!'

He and a boyhood friend, Willie Crossan, had a cycling competition, using George's bike. The game was to speed down Range Road from the Crosshill Avenue intersection, then turn right and finish at Willie's house in Meadows Avenue, where the one who wasn't on the bike would be waiting to time the effort. On one of George's runs, the bike skidded on gravel and he was thrown off. He was concussed and his right arm still bears the scar of a puncture wound. Willie was waiting and waiting for George's appearance, but he was lying in a heap, practically outside his own door, and ended up in hospital. After hearing that story, I began to think that perhaps I too should invest in a helmet.

We left the bikes past Largiebaan steading and headed out to the cliffs by the Kintyre Way. It was a fine day, but one vital element was absent – a breeze – and there were elements present – midges, clegs and flying ants – which wind was required to counteract. So we headed towards

Binnein Fithich in the expectation of catching a breeze higher on the cliffs. On our way up, I showed him the little clifftop colony of wood vetch I'd found six days earlier, and in the same gully, but lower, spotted clumps of yellow saxifrage, of which we saw eight or nine more colonies during our ascent.

The climb was justified, for we were soon in a brisk south-easterly breeze, which the lower land forms had blocked. We sat and ate on a knoll beside the Kintyre Way, not far below Binnein Fithich, but we had no view of the cliffs and sea from there, so, when the breeze began to strengthen, we moved to the cliff top and enjoyed an hour there, still free from the attentions of flying insects. Apart from a few goats and sheep, there was nothing moving on the landscape, and less in the air, but the sun was out again and we had a view I'd watch before any film that's ever been made or will be made.

A figure in the landscape

While we were sitting there, George broke the silence with an unexpected question: 'Is that somebody down there?' I trained my binoculars in the direction he indicated and saw, to my surprise, a figure ascending slowly on the skyline of Rubha Dùn Bhàin. Humans are one of the rarest of native mammals found at Largiebaan, and we began speculating on the identity of this one. Jimmy MacDonald was the obvious assumption, but I wasn't quite recognising Jimmy in the distant figure. The mystery man became an object of our scrutiny all the time he was in our sight. Every move he made was analysed for clues as to his reason for being there; for example, if he looked closely at the ground, he was a botanist; when he looked over the cliff, he was an ornithologist, or maybe a geologist ... Increasingly, however, he appeared to be Jimmy MacDonald, and when he cut inland from the coast I predicted to George that he would disappear into a forest ride which I knew to be his customary route to and from Dùn Bàn. He duly did disappear and, now ourselves on the move, we watched for his re-emergence. I was certain we'd then see him cross the expanse of marshy ground to the Kintyre Way and his waiting bicycle, but we didn't and were forced to revise our assumptions of where he had gone and if 'he' even was Jimmy.

We had our answers a couple of hours later when we stopped at Killeonan, where Jimmy and his wife Katrina had moved earlier that summer. I shouted at the back of the house and Jimmy emerged. First question: 'Did we see you at Dùn Bàn?' Yes, he had been there, and had not only seen, but also photographed us in our sitting place – he brought the indistinct but unmistakable image up on his camera – and assumed that I was there with Judy. We had simply failed to observe the final stage of his departure, and he had already eaten his dinner by the time we caught up with him.

Jimmy occasionally reminds me that I used to condemn Largiebaan as a 'shite-hole'. That would be about ten years ago, when my dog Benjie was ageing and I was content to walk him close to town. It was at Largiebaan, in October 1999, that Benjie had his only serious accident, when he fell during a descent to the shore.[150] It's a place one likes or doesn't like, or, in my case, a place one is drawn to at particular times for particular reasons. One wit who is familiar with that coast claimed that a Japanese soldier hid out in the caves for years, not knowing that the war had ended! Jimmy's own feelings about the place were expressed in an e-mail to me a couple of days after our conversation: 'It's some place Largiebaan. I always get the feeling that seeing just about anything is possible there. I also get a distinct sense of danger, especially on the shore. That's something I don't really get anywhere else, and it's quite addictive.'

On the day George and I saw him, he'd been on the shore below Dùn Bàn, a part of the coast rarely visited by humans, and I wondered what botanical rarities he might have passed by. I'd been pressing him for a couple of years to photograph interesting looking flowers or butterflies he encounters in remote places, but I know, from personal experience, that if one is not ready to venture into a new field of discovery, then it's difficult to perceive let alone evaluate what's around one.

I came late to the broad field of natural history, and even now my knowledge is restricted in every subject I engage with. Partly it's down to an unwillingness to confront the minutiae of species differentiation and partly it's down to that slow start. As a boy, I gravitated to the sea and shore and spent hours at a time gazing into rock pools at Kilchousland, but that was the extent of my engagement with nature. Unlike many proper naturalists, I had no mentors to educate me in the best way possible, by on-the-spot instruction, and I didn't read much either. Jimmy, whose ruling passion is birds, took early to books and matched his reading with observation in nature. He may extend his interests or may not. Heaven knows, it's hard enough to achieve genuine expertise in even one subject!

3 July 1987: Richard Branson's balloon

As George and I were walking back to the bikes, the conversation turned – via a discussion about telephone links in remote habitations and the prohibitive cost of installing them nowadays – to an historic event we witnessed together from the cliffs at Largiebaan ... well, almost witnessed. The date was 3 July 1987, though neither of us could have ventured even the year; but I remembered I had a dated slide I took of George that day, and I later looked it out. He was sitting, in his blue Coastguard boiler suit, gazing west, which was the sea, the north coast of Antrim, and Rathlin. In the nature of the call-out, we'd have stationed ourselves high on the cliffs, so we'd been sitting close to where we'd sat twenty-eight years before, and in my backward-looking life such correspondences matter.

We were watching for Richard Branson, who was heading our way, in his attempt to complete the first trans-Atlantic crossing by hot air balloon. He and his co-pilot, Per Lindstrom, had set out from Sugarloaf Mountain, in Maine, the previous day, and the Virgin launch crew had arrived at RAF Machrihanish awaiting news, because at 5 p.m. that Friday the balloon was on a direct course for Machrihanish. The air base had stayed open late 'with full facilities', Campbeltown life-boat had been launched, and George and I were sitting in sunshine on the heights of Largiebaan, binoculars in one hand and flask of tea in the other, doubtless the easiest money we ever made during our Coastguard service. George remembered having taken the Coastguard Land Rover out beyond Largiebaan farmhouse, which was tenanted then by Archie Ronald (p 29), whose telephone we were obliged to use after a stint on the cliffs had yielded no information. By then, Branson's progress towards land had been arrested, and we were directed, by H.M. Coastguard headquarters in Greenock, to go to RAF Machrihanish.

The balloon had touched down in the sea off the north coast of Ireland, beyond our vision. It bounced back up, but the gondola and its flotation gear had been damaged by the impact and Lindstrom jumped out from a height of seventy feet. Meanwhile, search and rescue helicopters and helicopters chartered by newspapers had refuelled at RAF Machrihanish and were heading towards the spot where Lindstrom was believed to have jumped. He was rescued, and Branson too – by a Sea King helicopter from HMS *Gannet* – when the balloon again struck the sea and he also jumped from the gondola. Momentous events in the history of a rich man's vanity, but the adventure paid off. At the time, the validity of the attempt was in doubt, but it was ultimately accepted as the first trans-Atlantic crossing by a hot-air balloon, and also broke the distance record of 913.8 miles, set in January 1985 by Canadian balloonist Harold Warner.[151]

15 August: Even in dreams I sound the same

I was going to Largiebaan again that day and woke before my alarm clock sounded. I drifted back to sleep and had a dream of the Learside, and when I woke from it, with the alarm ringing, the thought came to me that perhaps I was hankering subconsciously for a change of destination.

I am returning from the Learside with Judy, and at Kildalloig a mist descends. A strange brick-built hut at the roadside appears and we go inside it. Soon afterwards, a car's headlights appear and a man and woman join us in the shelter. He introduces himself as John MacCallum, a social worker, and I inform him immediately that I have MacCallum genes on both sides of my family. This is true but rather misleading, because both women are far back, one in the eighteenth and the other in the nineteenth century.

I notice little flowers growing from the walls inside the shelter and begin counting the species, but though I manage the count – which was four – to my discomfiture I can't identify any of them and it is left to Judy to provide the names.

We leave MacCallum and his wife there, but, to satisfy an afterthought, I return to the hut and ask him: 'Where did your MacCallums come from?' He replies, but I cannot make out his words and continue towards him. He repeats the answer again and again, but I still can't hear what he is saying. Finally, I hear him say that he doesn't care where his family came from. Suddenly dejected, I point through a window and appeal to his imagination: 'Wouldn't you like to know that your great-great-grandfather lived in a cottage on that shore?' MacCallum still doesn't care.

An imaginary encounter

The weather forecast was good for the day and I set off by bicycle at 11.45, stopping at the 'Parting Lay-by', where I ate a 'jeely-piece' and an even drier surviving coconut bun, and then pushed on. As I free-wheeled towards Glenahanty, I drifted into a reverie, in which I saw the Stewarts' car parked by the side of the track and then met them at the foot of the Bruach Dearg.

'Ye're early the day,' Agnes remarks.

'Well,' I reply, 'I wis up at twinty past ten and away at quarter tae twelve, and that's me at Glenahanty two oors later – naw bad for an ould fella!'

Agnes laughs and looks at Allister.

'Listen tae him – an "ould fella"! What age are ye?'

'Sixty-three,' I say.

Then the reverie shifts to the past, to my own boyhood, when all adults seemed old, even if they were only in their twenties and thirties. One of them reappears, as clearly envisioned as though he were standing with me on the red brae. He was a local miner, who loved football and lived around the corner from me in Range Road and always seemed to be smiling. Then he is gone. I wondered when he'd died and at what age. The answers were on a headstone in Kilkerran: August 1970, aged 44.

My father was 64 when a coronary thrombosis killed him in 1975; heart disease would kill my mother five years later at the age of 67. I was now 63, but I was heading to Largiebaan for the fourth time in eight days and, minor ailments aside, feeling as fit as I'd ever felt. I doubt if my father could have reached Largiebaan even once at my age. He walked everywhere he went, though seldom beyond town, but he was heavily built, probably overweight, and suffered badly from indigestion, a condition he blamed on his life at sea, particularly the frequent greasy fry-ups served aboard boats. He was also a heavy smoker, who broke the habit several times, only to lapse. 'Kensitas' was latterly his brand of choice. It's hard to believe now, but some cigarette companies offered gift coupons to encourage smoking. I remember the 'Kensitas' mail-order catalogue arriving and being perused, and the bundles of coupons carefully counted before a gadget was selected and ordered. Years later, I imagined at the end of every catalogue a selection of the most expensive gifts on offer: coffins.

A real encounter

While I was still in the past with memories, a real person appeared on the Bruach Dearg, walking downhill with a rucksack on her back. I was keen, as ever, to uncover a stranger's background and engaged her in conversation. Her English was fluent, and she appeared to master my version of English with little difficulty. I guessed that she was German and asked her where she came from. She works as a nurse in Cologne and her name is Rachel Hart, which could easily be a local name. She loves hill-walking and comes to Scotland to indulge her passion as often as she can. She was on the final stages of walking the Kintyre Way and was heading to Southend, to stay the night in the Argyll Arms Hotel.

Two days earlier, George McSporran and I had been discussing the Kintyre Way and agreed that we seldom saw walkers on the stretches of the Way with which we were familiar. Here was one, and there was a group of four – which she'd passed – heading north to Machrihanish. Her route, however, puzzled me, because the path to Southend, as I understood it, turned off before Largiebaan and crossed Amod Hill into Glen Breackerie. She explained that this was a shorter alternative route, and showed me it marked on an official Kintyre Way map she was carrying. She further explained that she was feeling tired that day, particularly after a demanding uphill section. I knew the bit she meant – from Innean Mòr to the Aignish – and mentioned that my wife had strained a knee ligament on that ascent back in April and still hadn't fully recovered.

After Kintyre, Rachel was going to Ballachullish to visit a friend. I congratulated her on having chosen the driest week of the summer for her Kintyre Way adventure, and, before we parted, asked her to write her address in my journal, so that I could send her a copy of my next book, with her in it.

Under the Aignish

While sitting on the cliff top with George two days earlier, I was scanning the Aignish with binoculars and noticed two clusters of intriguing white flowers in the scree below the collapsed rock face. The real motivation for the day's visit was to identify these flowers. I got there by the route I'd taken on 4 June, but greater caution was required on the rocky slopes, because the bracken was fully grown, and a broken leg out there was unthinkable. Above me, during the traverse, I saw colonies of yellow saxifrage all the way, and when I arrived at the foot of the Aignish I discovered colonies of wood vetch: each of these species, I learned that day, was common at Largiebaan.

A disappointment was in store for me when I looked at the white flowers which had drawn me to the foot of the cliff – they were umbellifers, a family of plants which tend to look the same to me and of which I am able to confidently identify only a few. There was, however, an amusing irony which I recognised at once. Earlier in the month, Agnes Stewart had asked me if I'd seen upright hedge parsley (*Torilis japonica*) growing at Kildalloig. It's a flower she admires, and when I responded irreverently that to me it was 'just another damned umbellifer', a rebuke followed. I readily admit that I'm not the complete botanist and never will be. These umbellifers were at the top of scree at the cliff bottom and not easily reached, so I photographed them from as close as I cared to get. There wasn't enough foliage detail in the images, but from a leaf sample I obtained four days later, she identified sea carrot – *Daucus carota* and possibly sub-species *gummifer* – of which *The Flora of Kintyre* (p 25) remarks: 'Well-marked material on the limestone near Largybaan.' Michael Scott in *Scottish Wild Flowers* (p 124) identifies this as 'The wild ancestor of the cultivated carrot', but Grigson in *The Englishman's Flora* (p 240) pointedly remarks that 'Garden carrots descend, not from the English plant, but from the Mediterranean *Daucus carota* ssp. *sativus*'. I looked in Richard Mabey's *Food for Free* to see if he classed 'my' *Daucus* as edible: he doesn't mention it. Even if it were, I doubt if there would be much of a root to chew on from specimens growing in thin soil and stones.

The roots of another umbellifer, hemlock water dropwort (*Oenanthe crocata*) – locally 'hech-how', for which a derivation from Gaelic *iteodha*, 'hemlock', has been suggested – were occasionally dug up and eaten, with fatal effects. In the mid-nineteenth century, three sailors, from a man-of-war anchored in Campbeltown Loch, died after eating the roots of *Oenanthe crocata*, having mistaken the plant for horse radish (*Armoracia rusticana*), which is actually absent from the flora of Kintyre. The last local fatality I know of was Dugald Robertson, Dalintober, in 1920.[152]

I sat on a slab of mica schist, surrounded by hundreds of other rocks, ate my last 'jeely piece', and drank several cups of tea, for I was thirsty after my exertions. It was another perfect day at Largiebaan: the sun shone and a cool breeze was blowing off the tide-whitened ocean.

As I approached the cliff, I'd heard a doleful bleat. This was a solitary billy-goat who headed up the scree to avoid the unwelcome biped. Just before I left, I heard a sudden loud sneeze, which momentarily alarmed me, and looking up I saw another billy crossing the cliff face on a path I hadn't thought could exist. (He had two companions, as I'd notice as I left.)

The silhouette of a bird on the lower ridge of the Aignish turned out to be, when I looked at it through binoculars, a pigeon – a rock dove probably – which was picking seeds from plants. Journal note: 'That's how the flowers spread: in one end and out the other, maybe miles away.' As proof of that observation, I later noticed several tendrils of bramble (*Rubus fruticosus agg.*), the seed for which must have come from a fair way off. That plant seemed almost 'exotic' down there among the rocks. Specialists can recognise 300 'micro-species' of the common bramble,[153] a statistic which nips in the bud the aspirations of this budding botanist.

I'd been hoping for an unusual butterfly sighting below the cliffs, but 21 meadow browns was my lot until I reached the bottom of the cliff, when three common blues fluttered into sight, a consolation of sorts. I was willing one of them to alight on a harebell, so that I could photograph blue on blue, but it didn't happen.

By 5 o' clock, I'd been two hours at Largiebaan and the day had turned grey, with spits of rain falling and midges emerging with a thirst for blood. I packed my rucksack and left.

Milestones

As I was pushing my bike up the hill past Glenrea road-end, I saw a white van approaching and had a strong intuition that it would stop. It did, and the driver, who was Norrie Lang, rolled down his window. His passenger was Duncan Brown, from Stewarton, who immediately said to me: 'We've jeest been talking about ye.' This was interesting, and triggered a chain of coincidences. He said that he and Norrie had noticed the fifth milestone that evening, when they pulled in at the roadside to allow an oncoming car to pass. That was the first co-incidence, because I too had looked at the stone on my way out and had noted in my journal: '5 milestone just before L/dale.' I had recently taken an interest in the milestones along that road, but I'll return to that.

Duncan asked me if I remembered some bother involving a milestone when bungalows were being built just past Kilkerran graveyard in 2001. I didn't remember his involvement in it, but he was one of the builders and remembered my enquiring 'Where's that milestone?' This was the first milestone, which had disappeared during the clearing of the site. The story is told in *By Hill and Shore in South Kintyre* (p 158) and it'll suffice to say here that the stone was recovered and taken into protective custody by Cecil Finn, who later erected it at the entrance to his former house, where it remains, still a roadside feature and as near to its original position – one mile as measured from the old post office in Main Street – as makes no odds nowadays.

We chatted for a while on the brae, but midges were out in force, and when Norrie asked me, 'Are the midges no' botherin' ye?', I replied 'Only when I stop', which signalled the end of the conversation. I used to meet Duncan occasionally on Saturday afternoons in the public bar of the White Hart Hotel when I stopped off there for a beer on my way home from Pupils' games at Kintyre Park. My youngest daughter Bella, who is still a football fan, was usually with me, and was almost invariably the recipient of a handful of coins from Duncan's pocket. Having mentioned Bella, I'll move on to another coincidence.

In January 2001, during a family walk from Homestone to Glenrea and on towards Glen Breackerie, I remarked on the milestone past the bridge at Clachan Ùr, which prompted from Bella the question: 'What's a milestone?' My response to her query has been recorded elsewhere;[154] but fourteen years on I was wondering where that stone had gone, because I'd failed to find it. Milestones are disappearing one by one from the roadsides, which saddens me, because they are historical monuments, albeit of a minor class, and deserve protection. Some are knocked over by mechanised verge-cutters and end up overgrown in ditches, while others, I suspect, are removed by visitors for garden ornaments or curios. The problem is that milestones are scarcely used anymore, so few people notice them and fewer still notice their disappearance.

During my evening walk through Glen Breackerie on the 7th, I examined one cemented to the end of a wall at the former Glen Breackerie School. A chunk is missing from the top of it, but its information – which was once of real interest to walkers and carters and cyclists – remains complete: '9 MILES 181 YDS FROM CAMP'TOWN/ 11 MILES FROM CAMP'TOWN.' (These are the distances for the journeys east and west.) By the Argyllshire Roads Act of 1816, anyone damaging, defacing or removing a milestone is liable to a penalty 'not exceeding Ten Pounds Sterling for each offence'. A huge sum of money then, but nothing much now, so perhaps the surest means of preserving some of these relics of an age of leisurely travel is to fix them securely somewhere close to where they belong and trust that a two-centuries-old law for their protection isn't invoked!

18 August: The Aignish again

'Nature punched a hole in the pretty picture I'd painted for myself.' I wrote that line in my journal while sitting under the Aignish on yet another lovely afternoon of sunshine and blue skies. On my way there, I had found a sheep lying on her back in a stream, which was running red with her blood. One eye, and maybe both, had been pecked at by a hooded crow, which I had seen fly off minutes earlier without realising the horror I had interrupted. I lifted her out of the stream and laid her against a bank beside the track and continued on my way. There was little else I could have done in the circumstances, but the encounter took the pleasure from the day. On my way back, four hours later, I expected – hoped – that the ewe would be dead, but found her sitting near the stream, shaking and shaking her head. While I stood looking at her, she managed to stand up and blunder into a thicket of rushes beside the track. I wanted to believe she still had partial vision, but suspect that she sensed rather than saw me. On my way home, I stopped off at Jimmy MacDonald's house at Killeonan, and he e-mailed the farmer and reported the attack and passed on my description of the ewe's location.

Later in the year, while proof-reading *A Night of Islands*, a selection of my poems published by the Shoestring Press in February 2016, the poem 'Lamb', which I hadn't looked at in many years, brought back the horror. On 3 June 1989, I'd found a living lamb, eyes 'half-stabbed from his head', in the Inneans Bay, and put the experience into the poem, which I wrote at Craigaig sheep-fank on my way home.

There were five cars parked at the end of the Glenahanty road on 18 August, the most I'd ever seen there, but I saw no one at Largiebaan during my three hours there, looking at flowers to try to resolve a couple of uncertainties from the previous visit. Alex Docherty from Stewarton was one of twelve walkers who went up the Bruach Dearg ahead of me that day, but he took the Kintyre Way to High Glenadale. He was still recovering from a nasty fall from his bicycle on Torrisdale brae earlier in the summer, and I was pleased to hear he was back in his old haunts, though he had still to reach the Inneans Bay.

One of the raptors I watched presented a vision of great beauty. As I was climbing out from the foot of the Aignish, a kestrel appeared and hovered quite close to where I'd stopped. As it hung in the air, tail feathers spread, the bright sunlight seemed to pass right through it, transforming it momentarily into a creature of ethereal unreality. It was a lovely image to take away with me from Largiebaan, but I knew I wouldn't be back there soon.

23 August: Learside

Daughter Amelia and I set off together by bike in the early afternoon, but she was to meet friends in Burnside Square, where live bands were playing as part of the local music festival, so she turned back at the Sheep Fanks. I continued only as far as the top of the Second Water brae, chained the bike to a fence and headed around the hill, looking in vain for mushrooms. Flying ants – some of them mating – were abundant in the lee of the hill, so I gained the top and sat close to the putative boundary-marking boulder which also marks events in my past.[155]

I was looking down into Balnabraid Glen and its splendid deciduous woodland, and also towards the site of one of the Coasters' huts which stood at the Second Water in the 1950s and '60s. Alastair Thompson had told me that during his own Coasting years, as a teenager in the mid-'60s, the huts had been taken over by motorbike gangs from Clydebank, 'Rocker guys', as Alastair described them.[156]

Though I didn't recall these gangs, I didn't doubt Alastair's information. His memory was confirmed in a Campbeltown

Burgh Court report I noticed in the *Campbeltown Courier* of 5 September 1968. A youth from Port Glasgow was discovered asleep in a public lavatory in Kinloch Road, after police noticed an attic hatch missing. Raymond Kirkpatrick admitted 'lodging in the attic, the property of Campbeltown Town Council, without permission', and was fined the maximum penalty of £1. The Burgh Prosecutor, Robert Graham, told the court that the town had been 'plagued' by youths from the Port Glasgow and Greenock areas, who would 'lodge anywhere'. (Bob Graham's defence of another offender in a Campbeltown court is still locally quoted: 'Your honour, my client was drinking wine of dubious vintage.')

24 August: Lochorodale

Place-names, like people, can be overworked, and I reckon 'Lochorodale' is overworked. If I said I'd been at Lochorodale, what picture, if any, would form in the reader's mind? Lochorodale is still, for me, the rather gaunt farmhouse facing south at the side of the hilly single track road from Auchencorvie to the head of Glen Breackerie, which was scenic before spruce forests choked the landscape. The McCorkindale brothers, Hugh, Donald and Lachie, and their sister Bella, were the last to farm there.

Yet, until the latter half of the nineteenth century, that farm was known as 'Glecknahavil' (perhaps *Glac na h-abhaill*, 'Hollow of the apple tree'). Lochorodale was a neighbouring farm, recorded as far back as 1502 and by 1874 amalgamated with Glecknahavil and Kerrafuar and reduced to a shepherd's cottage. It took its name from a nearby loch, the draining of which was ordered by Argyll Estates in the eighteenth century and completed in the nineteenth. In 1938, when the McCorkindale family moved to the renamed Lochorodale, all that remained of the loch was a marsh, fenced off to keep livestock out. Fifty years later, the subsequent owner dammed the marsh to restore the water level and converted the shepherd's cottage into a holiday home.[157] 'Lochorodale', like Loch Grunidale (p 192), is a Norse name with Gaelic *loch* added. The Norse specific is debatable, but for what my opinion is worth – which is very little in linguistic matters – the personal name *Orri* is tempting, therefore 'Orri's Valley'.

24. Amelia Martin with bicycles at Lochorodale, 24 August 2015. Photograph by the author.

I was at all three places known as 'Lochorodale': the former farmhouse, the restored shepherd's cottage and the loch itself. Amelia and I cycled out in the early afternoon and stopped for lunch at the farmhouse. I'd rather have stopped at the bridge downhill, because bridges offer the soothing music of the waters they span, but there was little wind and therefore a threat of midges. Amelia lay back for a while on the roadside, enjoying the sunshine, and then we cycled out to the loch by the forest tracks and spent a little time picking blaeberries overlooking the water. There weren't many, nor were there many ripe brambles to be found anywhere: they too were late, but ripened in abundance, at least in some parts of Kintyre, towards the end of September, when, in most seasons, they would be turning scabby.

On our way out, we'd stopped at Auchencorvie to look at the war memorial at the old school. The monument bears an invitation to travellers to stop and drink, but water has long since stopped flowing. The names of the fourteen former pupils killed in the First World War were difficult to read, and while I was peering at them, a dog appeared on the other side of the wall. Amelia took a great liking to his affectionate manner, and a little later his mistress also appeared, and told us his name was Ivan. We discussed the neglected state of the memorial and I suggested raising the issue with the British Legion, of which my sister Barbara is a member. On our way home, however, we saw the woman busy at the memorial with a pot of black paint, and the lettering of the bottom name, Gilbert Blackstock, was already once again plain to see. The memorial was unveiled in December 1920 by the Dowager Duchess of Argyll, Ina MacNeill,[158] who lived in seclusion at Macharioch House until her death five years later.

A lost place-name

Just as some place-names are 'overworked', other place-names are under-used. A name, unlike an animal, will never die of overwork, but if it isn't used it will surely die, unless preserved on a map. I'd guess that in Kintyre alone hundreds of place-names have disappeared in the past couple of centuries. The vast majority are classifiable as minor – attached to fields, hillocks, rocks and the like – and would be forgotten when the land was depopulated and the Gaelic language entered its terminal decline. A few of these names survive by chance in documents, but almost invariably can't be fixed to any specific location. One such is 'Garavalt', which emerged when I researched the story of a sudden death.

Peter McSporran left his house at Homestone on 26 March 1869, to cut a 'birch broom', and, when he failed to return, a search party went out to look for him. His body was found the following morning, lying near a stream. He was assumed to have fallen over a 'small precipice' nearby. 'A faithful dog stood by the old man's body when discovered, and would allow no person near it until he recognized a boy who lived in the same house with the deceased.'[159]

McSporran's death certificate stated that he had been 'Found dead at Garavalt on the farm of Lochorodale in the parish of Campbeltown'. The name represents Gaelic *Garbhallt*, 'Wild or rough burn', and two examples survive in Kintyre, one near the Mull and the other in Barr Glen, along with a third, on the north shore of East Loch Tarbert, which is in South Knapdale Parish.

The death registration, incidentally, was enigmatic in the extreme, for although Peter McSporran was earlier reported as living on the neighbouring farm of Homestone, no one there seems to have known who he was. No home address is given, no trade or occupation, no marital status, and no parental names. The doctors who examined his body, John Buchanan and William Gibson, concluded that death was from 'exposure to cold'.[160]

28 August: Tarbert

Judy and I took the 3 p.m. bus to Tarbert carrying a pot of paint. We were going to do a little work in the flat our daughter Isabella had bought at Easfield. I have never been keen on domestic chores of any kind, but until several years ago I found painting quite relaxing. Now I find it boring, and after coating a door and a half I escaped to the graveyard, which Bella's flat overlooks. Cill Andreis is probably my favourite burial-ground after Kilkerran, but I haven't spent much time in it over the years, which probably accounts for the unexpected revelation which awaited me there.

This was on the stone raised by George Hay to his first wife, Mary Macdougall. Hay was father of the novelist John Macdougall Hay, and grandfather of the poet George Campbell Hay, the centenary of whose birth was elaborately marked in Tarbert that year. I hadn't realised that Mary died young, aged 37 in 1889, or that George had remarried. His second wife's name was Flora MacLean, a surname which triggered a few associations.

The first of these, a missed opportunity, was unwelcome. In this book's predecessor, *Another Summer in Kintyre* (p 133), I had documented George Campbell Hay's visits in the 1930s to Donald MacDougall and his wife Annie MacLean at High Park, a sheep farm in the hills north of Campbeltown. I remarked on George's wearing a MacDougall kilt – his paternal grandmother's tartan – and Donald MacDougall's dismissive reaction to this choice, since George preferred Annie MacLean's Skye Gaelic to Donald's Lismore variant. Had I known that George's step-grandmother was a MacLean, I would have taken account of the coincidence, trivial though it is.

The second thought was a question: could Flora MacLean have been one of the MacLeans at Breaclarach, a family examined earlier in this book (pp. 129-132? MacLean certainly isn't one of the commonest of Tarbert surnames. Flora died on 7 September 1920, when George was just five years old, and he never mentioned her to me. Her death certificate revealed that both her parents were named MacLean: Malcolm, a mason, and Barbara. There was no clear link to the Breaclarach MacLeans.

Flora died in the Western Infirmary, Glasgow, aged 63, of peritonitis. Her home in Tarbert was Heatherknowe, and she was a widow; George Hay had died in 1911, aged 66. He must have married Flora soon after he was widowed, for in the census of 1891, two years after his first wife's death, Flora is with him in Tighclachbreac, with four of the children Mary bore. He – the son of an Ayrshire-born fish-merchant – is a Gaelic speaker, described as a steamboat agent and fish-buyer, while Flora, a Tarbert-born MacLean, has no Gaelic; but these seeming-anomalies were rife in Kintyre at that time.

Another stone I looked at commemorated a brother of George's, Robert, his wife Margaret Smith and their family. An unusual name, 'Dundonald', caught my eye, but I already knew the story behind it. A son was born on 1 March 1900, the day Ladysmith was liberated during the Boer War. The military commander was Lord Dundonald, and Robert decided to name his new-born son 'Dundonald Smith Hay' after the 'hero of the relief'. He sent a copy of the birth certificate to Lord Dundonald, who replied with a 'lengthy autograph letter thanking him for the honour'. His lordship hoped that the boy would 'wax and grow strong in spirit and that he may in time come to serve his country as a soldier of the Empire'. Hay, supposedly 'a bit of a humorist', remarked that 'it was lucky his youngest was born on a historic occasion, as his family, being so numerous, he had used up all the Christian names he could think of'.[161]

As it transpired, the boy with the distinctive name did join the Army for a time, but afterwards made the sea his career, attaining the status of master mariner. 'Dunny', as he was popularly known, died in 1950 at the age of 49.[162]

As Judy and I waited for the last bus home, an elderly man appeared and passed the time in conversation with another pensioner, who was going to Tayinloan. I overheard the idler pronounce: 'We've only had fifteen days of summer this year.' How he arrived at that calculation I had no idea, but it sounded just about right. A minute later, however, he amended it to 'fifteen and a half days', which didn't sound quite so right.

30 August: Kilchousland and names on rocks

Kilchousland is more of a winter driftwood-gathering shore for me and I hadn't been there all summer, though it's just a twenty-minute cycle from my house. It was once a popular picnic beach and on a sunny day the sands would be packed with families. That popularity ended in the late 1970s, by which time most families had the use of a car. There is no car-park at Kilchousland, therefore visitors now tend to arrive on foot; and I haven't seen anyone there in years.

When I arrived on the beach, below the Second World War gun emplacements, I discovered evidence of a past visitor; not litter, though there's plenty of that washed in by the sea, but initials carved in a rock. At first I thought the marks were natural, but when I looked closely I could discern 'TM L KG'. I had never noticed the initials before, but they've been there for years, and possibly decades, because lichen has been colonising the grooves. I tried to translate the initials into names, but failed; I have only local knowledge at my disposal, of course, and the couple may have been holidaymakers. Perhaps some reader can 'break the code'. Whoever TM was, he accomplished a 'labour of love', because the initials are in a hard rock, unlike other carvings I have recorded on the Learside, which are in softer red sandstone.[163]

That discovery at Kilchousland reminded me of another on 16 April. I was with my niece, Barbara Matheson (p 36), and it was she who noticed 'Saul' on a flat sandstone rock just south of the Second Water. The name was in large capitals – about four inches deep, I reckoned – and appeared to have been chipped rather than scraped out. I speculated that a visiting geologist might have left his mark with a geological hammer. As Barbara remarked, 'It's an unusual name', and I agreed; I'd never before encountered it in Kintyre in any context, though, near the end of the year, when Judy and I met Susanna Fee and her baby son in town, we discovered that his name was Saul! Jimmy and Katrina MacDonald also noticed the name on the rock, and he asked me if I knew anything about it. He reckoned it looked 'quite old', but I'd been on that shore quite frequently in the previous winter and hadn't seen it, so my guess is that it was recently done.

There is another name carved in red sandstone further down the Learside. It is 'Rock Hopper' and I first noticed it soon after Judy and I acquired a caravan in the Wee Holm, Polliwilline, in 1988. The rock is on the upper shore at the north end of the bay and has the year '85' below it, followed by '99' and '2000'. The carving was done by Iain McEachran, who was born and brought up in Greenock. He took the name as a Citizens' Band radio 'handle', a choice which he explained as follows. In his younger and fitter years, he enjoyed climbing and hill-walking and beach-combing, added to which, in the aftermath of the Falklands War he served as radio operator on the salvage tugs *Rollicker* and *Roysterer*, from September 1982 until May 1983, and became familiar with the Southern Rockhopper penguin. He first visited Polliwilline with a friend from Gourock, Gordon Hamilton, and now has his own little caravan in the Wee Holm, where, as a dedicated astronomer, he enjoys the clear night skies. The 'Rock Hopper' carving, thirty years on, is eroding and Iain considered restoring it, but decided it was 'just like graffiti', so didn't bother. His real name suggests an origin in Kintyre, but to his knowledge his McEachran family came from Morar.

I watched the *Isle of Arran* steam down the Kilbrannan Sound and into Campbeltown Loch on her Sunday run from Ardrossan, and wondered sadly, since this was the last of her three years contracted to the service, if I'd be seeing her in 2016. She reappeared about forty minutes later, this time heading for the south end of Arran, and before returning to my bike at Ballymenach road-end I watched her until she was just a dot on the horizon. (Later in the year, the Scottish Government announced that the ferry would continue, still as a limited summer service, but on a permanent basis.)

31 August: Knock Scalbert

This was another first visit of the summer, and I set off late in a sunny afternoon. In the first few years of this century, I was quite often on Knock Scalbert with Bella and Benjie, looking for horse mushrooms. August and September were the main gathering months, and by the end of September we usually found ourselves still on the hill close to sunset. Autumn evenings can be as lovely as spring evenings, but whereas in spring there is joy and promise, in autumn there is sadness and regret. But that's just my own romantic shorthand.

Those evenings on Knock Scalbert have merged and blurred into vague outlines, which only my journals would clarify, but for once I'm not going to consult them. In memory, Bella and I are sitting on a hillock south of Knock Scalbert as the sun sets, and seeing windows on the Ayrshire coast flashing back the light at us. I tried a couple of times to put these signals – remote and meaningless, yet somehow intimate and significant – into a poem, but failed. The idea was good, but its execution fell short.

While on top of Knock Scalbert, I noticed in a field to the south-west, beyond the town, long shadows cast by a hedgerow I recognised. I have been seeing that hedgerow since my boyhood in Crosshill Avenue, when it was visible from my bedroom window. I once painted a crude picture of the hawthorns silhouetted against a sunset sky, and had it tacked to my wall for years. Years after I had left that house, I wrote the poem

HAWTHORN HEDGE, KNOCKRIOCH

From childhood's window on the west
the final sharpest silhouette
was a ragged ridge of hawthorn
backlit by clouds' translucence
or a sunset's serene blush;
I pass it daily but the angle's wrong now.

> I've never placed myself there
> never that neighbourly earth walked
> never a gnarled stock stroked
> or blossom's odour breathed
> perhaps I'll leave these tributes to the last
> if in this world they need be paid at all.

While gazing on the hedge and its shadows, I heard a disturbance in the air and looked to my left and saw a ringtail – an immature hen harrier – banking away. It had obviously been skimming the summit flanks until it met me. If you sit on the top of Knock Scalbert for long enough – in my case, usually an hour – most days you'll see a harrier. Next to appear, travelling in the opposite direction, was a buzzard, and I'd already seen a kestrel.

1 September: Dalbuie to Feochaig

The heading should strictly read 'Campbeltown to Dalbuie to Feochaig and back to Campbeltown by the Learside', a roughly twenty-mile round-trip by bike with George McSporran, who, earlier in the year, had suggested it. By choice, I seldom walk or cycle on forestry roads, but I unexpectedly enjoyed myself on that overland road, which is as smooth as a plate until almost the end, and a credit to the road-makers.

During the first uphill push, above Dalbuie, I noticed a little clump of heavily berried blaeberry bushes crowning the roadside ditch. We got stuck into it immediately and were surprised not only by the quantity of berries, in what had been a poor fruiting season, but also by their generous proportions and sweetness. We agreed that we'd never before tasted better, though that response was likely conditioned by the unexpectedness of the find. As George remarked, 'We're like these animals that gorge themselves'. We saw plenty more blaeberry bushes, but none that tempted us to stop and pick.

At the first junction we reached, George was uncertain as to the direction to take, and I hadn't a clue where we were. He opted for left, and the further we travelled the quieter he became. I knew that he had begun to doubt the choice and reassured him that if we'd gone wrong then we could enjoy the day just the same and, if need be, abandon the Feochaig plan and return home the way we had come. But his doubts were at once dispelled when a big quarry appeared. It was the validation he'd been awaiting, and he explained that he 'could have sworn the quarry was nearer to Dalbuie'.

George supposed that I'd recognise the quarry, but I didn't, though he assured me I'd been there. I didn't remember the quarry, but remembered something within it, and later looked in my journals. For 15 October 2002, 'Dalbuie Forest', I'd noted: 'Have passed R W Munro's weather station – wrecked'. I remember a rain-gauge there, but nothing more, and when George looked for it a few years later, there was no trace of the installation. I'm sure there's an interesting story behind the 'weather station', and I hope to hear it some day. I also remembered our watching a hen harrier that day. It was hunting over tree-cleared ground close by, '... its colours illumined by afternoon sunlight with a vividness that neither photography nor painting – no matter how accomplished – could possibly convey'.

Four days later, George walked overland from Campbeltown to Southend. The journey, which began at Narrowfield and ended at Polliwilline, was made possible by recent timber-felling and the extension of forest roads, and took him a very creditable three hours and forty minutes, including a twenty-minute stop.[164]

Almost thirteen years later, at a high point on the road above the spruce plantations, George and I enjoyed clear views to the west and south. Cnoc Moy looked magnificent and Dunaverty stood out, with a silvery sea and the blue hills of Ireland beyond. After a long free-wheel, we reached a junction with which George was familiar from walks to his caravan at Polliwilline, and we stopped there for food and tea.

From where we sat, we were looking on to the south side of Arinarach Hill. On 24 July, with Jon Immanuel, we'd been looking at the north side. The hill takes its name from a farm, *Àirigh Nathrach*, 'Serpent Shieling', which was deserted by the time of the 1841 census. The hill was afforested by the time I might have been interested in visiting the ruin, and I have never seen it. The name is an old one, appearing first in a charter of 1481 as 'Arenarroch'. In 1792, John McMichael and Cathrine McArthur were there with five young children and two servant-girls, Isobel Campbell and Peggy Galbreath. Five years later, Duncan McCallum kept two horses there.[165] The last tenant was probably Alexander MacMillan, who erected a headstone in Kilkerran to his father Donald, who died on 18 May 1833, aged 73, and his brother Neil, who died on 14 July 1827, aged 19. The last Argyll Estate lease for the farm, dated 1820, contained the note: 'As presently occupied by Donald McMillan, uncle and guardian of the orphan grandchild of the deceased Alexander Crawford, the tacksman.'

George remembered sitting at the junction about ten years before, on an exceptionally warm day. When he brought out a bar of chocolate from his rucksack, he discovered it was entirely liquefied, but since it hadn't leaked from its wrapper, he drank it. 'Ye canna mind whoot chocolate it wis?' I asked him jocularly. 'Cadbury's Dairy Milk,' he replied immediately.

Here is an anecdote of my own which came up while we sat in conversation. On our way out the main road, we looked in a roadside quarry on Killellan brae. It has been thickly colonised by flowers, trees and shrubs, and I had counted a variety of butterflies there in July 2014, and hoped to repeat that success. The quarry was sheltered from the north-westerly wind that blew all day, but we saw only two butterflies, a green-veined white and a pristine peacock, one of that summer's hatch. Iain Russell, one of my class mates at Campbeltown Grammar School in the mid-1960s, lived at Killellan Park Farm, and, since there was a lime quarry and kiln on his father's land, I asked Iain if I could look for fossils there. I had no geological hammer and instead took a brand-new claw-hammer of my father's, which I remember was kept in the cupboard in the lobby which housed the gas-meter. By the time my geological efforts had ended in failure, the hammer was ruined. The head was made of a metal alloy of some kind, and I had knocked lumps out of it. If my Father ever reprimanded me for the folly, I don't remember. He probably let me off: innocence is sacrosanct!

5 September: Tòn Bhàn

I'm not sure what the place is really called. Tòn Bhàn would make the meaning 'Light-coloured Backside', and it does from north and south resemble a big arse thrust seaward. The name wasn't noted by the Ordnance Survey in 1866, surprisingly for such a prominent feature, but Duncan Colville recorded it around 1929 from a Gaelic-speaking shepherd, John McCallum, who gave it as Dùn Bàn, 'Light-coloured Hillock', adding that shepherds referred to it as 'Ballygroggan Dùn Bàn' and the other one, to the south, as 'Largiebaan Dùn Bàn'. William McTaggart, himself a Kintyre Gaelic speaker, put the headland into two of his major paintings, 'The Coming of St. Columba' (1895) and 'The Preaching of St. Columba' (1897), both of them set in the Galdrans, looking south. I wonder if he was familiar with the place-name and, if so, what his pronunciation was. In the past I have accepted John McCallum's interpretation, but it's now time to at least acknowledge the alternative, which may be a corruption and is generally pronounced 'Tin Van'.

I have stood on Tòn Bhàn, as I'll call it, but had never ventured down to the foot of its cliff. John MacDonald, a keen angler, has fished there and offered to take me. On 5 September, a sunny day with a strong north-westerly wind blowing, he contacted me and suggested an outing there. Mary Sinclair, who was brought up on Ballygroggan Farm and is in her early eighties now, was on the 1 o' clock bus with us and recalled that when she first started travelling on the Machrihanish bus, the fare was four pence ha'penny. I, like Mary, travel with a bus pass, but John paid £2.50p for a return fare, which seemed reasonable to me, particularly when the driver, who was listening to the conversation, informed us that the fare hadn't increased in about five years.

We headed down the coast through the Galdrans and, as we approached Tòn Bhàn, John pointed out a rock chasm, on the north side of the headland, for which he'd been given the undoubtedly modern name 'Leap of Faith', probably by James McPhee, who first took him there to fish in the mid-1980s. It's a short-cut to the foot of the headland and requires just one step to cross it, which his friend Martin McKellar routinely takes, but John, conscious of the drop below the cleft – about sixty feet, he reckons – has never attempted it and prefers to scramble round the rocks.

Our route to the foot of the headland was on the south side, and we descended a grassy slope to a pile of huge boulders. Our destination was a great, tilted slab of mica schist below the seaward-facing cliff, which John assured me would be sheltered from the wind. It was, but I had a moment of anxiety climbing on to it. John took a less direct approach, which I decided I'd use on our way back, but, when the time came, that route gave me an even bigger fright and I told him I wouldn't be returning. It's a condition of age: I'm comfortable walking on rocks, but not climbing them; I'm not as physically robust as I used to be, but my imagination is more robust than ever! John's imagination runs along different lines. He confided to me that his greatest fear at the foot of Tòn Bhàn was being crushed by a falling rock. 'See when I come down here, I feel insignificant, especially when I look up.' I looked up when we reached our destination, and we were right under a cliff.

John assembled a fishing-rod and was soon casting from the edge of a rock, using, as lures, a 'Costa' and a 'Muppet', names which meant nothing to me, since fishing doesn't interest me and I'd sooner kill a corrupt banker or businessman than a fish. John was in such a hurry to start fishing that he poured a cup of coffee from his flask and left it untouched. He had seen lythe up to 15 and 16 lbs. taken there, sometimes in large numbers. The biggest fish he ever saw there was caught by his brother Jimmy, who doesn't as a rule fish and who avoided handling the many fish he caught, all of which, John added for my benefit, were liberated. Conditions then were favourable for rock fishing, but on the day I was there the wind was onshore and the sea turbulent. John reckoned he had felt 'a couple of big hits', but no fish was landed, which suited me. I was content to sit, smoking my pipe and alternately watching the waves breaking on the rocks below me and John casting and re-casting, a timeless figure on his rock perch above the heaving sea. He reckoned, rightly I think, that this would have been a customary fishing spot right back into prehistory.

About fifteen years ago, while sitting there having his 'piece', he happened to turn round and saw a mink in the act of dragging one of the lythe he'd caught into its hole in the rocks. He quickly retrieved the fish from the animal, which hissed its annoyance before retreating into its lair, from which it occasionally 'keeked' out at him. He later gutted and filleted the fish on the rock, and left the remains for the thwarted mink.

Around the corner, to the north, there is another fishing station, but I declined his suggestion to pay it a visit. Access is by a narrow sloping rock, which, John assured me, opens on to an expanse of flat rocks, with a gully at the back of them, occupied by nesting shags, but the route looked forbidding to me. He was fishing there about eight years ago, when three boys appeared at his back. 'I nearly jumped out of my skin,' he said. They had come down the face of Tòn Bhàn by a route he hadn't known existed and has yet to investigate. They said they were 'rock jumpers', which John explained as a 'craze' – self-explanatory – at that time.

John pointed out another fishing rock a short distance to the south. Out from it, the seabed is sandy. Two years previously, when he and Martin McKellar were climbing off the shore, they saw an unforgettable sight – a small pod of Risso's dolphins hunting over the sandy patch. The sea was calm and they watched the dolphins throwing up sand from the seabed, catching flatfish, John assumed. I was reminded of a whale sighting my niece Barbara Matheson and her brother Malcolm Docherty had from the top of Tòn Bhàn. It was a big whale, and directly below them, but her memory of it is vague – she was a teenager at the time – apart from barnacle clusters on its back.

25. Bella and Angus Martin with ox-eye daisy, Ben Gullion, 7 July 2003. Photograph by George McSporran.

When I tired of watching John and the sea, I decided to explore our rather confined spot. I climbed under the cliff for as far as I could go and found myself on a rock platform under an overhang. It was carpeted with dried goat dung and was obviously a commonly used lair of the local goat flock, of which we had seen – and smelt – twenty members on the south side of Bun an Uisge. The commonest flower on and around the cliff was sea mayweed (*Tripleurospermum maritima*), a member of the daisy family. I used to confuse it with ox-eye daisy, until I sorted out the differences, which wasn't difficult when I got around to it – the leaves have little in common but their greenness!

I first noticed ox-eye daisy (*Leucanthemum vulgare*) on 7 July 2003, on a bend of the Ben Gullion trail. I was with George McSporran, daughter Bella and Benjie the dog. George had a brand-new camera with him that evening and photographed the flowers and Bella and me kneeling on the track looking at them (at 1902 hours, according to the camera's memory). Each summer thereafter, I made a point of paying my respects to the little colony. As Bella entered her teenage years, she accompanied me less often on walks, and finally gave them up; Benjie died in 2008; some years George was with me when I revisited the flowers, and some years not. These big, bright, smiling daisies became, for me, a reassuring and cherished link with past summers, but in 2014 and 2015 none appeared.

Recreational fishing

Being at Tòn Bhàn with John, who was fishing, brought back memories of Campbeltown Old Quay, to which I was attracted at a young age, probably eight or nine years. I remember encountering an uncle, Henry Martin, with other retired fishermen, outside the fish-shed, and his ordering me home. I resented his interference, as I saw it, and defied him, simply moving off and keeping out of his way. His concern, as I later realised, was real enough to him. Water is a danger to children, especially children who cannot swim.

I experienced only one fright on the quay and I haven't forgotten it. The underside was then largely open – it's since been sealed off by steel piles – and the immense wooden supporting beams that interconnected vertically and horizontally were easily accessible. That dark underworld of slimy green-weeded timbers was known as 'the skeegs', a peculiarly local word for which, to my knowledge, no etymological explanation has yet been delivered. It was a place of legendary horror in which huge conger eels thrived. These were said to have escaped from fishing-boats landing their catches. There may have been some truth in that, but I never saw even one of the awesome eels. Congers are unquestionably scary creatures: serpent-like, slimy, stealthy in free motion, coiling and writhing with demonic vigour when captured, and death-defying when subjected to prolonged exposure to air or to blows that would kill a horse.

Most of the boys I knew on the quay were often in the skeegs, to fish or just to explore that dank and dripping zone after the tide had left it. By nature timid, I persistently declined to accompany them, but one day curiosity overpowered caution. I was alone – a mistake which might have proved fatal – otherwise I wouldn't have gone, because if I 'chickened out' at some stage, only I would know my failure. I descended by one of the iron ladders on the side of the quay and stepped into the skeegs. I didn't like the place and soon decided I wanted out. I began my exit at the north-eastern corner of the quay, but when I reached the top of the ladder there, I found that the concrete bulwark between me and safety was alarmingly thick, and I began to panic in my efforts to grasp the top of it and haul myself over. In the end, I managed to 'sprachle' – or scramble – over the obstacle in a fear-driven surge, and lay on the ground panting and shaking. If I'd slipped and fallen, I'd most likely have drowned because there was no help near and I couldn't, and still can't, swim. I don't recall ever returning to the skeegs, but I occasionally revisit that corner of the quay and peer over at the sucking water below.

If I saw no congers around the quay, there were abundant other fish. These were mostly saithe, but they weren't called that – the smallest, at three or four inches long, were 'cuddies' or 'cuddins', and the rarer ones, not much bigger, were 'gleshans', names derived from Gaelic, though I didn't know that then. The cuddies were in their thousands if one looked over the edge of the quay, particularly on the north side. As a boy, in summers, I was content to observe these little fish. To be honest, they didn't do much else than swim unceasingly, but occasionally one would flip over and flash its silvery belly. The monotony of fish-watching could be broken by dropping some small object into the water and creating a momentary frenzy of interest – if some edible scrap, a gang of cuddies would pursue the morsel on its descent, snapping vigorously at it, and if a small stone, or something equally inedible, the deception would soon be recognised and pursuit abandoned.

I only once dropped a baited line over the quay and caught a cuddie, but having unhooked the fish I returned it to the sea and resolved never again to fish for 'pleasure'. I experienced no enjoyment in the act, and failed – and still fail – to understand what motivated boys to sit for hours at a time hauling up fish after fish with monotonous ease. In other parts of the West Coast, cuddies were caught for food. I didn't know that then, but had I known, I would have recognised a genuine motivation grounded in community tradition. What I couldn't understand was the pointless waste of life that I saw daily all around me on the quay.

Practically every young fisher kept his entire catch, and the custom was to arrange the fish in a row, from largest to smallest, until the end of the day, when the hoard would be ritually tossed to the gulls, each mid-air catch a cause for celebration. Witnessing those gleaming little fish quiver their lives out on the quay, reduced at last to lustreless wrinkled corpses, seemed criminal to me; but the boys who engaged in the pastime were oblivious to the cruelty I perceived. I suppose I must have been a sensitive child. I suppose, too, that the creed of vegetarianism, which I adopted in 1978, was latent in me even then.

There was more to my aversion than sentiment, for I knew that cuddies, if given the chance, grew into the big fish – almost a boy's length, some of them – which were netted in deep water and known as 'stainlock'. Indeed, the first fish presented to me on the quay was just that. One evening, while I was watching the quay-workers sorting and boxing fish that the boats had landed, one of the men, 'Tec' McEachran, glanced at me and asked if I wanted a fish to take home to my mother. He lived near us, in Ralston Road, and may have known me; I certainly knew him. The offer surprised me, but I accepted at once and received a stainlock, with advice that it should be boiled and made into fish-cakes.

At that time – the early 1960s – the market for saithe was scant. Along with monkfish, eels and other stray oddities, they were generally classed as 'rough' and boxed miscellaneously, unlike the more marketable species – whiting, haddock, cod and flatfish – which were graded by size and boxed accordingly. A time came, in the early 1970s, when saithe were targeted by mid-water trawlers in the Kilbrannan Sound, and when that intensive fishery had depleted the stock, cuddies were no longer so abundant around the quay.

10 September: Blaeberries and sloes

This was an evening walk on Ben Gullion, in breezy sunshine. I hadn't paid much attention to blaeberries all summer, supposing the crop must be poor. In fact, though late in the season, I got a decent picking around Fin Rock on the east side of the hill, but when I arrived home I found – not for the first time – that the lid of the container had come off and that berries had spilled out. They stain badly and I had to empty and clean the rucksack. (Nearly a month later, at the top of Polliwilline brae, Judy and I would collect substantial quantities of berries on two successive days.)

On my way across the top bike trail, two dogs appeared and faced me, barking. One of them nervously edged up to me and let me clap it, but the other raced past. I didn't recognise the dogs, but recognised their owner, Dougie Ferguson, when he appeared a few minutes later on his bike. I was in the Coastguard for years with Dougie and meet him occasionally on the hill. As we chatted, conscious of an increasing midge presence, he asked if I was retired. 'Coming up for four years now,' I replied. 'Ye'll be livin quite well on the money that's comin in fae the books,' he remarked, mischievously I suppose. 'Ye mean the money that's gan oot!' I corrected him. Later in the evening, I remembered a cheque delivered the previous week for a year's sales of *Always Boats and Men*, my collaboration with the artist Mark I'Anson: it came to £8.77p.

I sat in the middle of Crosshill Dam, which was catching the easterly breeze, until the sun set. George McSporran had mentioned, earlier in the month, that he'd checked the blackthorns north of Polliwilline and seen only a handful of berries. The Valley, at the back of the Dam, is my usual gathering place, and I decided to take a look there on my way home. The crop was abundant in 2014, and in the second week of October I filled a carrier bag for a woman I'd met outside Café Bluebell one day. She and a friend had gone looking for berries to make sloe gin with, but had been in the wrong places. Later in the year, she gave me a small bottle of her concoction, which I enjoyed and, with Judy's assistance, finished. I decided I'd like to try making it for myself, but when I looked in the Valley I found exactly one berry! Admittedly, light was then fading, but I'd picked sloes in low light in other years, as described in a poem from 2010, 'Sloe-Gathering', which ends with the berries themselves as 'the very darkness'. The poem's first verse evokes a feeling I often experience in the Valley in autumn, whether gathering hazel nuts or sloes. That narrow glen seems somehow to collect and distil the autumnal atmosphere, or maybe it's in my mind, my backward-looking mind.

I found a new serenity
deep in the Valley bottom
squelching dusk on dusk
on the edges of the flower-dead marsh
alone but for a chiding bird,
a drifting owl or people heard.

13 September: Balnabraid

Cycling along the track to Balnabraid, I absent-mindedly took a new section of road to a wind-turbine and was under its swishing, wheezing blades before I realised my error; but within half-a-minute I was back on track. A Canadian friend with Kintyre connections, Doug Cooper, had left a telephone message that morning to say that he and his wife Kelly were in town, and as I neared Balnabraid I recalled that he had been there with Jimmy MacDonald and me one evening. It was a spring, because I remembered Jimmy performing his mimicry to bring cuckoos into the trees, but what year was it? Prompted by Doug, I later found the answer in a journal – 2010, 25 May – and, additionally, that the number of male cuckoos duped was three.

As I sat in the shelter of a wall, I looked around me, and, as I occasionally do when I am alone and nothing's happening, I tried to imagine the landscape as it would have been hundreds of years back: harvest fields, flower-speckled fields in fallow, drystone houses with smoke meandering out through the thatched roofs, the sounds of sheep and cattle on the higher grazings, and Gaelic voices all around. It would have been a tough life, with few luxuries and death omnipresent, but these folk, unlike most folk nowadays, knew where their food came from and the labour involved in its production. There would have been no food wasted in those times – often enough there would have been no food!

A story I read in an old newspaper returned to me, but it was fragmentary and I had to go back to the source a couple of days later. On 2 October 1856, a Campbeltown fisherman

John MacEachran was found half-dead in 'Coraphin Glen', an alternative name for the Ordnance Survey's Balnabraid Glen. He had 'left home for the purpose of gathering herbs', but what herbs was he interested in and what did he intend using them for? Could he have gone all that way for food flavourings, or, as I suspected, were these unspecified 'herbs' for food? I checked 'herb' in *The Concise Scots Dictionary*, thinking there might be Scottish usages which would illuminate the mystery, but the word wasn't there, so I went to *The Concise Oxford Dictionary of Current English* and found: 'plant of which leaves etc. are used for food, medicine, scent, flavour, etc.' My guess is that he was foraging for sustenance.

He'd gone out on 1 October and failed to return. On the following day, several search parties went looking for him and he was found by a Campbeltown shoemaker, James Kerr, lying in the glen 'on his back, with a very firm grasp of a bush, so that it was with difficulty he was made to let go'. He was taken to 'Ballinabrad farm house', where he was warmed and his wet clothes dried. He was 'too weak to account coherently for his condition', but he was known to be 'subject to weakly turns', and the assumption was that he had been 'seized by a fainting-fit' and collapsed. He was taken home by horse and cart and was 'still in a dangerous state' when the *Argyllshire Herald* went to press.[166]

When Bill Pursell (p 191), as a boy of 12, visited Balnabraid ruins in April 1942, there was a 'rusty iron bed-stead' inside the walls, a poignant reminder of lives lived there. And on the walls, the number of adders sunning themselves amazed and unnerved him. He had stopped at the ruins during a solitary expedition at the start of the trout-fishing season. With the first spate, he would head for the top of Balnabraid burn and fish the pools all the way down to the sea, which normally took most of the day.[167]

He'd see basking adders again on one of his trout-fishing outings, but in unusual circumstances – several of them curled on a rock in the middle of the burn! 'This amazed me,' he recalled, 'and I proceeded to tip them into the water with the end of my fishing rod and they started to swim easily to the bank. I took off immediately, having learned that they are very good in water!'[168] Reports of adders at sea appeared occasionally in local newspapers. One evening in April 1901, when the Dunmore ferryman was crossing West Loch Tarbert, he saw an adder 'swimming for the Kilchamaig shore on the other side'.[169] In 1908, about a quarter of a mile off Iorsa Water, Arran, the crew of Dennis McKay's *Annunciata* saw what they took to be an eel in the water. 'When they recognised what it was they got it on board the skiff and ended its career. It is thought that the reptile in attempting to swim the stream was swept out to sea.'[170]

15 September: Lagloskin

Doug Cooper, his wife Kelly and I took the 11.30 bus from Campbeltown and got off half-an-hour later, just north of Tayinloan, to walk to Lagloskin. Doug's great-grandfather Duncan Mitchell had been shepherd there in the late nineteenth century and his great-grandmother, Jane Greenlees, died there in 1894. Lagloskin was one of the many places in North Kintyre I hadn't visited, and I'd assumed it would be Doug's first time too, but on the way there he described a visit in 2003. Around the time he was telling me this, we heard a vehicle approaching. It was the farmer, John Casey, with dogs, driving a small flock of sheep which sensibly ignored us when we stepped off the track. John stopped and switched off the ATV's engine and we had a chat, during which he mentioned that about five years ago on the track he'd met another Canadian whose ancestor had emigrated from Lagloskin and who had met and married in Canada a woman from a farm 'over the hill' from Lagloskin. He couldn't recall the name of this other farm or the surname of the Canadian visitor. Doug was intrigued, thinking there might be a Mitchell connection there too, but he couldn't figure one out.

The track we were on was not the one Doug's ancestors would have walked, which passed Largie Castle. It is a forestry track, dating to the late 1980s, and, like most such tracks, has enhanced the botany of the area. In the roadside ditch we encountered a long chain of Grass-of-Parnassus (*Parnassia palustris*), a late-flowering white beauty and a favourite of mine, plus water mint (*Mentha aquatica*) in flower, bog asphodel (*Narthecium ossifragum*), whose yellow flower-spikes had aged to orange, and bog myrtle (*Myrica gale*), which I hardly see in South Kintyre, where I do most of my walking, but see in abundance almost everywhere I go in North Kintyre.

Doug mentioned that, on his first visit to Lagloskin, he had noticed growing on top of the ruined walls a flower which he knows in Canada as 'fireweed', from its being one of the first species to flourish in ground which has been swept by forest fires. When we reached the ruin, we saw the flowers on one of the walls; they were my rosebay willowherb (*Epilobium/ Chamerion augustifolium*).

Even with all the seasonal wild flowers around them, many country women liked to plant garden flowers at their cottages. I have seen, or know of, daffodils, snowdrops and 'Easter lilies' (*Narcissus poeticus*) which flourished long after a house was ruined and its garden overgrown. An hour or so after we arrived at Lagloskin, Kelly rather surprised me by saying she'd been looking for rhubarb as a sign of a former garden. I thought to myself: you've done this before. In 2011 she'd gone to Cayuga in Southern Ontario to search for the farm-stead of her paternal great-grandparents, John Toohey and Mary Downie, who had come from Ireland. The house itself was gone, but Kelly found snowdrops growing close to the site and took away a few bulbs for sentiment's sake. She'd heard that Mary had planted the snowdrops against her husband's wishes; masculine logic, I suppose, would dictate that if it couldn't be eaten, it wasn't wanted. Mary, however, had the last word: 'I'm taking my egg money and I'm buying some flowers and I don't care what you say!'

In 1887, during a visit to his birthplace, Achavallich, near Clachan, James McEwing dug up daffodil bulbs from the garden there, took them away and transplanted them in his garden in Ontario, where they flowered in Easter week, year after year, and were still flowering when he died in 1950. His parents had emigrated to Canada around 1858, when he was a baby.[171]

Doug's great-grandparents, Duncan Mitchell and Jean Greenlees, had a large family – there were nine children with them at Lagloskin in 1901 – eight of whom, including Doug's grandfather, Robert, emigrated. He left in 1901, having appeared in the population census of Scotland, and arrived in North Dakota in time to appear in the U.S. census; but he and his seven siblings all ended up in Canada, and Robert and his three brothers 'homesteaded' close to one another in central-eastern Alberta.

Robert's brother Archibald, one of the two Mitchell brothers who remained in Scotland, was named after his grandfather, a shepherd who was ceremonially presented with a bag of gold sovereigns in 1874 and mysteriously died in Campbeltown harbour the year after.[172] In 1906, while still at Lagloskin, Archibald applied for a patent for an 'adding apparatus' he had invented. The device was described in detail by the *Argyllshire Herald*'s Tayinloan correspondent,[173] but I could make no sense of it, and neither could Doug. It remains, however, an intriguing achievement, even if it never progressed beyond the design stage, and Doug was able, through the British Library, to find the patent application, with accompanying diagram, on an internet website.

Lagloskin is Gaelic *Lag losgainn*, 'Toad hollow'. The eponymous hollow may be the marshy area to the south of the shepherd's cottage, but I'm guessing. The cottage was occupied within living memory. Mrs May Currie in Tayinloan was born in 1924, the year her father John Gillies moved to Lagloskin as shepherd. In 1939 John Gillies was succeeded by James Strang, who in turn was succeeded two years later by Alexander MacPherson, who came into the district from

Kilbirnie, Ayrshire. He, too, appears to have moved on after a few years, so Lagloskin has lain empty since the 1940s.

The house is roofless now, with a small rowan growing from the top of one of the walls and a crown of ivy on the south gable. That gable had a big window – of concrete construction – built into it as a later modification, and a small brick fire-place added within the room, probably at the same time. My assumption is that the compartment – one of three – was originally a byre and was converted into a second bedroom. Poignantly, at a corner of the window there was a fallen swallows' nest and a pile of droppings.

The sprawling ruins close by constitute, I presume, the older Lagloskin, replaced in the latter half of the nineteenth century. The house there is of an earlier type, having tiny windows and no evidence of chimneys; a sheep-fank was built alongside. The Lagloskin shepherd in 1820 was John MacCallum. He had been 'missing sheep from his flock', and the suspected thief was John Campbell, a cottar at Auchavraulladale, a now-obscure settlement nearby.[174]

In the early 1870s, there was a recurrence of sheep-stealing on Lagloskin, which led to the offer of a £50 reward for information leading to an arrest. Between November 1873 and 1 March 1874, 21 Cheviot and 16 black-faced ewes and wedders went missing. The distinctive markings – ear-notches, blue keel on near hip, and nose and horn brandings in 'L' and 'A', in various combinations – were described. The notice, which was inserted in the *Argyllshire Herald* by D. McKechnie, superintendent of police in Campbeltown, ran from 14 November until 12 December 1874, evidently without result.

The Lagloskin shepherd at that time was John Robertson, who belonged to Moffat in Dumfriesshire. Censuses show him at Lagloskin from 1861 to '81, but he could well have been 30 years or more there. From the ages and birthplaces of his children, his arrival in Kintyre can be computed to around 1848, but he wasn't at first in Lagloskin, which in 1851 was occupied by another Borders shepherd, Samuel Stewart.

The year the Mitchells moved to Lagloskin is known from the Rhunahaorine School admissions' register, which shows that on 4 June 1890 four of the children – John, Robert, Mary and Neil – were enrolled; their previous school was given as Drumlemble.

In *Another Summer in Kintyre*, I examined the Mitchell name in an account of the life and the death of Archibald Mitchell, Duncan in Lagloskin's father. To summarise: though the Mitchell families in South Kintyre are demonstrably of seventeenth century Lowland plantation origin, there were Gaelic-speaking Mitchell families in North Kintyre whose origin is not so certain and whose surname may be the final Anglicised form of a native Gaelic surname. Doug's Mitchell ancestors belonged to that group.

Concerning Duncan Mitchell's wife, Jane Greenlees, there is no such doubt. The Greenlees families in Kintyre all descend from seventeenth century Lowland stock. Like their Mitchell counterparts in South Kintyre, with whom they intermarried, they began in farming and diversified – some of them, at any rate – into whisky-distilling. The London-based brothers James and Samuel Greenlees, indeed, were nineteenth century pioneers in whisky-blending and in the popularising of Scotch whisky world-wide.[175]

Jean's family, however, remained in farming and accrued no fabulous wealth. The family was in Putechan/Putechantuy farm, near Bellochantuy, by 1814, and was soon riven by disputes. The lease was held by two elderly brothers, John and Robert Greenlees. In 1821, John wrote to the estate chamberlain – the Duke of Argyll's factor – complaining that his children were 'disgusted' with Robert, their uncle, and threatening to 'go elsewhere'. Two years later, with the rent in arrears, Robert and his son Hugh moved out after disputes with John. In 1867, Thomas Greenlees's stock was seized to pay arrears of rent for 'Putechantuy', and he assigned the lease to Angus MacKeich in Campbeltown, who gave him a house and 'cow's grass' for the remainder of the lease.[176] This Thomas was Jane Mitchell's father. She appeared at 'Putachan', aged four, in the 1851 census, along with her parents, two younger sisters, and five servants. By 1861 Thomas Greenlees was a 66-year-old widower in 'South Putechan', with 14-year-old Jane, four siblings and four servants. In 1871, Thomas, having lost the farm, was still living there in retirement, alone but for a daughter Margaret.

Thomas was involved in a sheep-stealing case in 1837, after his father John's stock on Putechan farm had suffered the loss of six animals. From remains shown to him, he identified a skin and a head which bore the Putechan marks: a spade haft on the right ear and an inverted 'T' branded on the left side of the nose. The accused, Hugh MacIntyre, shepherd at Margmonagach, fled Kintyre by the Skipness ferry, having spun the boatman a yarn about beating up an Exciseman who tried to seize smuggled goods from him.[177] (Some time after I published that story in *Kintyre Country Life*, I received a letter from a descendant of Hugh MacIntyre's, explaining that the fugitive made a new life for himself in Lowland Scotland, but I omitted to file the letter and forget the details.)

In the 1891 census, Jane, as well as her husband Duncan, is marked as bi-lingual in Gaelic and English, no great surprise considering she was brought up in the southern end of Killean and Kilchenzie Parish at a time when Gaelic was still widely spoken there and a Lowland surname signified little in the prevailing cultural milieu. Further, her mother, who was born in Killean Parish, would almost certainly have been a Gaelic speaker. She is named in Jane's death certificate as Mary 'Keith', but the surname was earlier MacKeich, and the Angus MacKeich who helped her husband Thomas, when he was in trouble with the farm, was probably a relative.

In that 1891 census, none of the 11 children at Lagloskin is credited with having Gaelic. Ten years later, however, Duncan's sons Archibald (27), Robert (21) and Neil (18) appear as bi-lingual, while siblings and cohabitants Mary

(20), Maggie (15), Hugh (13) and Isabella (11) do not, an inconsistency which could have several explanations, including how the enumerator, or the head of the household, Duncan Mitchell, chose to define fluency in the language. By 1901 Duncan was a widower, Jane having died from liver cancer on 12 May 1894 at the age of 47. In 1911, their eldest son Archibald was at Lagloskin with his wife Amelia McMillan– they had no children and never would have – and an assistant shepherd, Gilbert MacCallum.

Robert Mitchell, Doug's grandfather, appears to have kept his Gaelic alive. Doug was told by a brother-in-law, who visited the old man in Vancouver Island in the early 1970s, that Robert frequently spoke on the telephone to a friend, using a language which was unintelligible to everyone but the man on the other end of the line. With the death of Kintyre Gaelic, abroad as well as at home, I'll leave Lagloskin – one of a multitude of ruined homes – to the silence of the hills.

References

1. G. Grigson, *The Englishman's Flora*, 1975 edition, p 42.
2. D. Clyne, *Gaelic Names for Flowers and Plants*, 1989, p 61.
3. A. Martin, *A Summer in Kintyre*, pp. 188-95.
4. Mick Houghton, *I've Always Kept a Unicorn: The Biography of Sandy Denny*, p 407.
5. 'Siol Chuinn', quoted in A. Martin, *Kintyre Places and Place-Names*, p 295.
6. *Campbeltown Courier*, 30/7/1938.
7. A. Martin, *Kintyre: The Hidden Past*, p 213.
8. *Argyllshire Herald*, 22/2/1913, 'Sheep Stealing/ Farmer Convicted/ An Extraordinary Story'.
9. *Campbeltown Courier*, 30/12/1911, death notice.
10. Register of Poor, Campbeltown Parish, 2574, Argyll & Bute Council Archive, CO 6.
11. Philip Lusby & Jenny Wright, *Scottish Wild Plants*, 2001 edition, p 98.
12. Alexander Macbain, *An Etymological Dictionary of the Gaelic Language*, 1911, p 319.
13. I. A. Fraser, *The Place-Names of Arran*, 1999, p 142.
14. D. Colville and A. Martin, *The Place-Names of the Parish of Campbeltown*, 2009 edition, p 21.
15. A. Martin, *Kintyre Families*, pp. 30-31.
16. A. Martin, *Kintyre Country Life*, p 72, & *Sixteen Walks in South Kintyre*, pp. 37-38.
17. *Campbeltown Courier*, 24/11/1928 & 18/10/1947.
18. A. Martin, *By Hill and Shore in South Kintyre*, pp. 79-80.
19. Archie Ronald, by C.B. radio, 24/10/1996.
20. *Campbeltown Courier*, 26/3/1935.
21. James MacDonald, *Kintyre Magazine* 69, pp. 30-31, 'Observations on Ravens'.
22. Quoted in A. Martin, *Kintyre Birds*, 2008, p 49.
23. *Campbeltown Courier*, 13/6/1896.
24. *Ibid.*, 20/6/1896.
25. *Kintyre Magazine* 63, pp. 24-25, 'Falcons at the Mull'.
26. From Argyll Estate Archives, via Murdo MacDonald, letter, 9 July 2015.
27. A. Martin, *Fishing and Whaling*, p 62.

28. A. Martin, *Kintyre Magazine* 71, p 26.
29. John Gerard, 1597/1633, quoted in Grigson, *The Englishman's Flora*, 1975 edition, p 50.
30. A. Martin, *Kintyre Places and Place-Names*, p 75.
31. *Campbeltown Courier*, 6/1/1966, 'Australia's Footballer of the Year'.
32. *Kintyre Magazine* 71, p 27.
33. C. Bannatyne, 12 June 1977.
34. G. Grigson, *The Englishman's Flora, op. cit.*, p 463.
35. *Ibid.*
36. *Campbeltown Courier*, 6/8/1938, & A. Stewart, by e-mail, 29/2/2016.
37. For an account of the castle's history, and in particular its connection with the MacDonalds of Smerby, see my 'Smerby Castle and its Historical Associations' in *Kintyre Magazine* 73.
38. A. Martin, *A Summer in Kintyre*, p 133.
39. A. Martin, *Ibid.*, p 27.
40. *Campbeltown Courier*, 15/9/1966, both reports.
41. A. Martin, *Kintyre Magazine* 56, p 22.
42. A. Martin, *Kintyre: The Hidden Past*, pp. 6-9.
43. A. Martin, *The Ring-Net Fishermen*, pp. 250-52.
44. M. MacDonald, *Kintyre Magazine* 65, p 9, 'Archibald MacKinnon and his Cave Picture Revisited'.
45. *Campbeltown Courier*, 18/8/1923, reprinted from *Campbeltown Journal*.
46. *Argyllshire Herald*, 2/6/1896.
47. J. Boyd, *Memorial Volume of the Bi-Centenary of Longrow Church of Scotland, Campbeltown, 1767-1967*, pp. 22-24.
48. *Campbeltown Courier*, 27/10/1923, 'Campbeltown War Memorial'.
49. G. Robinson, by e-mail, 19/10/2010.
50. *The Englishman's Flora*, 1975 edition, p 150.
51. Douglas Clyne, *Gaelic Names for Flowers and Plants*, p 43.
52. *The Flora of Kintyre,* p 18.
53. *Campbeltown Courier*, 4/1/1930.
54. *Ibid.*, 27/2/1904, 'Campbeltown's Fishing Fleet: List of Boats'.
55. *Ibid.*, 13/1/1933.
56. *Ibid*, 7/2/1974.
57. A. Martin, *Another Summer in Kintyre*, pp. 18-19.
58. *Campbeltown Courier*, 24/4, 18/7/1974, & 16/1, 24/4, 15/5, 8/7/1975.
59. *Ibid.*, 5/8/1922, 'Sudden Death of Mr J. Macalister Hall of Killean and Tangy'.
60. *Ibid.*, 12/8/1922, 'The Late Mr J. Macalister Hall, Impressive

Funeral at Killean'.
61. *Ibid.*, 24/5/1947, 'Gaelic Concert'.
62. A. Martin, *Kintyre Families*, p 72.
63. *Campbeltown Courier*, 17/8/1912, 'Opening of Grouse Shooting'.
64. *Ibid.*, 12/8/1922.
65. *Ibid.*, 3/5/1913, 'Marriage Celebrations at Killean and Tangy'.
66. *Ibid.*, 27/4/1940.
67. *Ibid.*, 23/3/1940, 'Death of a "Model Landlord"'.
68. *Ibid.*
69. *Ibid.*, 20/9/1930.
70. Murdo MacDonald, letter, 1/6/2015.
71. A. Martin, *Kintyre Places and Place-Names*, p 33.
72. A. Martin, *Place-Names of the Parish of Killean and Kilchenzie*, p 72.
73. D. Williamson, *The Horsieman*, p 3.
74. Register of Poor, Campbeltown Parish, *op. cit.*, 2083.
75. M. Burgess, letter to author, 7/12/2015.
76. A. Stewart, *Kintyre Magazine* 72, p 30.
77. *Ibid.*, p 29.
78. A. Martin, *Kintyre: The Hidden Past*, pp. 149-51.
79. *In Pharaoh's Army: Memories of a Lost War*, 1995 edition, p 19.
80. A. Martin, *Place-Names of the Parish of Saddell and Skipness*, p 26.
81. *Campbeltown Courier*, 30/1/1932.
82. A. Martin, *Kintyre Places and Place-Names*, p 63.
83. *Campbeltown Courier*, 25/2/1933.
84. *Argyllshire Herald*, 20/10/1888.
85. *Campbeltown Courier*, 14/7/1934.
86. *Ibid.*, 5/3/1938.
87. *Ibid.*
88. Campbeltown Parochial Board letter-book, Argyll & Bute Council Archive, CA/7/4/200 6, pp 217-19.
89. *Ibid.*, p 113.
90. A. Martin, *Kintyre Places and Place-Names*, p 89.
91. Hearth Tax List, Scottish Record Office, E 69/3, pp. 42 & 47.
92. A. Martin, *Place-Names of the Parish of Killean and Kilchenzie*, p 54.
93. A. Martin, *Kintyre Magazine* 73, p 32.
94. A. Martin, *Kintyre Country Life*, p 35.
95. A. Martin, *Place-Names of the Parish of Saddell and Skipness*, p 22.
96. F. Bigwood, *Justices of the Peace in Argyll*, 2001, p 60.
97. A. Martin, *Place-Names of the Parish of Kilcalmonell*, p 30.

98. *Kintyre Magazine* 75, pp. 9-11.
99. *Argyllshire Herald*, 4/10/1902, 'Death of Mr Hugh McLean'.
100. G. Grigson, *The Englishman's Flora, op. cit.*, p 463.
101. A. Martin, *Kintyre Places and Place-Names*, p 172.
102. A. Martin, *By Hill and Shore in South Kintyre*, p 112.
103. *Campbeltown Courier*, 29/8/1957.
104. *Ibid.*, 19/9/1957.
105. *Ibid.*, 18/5/1961, 'Southend War Hero Dies at 42'.
106. A. Young, *A Prospect of Wild Flowers*, Penguin Books edition, 1986, pp. 160-61.
107. J. Wigmore, letters, 7 November 1990 & 1 March 1991.
108. 3/8/1912.
109. 3/8/1912.
110. *Campbeltown Courier*, 26/6/2015, 'Craft Cross the North Channel'.
111. A. Martin, *Another Summer in Kintyre*, p 78.
112. *Guide to Modern World Literature*, Vol 1, 1975 edition, p 238.
113. *A Prospect of Flowers, op. cit.*, pp. 146-47.
114. R. Fulton, *The Way the Words are Taken*, p 77.
115. Letter to the author, 23/5/1990.
116. Full account in A. Martin, *By Hill and Shore in South Kintyre*, p 132.
117. A. Martin, *Fishing Boats*, No. 30, 2004, & *Fish and Fisherfolk*.
118. *Campbeltown Courier*, 8/2/1908.
119. Carol Crossan (*née* McAulay) 13/1/2005.
120. Jean Crowther (*née* Martin) 23/1/2005.
121. Quoted in P. Lusby & J. Wright, *Scottish Wild Plants*, p 61.
122. A. Stewart, *Kintyre Magazine* 72, 'Botanical Report', p 31.
123. Rupert Hart-Davis, 1960.
124. A. Martin, *The Place-Names of the Parish of Southend*, p 41, 'Tomb Park'.
125. Rev Angus MacVicar, *Campbeltown Courier*, 5/3/1927, 'Church Affairs in Kintyre, 1655-1660'.
126. *Campbeltown Journal*, 23/5 & 6/6/1851.
127. Martin C. Strong, *The Great Psychedelic Discography*, p 281.
128. A. Martin, *Kintyre: The Hidden Past*, 1999 edition, pp. *x-xi* &144-45.
129. *Campbeltown Courier*, 10/9/1964.
130. A. Martin, *Kintyre: The Hidden Past*, p 145.
131. G. Grigson, *The Englishman's Flora, op. cit.*, p 208.
132. *Campbeltown Courier*, 21/5/1935, 'District Rich in Memories of St. Columba and Robert the Bruce'.
133. *Times Literary Supplement*, 30/10/2015, p 36, James Campbell

reviewing Margaret Willes's *A Shakespearean Botanical*.
134. A. Martin, *A Summer in Kintyre*, p 102.
135. A. Martin, *Kilkerran Graveyard Revisited*, p 61, J. Immanuel, e-mail 25/2/2016 (quotation) & M. Davey, *Campbeltown Courier*, 18/9/2015, 'Kintyre wartime air crash sparks an emotional pilgrimage for Jon'.
136. *Kintyre Magazine* 34, p 27.
137. *Ibid.*, 42, p 32.
138. *Ibid.*, 55, p 13.
139. *The Scotsman*, 4/9/1941.
140. A. Martin, *Kilkerran Graveyard Revisited*, pp. 61 & 63.
141. *The Scotsman*, 4/9/1941.
142. Alastair Thompson, Gilbert Muir's nephew, by e-mail, 1 August 2015.
143. By e-mail, 24/9/2015.
144. *Campbeltown Courier*, 7/6/1962.
145. *Ibid.*, 31/5/1962.
146. Laura Thompson, *Agatha Christie*, 2007, p 9.
147. Patrick Evans, *Times Literary Supplement*, 25/9/2015.
148. A. Stewart, by e-mail, 10/8/2015.
149. A. Martin, *By Hill and Shore in South Kintyre*, pp. 266-67.
150. *Ibid.*, p 133.
151. *Campbeltown Courier*, 10/7/1987.
152. A. Martin, *By Hill and Shore in South Kintyre*, p. 207-8.
153. Michael Scott, *Scottish Wild Flowers*, p 20.
154. A. Martin, *By Hill and Shore in South Kintyre*, p 157, & *Another Summer in Kintyre*, p 97.
155. A. Martin, *A Summer in Kintyre*, pp. 120-24.
156. A. Martin, *Another Summer in Kintyre*, p 9.
157. A. Martin, *Kintyre Places and Place-Names*, pp. 200-1.
158. *Campbeltown Courier*, 18/12/1920.
159. *Argyllshire Herald*, 3/4/1869.
160. Murdo MacDonald, letter to author, 27/8/2015.
161. *Argyllshire Herald*, 23/6/1900.
162. *Campbeltown Courier*, 9/2/1950, obituary.
163. A. Martin, *A Summer in Kintyre*, p 184.
164. *Kintyre Magazine* 53, p 23, 'By Hill and Shore'.
165. A. Martin, *Kintyre Places and Place-Names*, p 232.
166. 3/10/1856.
167. Bill Pursell, e-mail 15/10/2015.
168. *Ibid.*, 30/10/2015.
169. *Campbeltown Courier*, 4/5/1901.
170. *Ibid.*, 11/7/1908.

171. *Ibid.*, 4/5/1950.
172. A. Martin, *Another Summer in Kintyre*, pp. 58-59.
173. 25/8/1906.
174. A. Martin, *Kintyre Country Life*, pp. 70-71.
175. A. Martin, *Kintyre Families*, p 19.
176. Kintyre leases, extracted by Duncan Colville from originals, pp. 167 & 166A.
177. A. Martin, *Kintyre Country Life*, pp. 71-72.

Index

Owing to the frequency of references, 'Campbeltown' and 'Kintyre' have been omitted.

Achavallich (768 564), 248
adders, 127, 181, 204-5, 245-46
'adding apparatus', Lagloskin, 248
Adventures of Angus Og and Other Tales, 92
afforestation, 5, 35, 96, 120, 122, 127, 195, 233
agricultural shows – see Kintyre Agricultural Show
Aignish (596 152), 19, 20, 27, 29, 30, 52, 53, 113, 138, 141, 201, 208, 216-18, 222
aircraft crashes, 69, 179 *et seq.*
Air Training Corps, 135-36, 181
Ancient Mariner, 173
An Cirein (598 161), 68
Anderson, Gary, Campbeltown, 63
A Night of Islands, xiii, 221
Another Summer in Kintyre, 3, 93, 156, 163, 165, 168, 180, 204, 227, 250
Antares, MFV, 43
ants, 176, 222
aphrodisiacs – see love potions
archaeology, 74, 87, 100-101
Argyllshire Herald, 131, 145, 245, 248, 249
Arinarach (724 150), 234

Arinarach Hill (731 161), 184, 186, 191, 192, 234
Arran, 20-21, 55, 152-55, 167, 230
A Summer in Kintyre, 33, 70, 164, 166, 172
Auchencorvie (679 169), 10, 54, 55, 199, 223, 225
Auchenhoan Farm (760 168), 186, 188, 189, 190, 191
Auchenhoan Head (764 170), 44, 196
Auchenhoan Hill (739 167), 179, 186
Ayrshire, 187, 228, 231

Bàgh mu Dheas (868 712), 60
Bailey, Ian and Patricia, Isle of Lewis, 91-92
Baillet-Latour, Count Guy de, 190
Baird, Tom, Baltimore, 42
balloonists, 212-13
Ballygroggan (622 191), 24, 29, 63, 68, 69, 126, 166, 170, 235
Balnabraid (753 158), 244-45
Balnabraid Glen, 180, 181, 182, 189, 191, 192, 222, 245
Balnabraid Water, 245
Bannatyne, Calum, shepherd, 57, 183, 186-190

259

Bannatyne, John, Campbeltown, 183, 186, 187, 189, 190
Barbour, Catherine (*née* Young), Keil, 160, 163
Barley Bannocks Hill (715 196), 162
Barr Glen, 76, 95, 220
bats, 104
Beachar (693 432), 102
Bealach a' Chaochain (672 385), 103
Bealach Ghillean Duibh (597 147), 134
Beatson, Sir George, 91
Beattie, John, Largiebaan, 29
Bede, 93
Ben Gullion (721 181), 2, 3, 8, 71, 161, 178, 192, 193, 194, 195, 211, 231, 239
Benjamin, Dr Mark, 182
Benjie, author's dog, 1, 109, 193, 194, 195, 211, 231, 239
bicycles – see cycling
Beinn na Faire (603 171), 53
Big Corrie/Corrie, Largiebaan (599 150), 19, 52, 53, 116, 138
'binmen', 10, 49, 203
Binnein Fithich (599 152), 210
birch, 71, 226
birdsfoot-trefoil, 89, 117, 139
Black, Joe, baker, 85
blackbird, 63
Black Loch, The (716 176), 192, 193, 195
Blackstock, Gilbert, 225
blackthorns, 243
Blackwaterfoot, 152
Blue, Archibald, Deuchran, 121

Blue, Donald, Campbeltown, 77
Blue, John, Deuchran, 122
bluebells, 90, 105, 177
blaeberries, 178, 179, 225, 232, 242
Boer War, 228
bog asphodel, 199, 247
boulders – see rocks
Boy Scouts, 160
bracken, 27, 217
Braids (718 447), 96, 122
brambles, 218, 225
Branson, Richard, 212-23
Breaclarach, Carradale Glen (c778 450), 127-29
Breaclarach, Tarbert – see Maclean, Sheila
Brodie, John, Campbeltown, 8-10, 109
Brown, Duncan, Stewarton, 219-20
Brown, John, Drumlemble, 173
Brown, Neil, 23
Brown, Robert 'Rab', 10, 11, 172-73, 175
Brown, Willie, Drumlemble, 172
Bruach Dearg (629 143), 8, 12, 28, 116, 133, 216, 222
Buchan, Tom, 47, 48
Bulletin, The, 187
bullets exploding, 204
Bullets Through the Barrier, 11
Bun an Uisge (623 197), 107, 239
Burgess, Moira, 50, 106
Burnet, J. J., architect, 102
buses, 23, 53, 54, 55, 114, 158, 197, 201, 203, 208, 235-36, 246

butterflies, 92, 133, 159, 192-93, 197, 200, 218, 234
butterwort, common, 175
By Hill and Shore in South Kintyre, 181, 193, 219

Cado Belle, 72
Campbell, Bella, Deuchran, 121
Campbell, Dugald, Bailie of Kintyre, 40
Campbell, Iain, Campbeltown, 164
Campbeltown Courier, 12, 47, 90, 92, 99, 101, 130, 135, 143, 144, 160, 169, 182, 223
camping, 23, 64-68, 77, 109-10, 114, 164
Canada, 132, 141-45, 181, 187, 213, 246, 247, 248, 252
Canada Steamship Lines, 145
canoes, 148
Carradale Glen, 119-29
cars, 24-25, 63, 158, 229
Carskey, 155
Casey, John, shepherd, 246
Castles, The (746 101), 89
cattle, 68, 104, 121
caves, 80, 93-94, 103-104
Cave Picture, Davaar – see Picture Cave
celandine, lesser, 28, 51-52, 53
Chinook helicopter crash, 180
Chiskan (680 189 & 730 102), 153
Chomsky, dog, 2, 3, 6, 161
choughs, 33
Christie, Agatha, 200-201
Cill Andreis, Tarbert (863 684), 226

cinemas, 77, 82, 198, 199
Clachan Ùr Bridge (646 135), 200
climbing alarms, 27, 41, 70, 112, 207, 236
Cnoc Moy (611 152), 22, 64, 233
Cnoc nan Gabhar (668 146), 51
coal-miners, 55, 69, 215
Coastguard, H.M., 69, 180, 212-13, 243
Cole, Jon, The Movies, 11
Coleridge, S. T., 173
Colville, Duncan, 99, 235
Colville, Willie, Machrihanish, 110, 134, 172
Coming of Judith, The, 128-31
conger eels, 240
coniferous plantations – see afforestation
Consider the Lilies, 48
Cooper, Dr Doug, Canada, 244, 252, 246-48
Cooper, Kelly, wife of above, 244, 246, 247
copper coin found and lost, 203
Cork, City of, 168
corn-kilns, 128
Corphin (769 146), 26, 163
Corphin Brae, 25, 149, 156
Corphin Glen – see Balnabraid Glen
Corrie (Largiebaan) – see Big Corrie
Cowan, George, 28
Craigaig (610 184), 10, 63, 71, 107-110, 126, 174, 176, 221
Craigaig Waterfall & Water (613 187), 107, 108, 179
Crossan, Willie, Campbeltown, 209

261

Crosshill (717 193), 195
Crosshill Dam (718 191), 243
Crosshill Reservoir (715 192), 7, 161-62, 193, 195
'Crossing Point, The', poem, 193
Crossley-Holland, Kevin, 93, 156
crows, hooded, 31, 33, 35-36, 221
Crowther, Jean (*née* Martin), 155
cuckoo flowers, 207
cuckoos, 55, 156, 244
'cuddie'/'cuddins', 241
Cuilleam (763 200), Davaar Island, 80, 90
Cunningham, M. H. 'Madge', botanist, 18, 71, 89, 116, 117, 118
curach – see *naomhóg*
cycling, 5, 6, 28, 43, 51, 55, 64, 76, 116, 133, 178, 205, 208, 209, 222, 232

daisy, ox-eye, 239
Dalbuie (691 139), 232
Dalsmirren Bridge (644 131), 11, 203
Davaar Island, 40, 41, 75-94, 162-63
Davies, Ian, aviation historian, 186
Denney, Eileen, 65-66
Denny, Sandy, 11
Deuchran (776 433 & 779 432), 120-22
Deuchran Hill (762 442), 121
Devil's Riddlings, Davaar (761 205), 21, 80
Docherty, Alex, Stewarton, 222
Docherty, Barbara, Drumlemble, 16, 148, 160, 225

Docherty, Barbara, Glasgow – see Matheson, Barbara
Docherty, Donald, 67
Docherty, Lewis, Skye, 16-17, 148-49
Docherty, Malcolm, Skye, 67, 148-49, 238
dog bite, 59
Doirlinn (745 200), 77, 84, 91, 95, 194
dolphins, 150-51, 238
Donegal, 142, 168
dream, 213
Drumlemble, 55, 110, 250
Duff, Tommy, Rex Cinema, 198
Dummy's Port (771 143), 26, 36-39, 42-44
Dunaverty beach, 158-59
Dunaverty, massacre at, 157
Dùn Bàn (c594 140), 89, 204, 210, 211
Dundonald, Lord, 228
Dunn, Douglas, poet, 45-46, 47, 48, 151

Eadie, Douglas, 48
eagles, golden, 33, 185
eagles, sea-, 53
Earadale Point (596 173), 64, 67, 68, 72
Easter egg-rolling, 25-26
Edinburgh, 45, 51, 114, 130
eels, conger – see conger eels
Englishman's Flora, The, 18, 57, 118

Faber Book of Twentieth-Century Scottish Poetry, The, 151

face on rock, 3
Fairy Dell, Arran, 154
falcons, 20, 36, 39-40, 96, 184
falconry, 39-40
Falklands War, 230
fantasies, 149-50, 214-15
fasgadair, 197
Feochaig (763 133), 150
Ferguson, Dougie,
    Campbeltown, 243
Finn, Cecil, Campbeltown, 219
Fin Rock (728 187), 6, 242
Fionnphort (625 202), 10, 160
fishing, 77, 158, 236-37, 241, 245
fish-traps, 59-62
Fleming family, Keil House, 40
Flora of Kintyre, The, 18, 54,
    57, 71, 107, 117, 118, 134, 139,
    147, 155, 202
football, 55-56, 215, 220
Forestry Commission, 119, 122
Four Points of a Saltire, 73
form poetry magazine, 151
foxes, 17, 31, 113-14
Fraser, Ian A., 103
Fulton, Robin – see
    Macpherson, Robin Fulton

Gaelic, 59, 60, 89, 98, 108, 118,
    123, 127, 132, 192, 196, 206,
    228, 235, 241, 248, 250, 251,
    252
Galbraith, Squadron-Leader
    John McLaren Galbraith,
    135-37
Galdrans, The (624 197), 10,
    107, 111, 160
Gallagher, Catherine, 18
Gallagher, Frank, 168

Gallagher, Rory, 167-68
Gannet, HMS, 213
gannets, 196
Gap, The (600 080), 54
'Garavalt' place-name, 226
Garioch, Robert, 47
Gartnacopaig (627 145), 9, 14,
    28, 53, 126
Garvachy (686 169), 21, 22
Gelder, Barry, Southend, 28
geocache, Largiebaan, 16-18
Gillies family at Lagloskin, 248
Gillies family at Largiebaan, 29
Gillies, Lachlan, author's
    grandson, 178
Glasgow, 35, 50, 69, 79, 82, 91,
    174, 178
Glecknahavil (666 155), 223
Glenadale (High, 627 115, Low
    648 117), 29, 204, 205, 222
Glenahanty (630 143), 11-16,
    17, 28, 64, 66
Glenahervie (747 107), 108
Glenbarr (670 364), 95
Glen Breackerie (659 106), 11,
    55, 57, 59, 203-4, 220
Glen Breackerie School, 220
Glen Caol (728 450), 95, 98
Gleneadardacrock (621 156),
    8, 66
Glenmurril Hill (734 156), 189,
    192
Glenramskill (734 185, High),
    91, 183
Glenrea (657 134), 219, 220
'gleshans', 241
goats, 19, 218, 238-39
Goings, The (601 069), 205
Graham, Robert, solicitor, 223

grass-of-Parnassus, 199, 247
Greenlees families, Putechan, 246, 250-1
Greenwood, Charlie, 104-6
Grigson, Geoffrey, 2, 18, 57-59, 89, 118, 119, 134
grouse, red, 99, 179
Guevara, Che, 80-81
gulls, 34, 61, 66, 67, 112, 241
Gulls' Den (594 155), 30, 112

Hall, Allan, Tangy, 98
Hall, Stuart, Killean, 98
Hamilton, Gordon, Gourock, 230
Hamilton, Ian, brother of Malcolm and Stewart, 110
Hamilton, Malcolm, Campbeltown, 68-70, 110
Hamilton, Robert, Trodigal, 70, 172
Hamilton, Stewart, Campbeltown, 68-70, 110
harebells, 163, 207, 219
hares, mountain, 33
Harrer, Heinrich, 112
harrier, hen, 185, 232
Hart, Rachel, Cologne, 210
Haunted Landscapes, 194
'Hawthorn Hedge, Knockrioch,' poem, 231
hawthorns, 71, 231
Hay family, Tarbert, 130, 227-8
Hay, Dundonald Smith, Tarbert, 228
Hay, George Campbell, poet, 60, 73, 130, 227
hazels, 76
'hech-how' – see hemlock water dropwort

hedgehog, 77
hedge parsley, 217
hemlock water dropwort, 218
Herald (*Glasgow*), 48, 131
'herb'-gathering, 245
herb-Robert, 90
Herring Fishermen of Kintyre and Ayrshire, 158
hoary whitlowgrass, 40
Holland, Lee, Glasgow, 27
Holland, Sue, Campbeltown, 197
holly, 71, 176
Homestone (673 155) & road, 10, 26, 54, 205, 220
honeysuckle, 147, 163, 177, 207
Hood, Frances, Peninver, 60, 76, 101
Hood, John, tender of falcons, 40
Horse Bay (762 200), 80, 84, 90

I'Anson, Mark, artist, 243
Immanuel, Jon, 182-86, 234
Innean Beag (605 166), 21, 22, 126
Innean Gaothach (595 133), 71, 116
Innean Mòr (601 162), 15, 21-22, 53, 126, 216
Inneans (Bay), The (599 165), 9-10, 67, 68, 69, 70, 114, 164, 166-68, 179, 221
Inneans Glen (605 165), 22, 52, 63, 89, 175
Innean Seilich (594 138), 116
Innean Tioram (592 135), 116
Inside Out, 165,
Isle of Arran, 76, 230

Its Colours They are Fine, 174
Ivan, dog, 225

jackdaws, 34-35
jays, 33
Johnstone, Ewan, 28
Johnston's Point (769 129), 147
Junction Pool (765 459), 127
Jura, Paps of, 152

Keil (672 076), 104, 155, 159, 163, 203
Kelly, John, Machrihanish, 10, 173, 178, 179
Kelly, Peter, Machrihanish, 10
kelp-kiln, Davaar, 87
Kenneth, A.G., botanist, 18, 116, 117
Kerr, Eddie, Campbeltown, 51
Kerr, James, Campbeltown, 295
kestrels, 20, 222
Kilchousland (752 220), 212, 229
Kildalloig, 94, 214, 217
Kilkerran Graveyard Revisited, 154, 180, 186
Killean (695 445), 92, 98 *et seq.*
Killellan Park Farm (680 158), 234
Kilwhipnach (674 165), 13
Kintyre Agricultural Show, 197-99
Kintyre Agricultural Society, 97, 132
Kintyre Antiquarian (& Natural History) Society, 99, 100, 101, 102
Kintyre Country Life, 186, 251
Kintyre Places and Place-Names, 116, 192, 206

Kintyre: The Hidden Past, 67, 109, 170
Kintyre Way, 16, 17, 20, 21, 22, 59, 63, 96, 114, 116, 141, 166, 208, 209, 216
Kirkpatrick, Raymond, 223
Knockbay (724 192), 1, 2, 7-8
Knock Scalbert (730 222), 231, 232
Kyle, Danny, 75

Ladysmith, Relief of, 228
Lafferty, Teddy, Campbeltown, 41-44, 64, 65-66, 75, 84, 179
Lagloskin (726 468), 246 *et seq.*
Lambie, John, Drumlemble, 170
Landscapes of Scotland, The, 60
Lang, Norrie, Campbeltown, 219
Larch Plantation, The, 42, 44-45, 152, 193, 194
Largiebaan (614 143), xiii, 16, 18-20, 25, 26, 27-32, 33, 51-59, 64, 111-16, 117, 126, 133-36, 138-39, 141-42, 201-2, 205-13, 217-18, 221-22
'Last Illusion', poem, 195
Leac a' Chreachainn (598 144), 200, 206
Learside, 24-25, 222-23, 232
Lee, Rob & Jennifer, 163-64
Liberator AM915, 179-92
Lindstrand, Per, 212, 213
Lochan Dùghaill (790 586), 132
Loch Grunidale – see Black Loch
Lochorodale (659 160), 193, 199, 200, 223-25, 226
Longrow Church, 86
'Looking from Point to Baraskomel', poem, 193

love potions, 57
Lowell, Robert, 48
Lurgan (764 458), 120, 123-27
lythe, 77, 237

McAllister, David, Campbeltown, 27
McAlister, Iain, Campbeltown, 119-123, 127-28
McAlister, Jim, Carradale, 119-20, 123, 127
McAllister, Scott, Campbeltown, 24
Macalister Hall, Enid, Killean & Tangy, 100-102
Macalister Hall, Grace, Tangy, 98
Macalister Hall, James, Killean & Tangy, 97-100
MacArthur, Neil, builder, 87
MacArthur, Willie, Campbeltown, 110, 172
McBride family, Pirnmill, 154-55
MacCaig, Norman, 45, 47, 48
McCallum, Archie, author's uncle, 203
McCallum, John, shepherd, 235
McCartney, Linda, 165
MacConnachie families, 21, 120, 124-26
McCorkindale family, Lochorodale, 223
McCulloch, William, monologist, 90
Macdonalds of Sanda, 157
MacDonald, Alasdair 'MacColla', 157
MacDonald, Rev Donald, Killean, 103
Macdonald, Rev D. J., Killean, 99, 100
MacDonald, Duncan, Largiebaan, 29
MacDonald, Ian, 95, 97, 104, 122
MacDonald, Jimmy, Killeonan, 6, 8, 17, 19, 23, 31-32, 41-42, 53, 56, 64, 71, 116, 210-12, 221, 229, 237, 244
MacDonald, John, Campbeltown, 36, 37, 168, 235-38
MacDonald, John, Culfuar, 122
MacDonald, PC John, Machrihanish, 171
MacDonald, Katrina, Killeonan, 53, 211, 229
MacDonald, Murdo, Lochgilphead, 54, 56, 80
MacDougall families, 227
Macdougall, Duncan, Glenbarr, 95-97, 100, 102-104
McEachran, Iain, Greenock, 230
McEachran, John, fisherman, 245
MacEachran, John 'Tec', Campbeltown, 242
McEachran, Neil, Campbeltown, 76-78, 87, 90
McEwing, James, emigrant, 248
MacFarlane, Hugh, Tarbert, 60, 196-97
McFater, Neil, Killean, 100
McGeachy, Edward, Dalintober, 165
McGeachy, Michael, Campbeltown, 166
McGougan, Flight Lieutenant Archie, ATC, 135

McGregor, Chrissie, Campbeltown, 85
MacIlglash, Neil, 21, 22
McInnes, Robert & Isobel, 209
Macintyre, Charles, 91
MacIntyre, Hugh, Margmonagach, 251
Macintyre, Dugald, writer, 33, 177
McKay, Dennis, Campbeltown, 246
MacKeich, Angus, Campbeltown, 250
McKellar, Martin, Southend, 236, 238
McKellar, Neil Mathieson, Glenahanty, 13-16
McKendrick, Dugald, Glenramskill, 55, 183
McKerral, Mary, wife of Neil McEachran, 77-78
MacKinnon, Archibald, artist, 80, 82
MacKinnon, John, Achnasavil, champion ploughman, 121
McLachlan, Duncan, Campbeltown, 150, 172, 173
Maclean, Alasdair, poet, 153
Maclean families, Tarbert, 132, 227
Maclean, Hugh, Tarbert, 131-32
McLean, John, Blary, 39
Maclean, Sheila, Tarbert, 129-31
Maclean, Sorley, 73
Maclean, Will, artist, 73
Macmaster, Jim, 50
McMath family, Glenahanty, 13, 16
MacMhuirich bardic family, 79

MacMillan family, Arinarach, 234
McMillan, George, Campbeltown, 94
McMillan, Dr Sandy, Campbeltown, 54
McMurchie, Jake, jazz-rock musician, 79
McMurchy families – see MacMhuirich
McNachtan, Alexander, falconer, 40
McNaughton, David & Katie, Campbeltown, 158
McNaughton, Dugald, son of above, 73
McNeill family, Amod, Glen Breackerie, 14, 28, 57
MacNeill, Ina, Dowager Duchess of Argyll, 225
MacNeill, Iona (*née* Pursell), 191
McNeill, Marie, widow, 157
McPhail, Duncan, Drumlemble, 170
McPhee, James, Campbeltown, 236
McPhee, Maureen – see O' Driscoll
Macpherson, Robin Fulton, 47, 151-53
MacPherson, Tommy, Campbeltown, 55-56
MacQuilkan family, Deuchran, 120-21
MacQuilkan, Angus, Ballochgair, 120-21
MacQuilkan, Robert, Low Ugadale, 13, 15, 121

MacRingan's Point (754 213), 94
McSporran, George,
  Campbeltown, 1, 5, 6, 59, 75, 76, 80, 82-84, 88, 91, 95, 103-104, 106-115, 174, 178, 179, 180, 181, 182-85, 196, 208-13, 216, 232-34, 239, 243
McSporran, Helen Revie, wife of Calum Bannatyne, 186
McSporran, John, brother of George, 181
McSporran, Margaret (*née* Thomson), 80, 185
McSporran, Peter, Homestone, 226
McSporran, Sandy, son of George, 27, 59, 109, 181
McTaggart, William, 235
MacVoorie's Rock (755 198), 79

Mabey, Richard, 135, 217
Machrihanish, 10, 53, 106, 114, 170, 171
Maley, T.P., 90
Manx shearwaters, 90, 196
'Marilyn' (726 185), 3-5
Martin family, Lurgan, 124-26
Martin, Amelia (*née* McKenzie), author's mother, 49, 159, 198, 215, 242
Martin, Amelia, author's daughter, 8, 35, 45, 54, 63-64, 70, 77, 153, 193, 222, 224-25
Martin, Angus, author's father, 73, 145, 159, 160, 204, 215, 235
Martin, Angus 'Longpipe', 155
Martin, Caroline, author's grandmother, 160
Martin, Carol, author's sister, 159, 160, 178
Martin, Colin, author's great-uncle, 143-47
Martin, David, Lewiston, 141-42
Martin, Elizabeth (Mrs Donald Munro), 86
Martin, Henry, author's uncle, 239
Martin, Isabella (Mrs Willie McBride), author's grand-aunt, 154
Martin, Isabella, author's aunt, 160
Martin, Isabella 'Bella', author's daughter, 153, 154, 195, 220, 226, 231, 239
Martin, John, author's great-grandfather, 143
Martin, Judy, author's wife (*née* Honeyman), 1, 4, 7, 19, 23, 45, 51, 52, 53-54, 57, 77, 89, 115, 116, 134, 139, 141, 178-79, 200, 202, 207, 208, 216, 229, 242, 243
Martin, Sarah (*née* Campbell), author's great-grandmother, 143
Martin, Sarah, author's aunt, 145, 160
Martin, Sarah, author's daughter, 2, 8, 35, 45, 77, 178-79, 193
Martin, Victoria 'Tory', author's aunt, 155
Martyn, John, 165
Matheson, Barbara, 36, 229, 238
Mathieson family, Glenahanty – see McMath family

Mathieson, Neil – see McKellar, Neil
Mati, Lucas, 63, 64, 70-71
mayweed, 200, 239
Meal Kist Glen (726 165), 184
Mewse, David, 154, 179
milestones, 148, 219-21
Miller, Arthur, 4
mink, 237
mint, water-, 247
Mitchell family, Lagloskin, 246, 248, 250, 251, 252
Mitchison, Naomi, 50
Monroe, Marilyn, 3
Moreton Macdonald of Largie, 124-25
Morgan, Edwin, 45, 46, 47
Morris, Craig, Campbeltown, 6
Morrison, Norman, 92-93
Morton, Rab, ornithologist, 90, 184, 196
Moss Road, 57
mountain avens, 116-119, 140
Movies, The, 11
Muasdale (676 401), 102, 104
Mull, Island of, 60
Mull of Kintyre, 69, 136, 179, 180, 186
Munro, Alexander, Dalintober, 85
Munro, Donald, Drumlemble, 170
Munro, Dr Robert, 132
Munro, R. W., 'weather station', 233
Murphy's Rock – see MacVoorie's Rock
mushrooms, 42, 77

names carved on rocks, 229-30
naomhóg, 148, 149
Narrowfield (710 195), 193, 233
navelwort, 163-64
New Orleans (757 179), 156, 196
Night Falls on Ardnamurchan, 153
Nimrod, HMS, 191
Nobles, MFV, 158
Norse, 20, 192, 224
North Sea oil, 93-95
Nye, Robert, 50

Oban, 46, 47, 48, 114
O'Driscoll, Don, Kinlochbervie, 160, 166-68, 175-76
O' Driscoll, Maureen (*née* McPhee), 168
Off Davaar, broadcast dialogue, 90
Oitir Buidhe (761 206), 77, 80
Oldfield, Mike, 72
Old Man of Storr, 70
Oman, Ellen (*née* McBride), 154
Oman, Les, Campbeltown, 165, 166
orchid, early purple, 56-57, 105, 112
Ordnance Survey, 79, 103, 123, 235, 245
otters, 82
owls, 23
oyster-catchers, 93
oyster-plant, 152, 155-56

paddling-pool, Kilkerran, 61
Paper Archipelagos, 193
'Parting Lay-by', 208
Paterson, Lachie, Carradale, 166

Paterson, Phillippa, Aberdeen, 82-83
Peninver, 76, 94
Perspex, 181, 190
photography, 3, 9, 12, 24, 27, 31-32, 42, 64, 80, 89, 103, 151, 200, 239
picnics, 158-59, 229
Picture Cave (759 198), Davaar Island, 80-82, 91, 92
pigeons (includes racers & rock doves), 33, 39, 103, 104, 218
Pinnacle/Needle Rock (597 166), 168
Pirnmill, Arran, 154, 155
Place-Names of the Parish of Killean and Kilchenzie, 95
poetry, xiii, 5, 42, 43, 44-51, 132, 156, 172-73, 174, 193-95, 231-32, 243-44
Point (745 193), 194
police, 69, 223, 249
pollack – see lythe
Polliwilline (735 100), 27, 185, 230, 233, 242, 243
Portan Àluinn (655 071), 107
Portavadie, 94
Port Glasgow, 223
Port na h-Olainn (592 131), 71
porphyry, 85, 86
'ports', 84
primroses, 52, 90, 105, 138
Pursell family, Davaar House, 190-91
Pursell, Bill, Canada, 191, 245
Pursell, Duncan, Australia, 186, 190
Putechan/Putechantuy (South, 665 314 & North, 667 318), 250-51

quarries, 84-87, 235
Queen Esther's Bay (767 165), 41, 44
quern-stone, Breaclarach, 128

rabbits, 67, 77
Rae, Robert, fisherman, Pans, 171
RAF Machrihanish, 213
ragworms, 61-62
Rathlin Island, 66, 141, 142, 208, 212
rats, 77
'Ratton, The', poem, 78
ravens, 29-32, 84
Reid, David & John, Kilwhipnach, 13-15
Reilly, Maggie, 72
Rhunahaorine School, 250
ribbons, 8, 200
Riddell, Murphy, Campbeltown, 79
Riddlings, Davaar – see Devil's Riddlings
Ring-Net Fishermen, The, 60, 73, 154
Robertson, Dugald, Dalintober, 218
Robertson, John, shepherd, Lagloskin, 249
Robertson, Robert, shepherd, Kilmory, 97, 99
Robinson, Dr Gary, archaeologist, 87
Rockhopper penguins, 230
'rock jumpers', 237
rocks, 20, 22, 63, 64, 70-71, 88, 110, 111, 196, 229-30
Ronald, Archie, Largiebaan, 29, 213

rooks, 34
rose, burnet, 177
rose, dog-, 176, 177
rose-root, 133-34
rosebay willowherb, 247
rowans, 6, 71, 249
Rubha Dùn Bhàin (590 144), 17, 116-18, 135, 175, 210
Ruesgen, Nona, Campbeltown, 109
rushes, 4
Russell, Iain, 234
Ru Stafnish (771 139), 25, 36, 147, 148

Sailor's Grave (598 166), 168-74
Saint Kieran's Cave (765 170), 33, 93, 104
saithe, 240-42
sand tracks, 68
saxifrage, cross-leaved golden, 2
saxifrage, mossy, 19, 115-16
saxifrage, purple, 18-19, 25, 27, 53, 54, 56
saxifrage, yellow, 19, 176, 207
Schutz, Hartwig, Germany, 1, 72
Scotsman, The, 50, 186, 188
Scott, D. Rankine, 25
Scottish Arts Council, 44-45
Scottish Poetry anthologies, 46-47, 49-51
Scottish Wild Plants, 115, 119, 140
seals, 62, 179
sea carrot, 217
sea kale, 159
sea pink, 108
sea radish, 147, 159-60, 163
sea sandwort, 159
seaweed, 67, 87, 88

Second Water (769 154), 26, 36, 43, 137, 173, 181, 191, 222, 229
Second World War, 76, 147, 179 *et seq.*, 229
Semple family, Dippen, 121
Seymour-Smith, Martin, 151
Shakespeare, 177
sheep, 13-15, 20, 21-22, 35, 68, 113-14, 121, 183, 194, 199, 221
Sheep Fanks (755 184), 222
Sheep Hoose (756 199), Davaar Island, 76, 80, 87
sheep markings, 15, 249, 251
sheep-stealing, 13-15, 21, 22, 249, 251
Shiskine, Arran, 152, 153
Sinclair, Donald, Ballygroggan, 69
Sinclair, Duncan, Ballygroggan, 170-71
Sinclair, Mary, Machrihanish, daughter of above, 235
Sinclair, Neil, Deuchran, 121
Siol nan Gaidheal, 157
'skeegs', 240
skuas, 196-97
Skye, 70, 73
Slate, The (633 164), 178
sloes & sloe gin, 243
'Sloe-Gathering', poem, 243
Smerby (Low, 753 229), 59-62
Smith, Iain Crichton, 46, 47-49
snails at Largiebaan, 135
snowdrops, 247
Song of the Quern, The, 77
South Kintyre Botany Group, 107, 202
Southend, 157-60, 216
Spence, Alan, 173-75

Spindrift poetry magazine, 174
squill, spring, 106-107
Sròn Gharbh (600 178), 70, 71, 89, 108, 110
Stackie (759 237), 76
Stacs, The (597 174), 66, 67
starlings, 168
Stewart, Agnes, Campbeltown, 2, 9-10, 19, 54, 55, 57, 61, 89, 106, 107, 108, 115, 116, 118, 133, 134, 155, 156, 159, 172, 202, 215, 217
Stewart, Allister, Campbeltown, 2, 41, 55, 156, 215
stonecrop, English, 62, 163
strawberry, wild, 134-35
'Strong Love', 167
Stuart, Rev John, 99, 100
sundew, round-leaved, 175-76
swallows, 52, 53, 249
Sweetie Bella's Quarry (767 160), 24

Tarbert, 17, 129-32, 152, 196, 226-28
Teesdale, Ian, Campbeltown, 202, 206, 207
'The Way the Wind Blows', poem, 49, 51
Thomas, Ann, Tarbert, 17
Thompson, Alastair, 168, 180-81, 222
Thomson, James McArthur, 109-10
tits, long-tailed, 181
Togneri, Ronald, Campbeltown, 13, 80
Togneri, Veronica, Southend, 107, 155

Tomaig Glen (707 186), 197
Tòn Bhàn/ Dùn Bàn Ballygroggan (612 191), 110, 177, 235-38
tormentil, 139
Torrisdale, 163, 222
Traffic, 164, 165, 166, 167
tramps, 102
Travellers, 104
Trodigal Cottage (652 202), 70
Tully, Colin, musician, 72
Tuttle, Lisa, 130

Uamh Bealach a' Chaochain (673 387), 102-104
Uamh Fhliuch, An (680 404), 104
umbellifers, 217-28
upright hedge parsley, 217

Valley, The (720 192), 243
vetch, kidney, 88-89, 133, 139, 159, 163
vetch, wood, 202, 207-208
violets, dog, 52, 53
voles, 4
Vulcan, 165

Walker, Steve, Campbeltown, 197
warbler, sedge, 63
warbler, willow, 53
war memorials, 87, 97, 225
Warren, Carol – see Martin, Carol
Warner, Harold, balloonist, 213
Watson, Lawrence, Campbeltown, 85

Watson, Willie, Campbeltown, 104
Wee Man's Cove (760 176), 196
Wee Wud, Glenramskill (742 191), 2, 57
Weir, John, sheep-stealer, 21-22
wells/springs, 97, 148, 167
whale, 238
wheatear, 53
White, Captain T. P., 33
White Spider, The, 112
Wickham-Jones, C. R., 60
Wild Flowers ('Observer's'), 1, 52
wilk-picking, 25, 44
Williamson, Duncan, 104
Williamson, Robin, 62
Willing Lass, skiff, 90
willows, 71, 116
wind turbines, 95, 122, 244
Winny Corner (766 136), 148
Winwood, Steve, 164, 167
Wolff, Tobias, 114
wood anemone, 1, 2, 57
Wood, Chris, 164-68
wood (for fire), 10, 26, 36, 75, 84, 92, 229
woodlice, 5
wood sage, 177
wood sorrel, 1, 53

yellow oxytropis, 138-141
Young, Andrew, poet and botanist, 140-41, 151-52, 156